South Africa

and U.S.

Multinational

Corporations

South Africa
and U.S.
Multinational
Corporations

Willcox

ANN & NEVA SEIDMAN

LAWRENCE
HILL & CO.

Westport, Connecticut

First published in Tanzania in 1977 by
Tanzania Publishing House, Dar es Salaam

Library of Congress Catalog Card Number: LC: 77-99205

ISBN: 0-88208-084-9 (cloth edition)
ISBN: 0-88208-085-7 (paperback edition)

First U.S. Edition, January, 1978

1 2 3 4 5 6 7 8 9 10

Manufactured in the United States of America

South Africa

and U.S.

Multinational

Corporations

THIS BOOK IS DEDICATED TO J.D.,
AND TO THOSE WHO ARE CARRYING
HIS STRUGGLE FORWARD.

Contents

CONTENTS Pages:

CONTENTS

CONTENTS

List of Charts, Maps and Tables

Charts

Maps

Tables: *Pages:*

Tables: Pages:

Foreword

Two separate, but intertwined, analytical strands were tied together in writing this book. Neva had written a comprehensive paper to explain the apparent paradox of South African industrial growth in the midst of the worsening impoverishment of the vast majority of the population. Ann, while coordinating an international research project on copper mining* at the University of Zambia, had become concerned with the expanding penetration by U.S. multinational corporations in Southern Africa. As they discussed their research together, it became increasingly apparent that they were exploring two sides of the same story.

That story is only partially told here, primarily for two reasons. First, as those concerned with human liberties in the U.S., as well as throughout the world, have expressed growing protests against the brutal oppression of Southern African peoples, the expanding involvement of U.S. interests there has become increasingly shrouded in secrecy. U.S. corporated reports no longer separately describe their Southern African holdings. South African sources print only what they wish their supporters to know. The fragmentary information contained in this book has been pieced together primarily from U.S. and South African governmental and corporated documents available in the Harvard Business School Library in Boston, U.S.A. It will probably remain almost impossible for researchers to find this type of essential information in Africa itself until the files of the South African governmental-business complex are liberated.

The second reason why this story remains unfinished here is that it is still being told. Nor will its outcome be determined by decision-makers working behind the doors of multinational corporated board

*A. Seidman, ed. *Natural Resources and National Welfare: The Case of Copper* (New York: Praeger, 1975).

xv

rooms or governmental edifices in the U.S. or South Africa. The conclusion to the story is still being written by the thousands, tens upon tens of thousands, of unknown heroines and heroes of the Southern African Liberation movement.

We would like to express our sincere appreciation to Davidson Anyiwo, who painstakingly perused lists of boards of directors of major U.S. multinationals with investments in South Africa to discover their linkages with U.S. governmental agencies and each other; to the University of Massachusetts-Boston for a grant to finance part of that search; and to Ray Torto for his support. We would also like to thank Arthur McEwan for his help and criticism; Ray Simon, whose friendship and insights have been invaluable; and Bob Seidman, who has encouraged us to report as much of this incomplete story as we could.

Boston, 1976   Ann and Neva Seidman

Preface

Since this book was completed in 1976, many changes have taken place in southern Africa. The victory of the MPLA (Popular Movement for the Liberation of Angola) in Angola and increased resistance in South Africa, Zimbabwe and Namibia reflect the growing strength of African liberation movements throughout the region. The presidents of the front-line states—including Zambia*, despite earlier waverings—have united to support the armed struggle against white minority rule.

South Africa has once more exploded into front-page headlines as this book goes to press in the United States. The South African regime, faced with continuing mass demonstrations and mounting guerilla activity, has continued to clamp down on all opposition. In the early sixties, the regime outlawed the African National Congress and its allies, forcing the liberation movement under ground. Now it has banned the parties which emerged to replace the ANC in the legal arena and which had been growing increasingly militant: the Black People's Convention (BPC), black student organizations, the Christian Institute, the largest black newspaper and other groups. Since June, 1976, thousands of South Africans have been jailed without trial, tortured or shot because they fought for their rights. Nevertheless, the growing unity and strength of the liberation forces spells the eventual end of the white regime.

At the United Nations, African states in 1977 demanded an effective economic and military blockade against the South African regime. The U.S., Britain and France once again vetoed African-sponsored Security Council resolutions for implementation of effective sanctions on investments and credits, prohibition of arms sales, revocation of licenses to manufacture weapons and an end to cooperation in nuclear development. They then voted for an arms embargo which banned shipments of military

---

*Zambia's case is described in Chapter XV to show some of the unseen ways in which U.S. and South African interests may exert pressure to influence politically independent African states.

supplies, including spare parts and the licensing of the manufacture of military equipment in South Africa. The embargo did not extend to investments, loans or collaboration in allegedly peaceful developments of nuclear power.

The Western powers' actions, under U.S. leadership, show a cynical disregard for the fact that multinational corporate investments in South Africa have already built the advanced industrial base needed to produce all but the most sophisticated weapons. United States based multinationals, assisted by the U.S. government, have enhanced South Africa's capacity to produce nuclear weapons, which may even now be available for use.

Close scrutiny reveals that the Carter Administration's policies relating to South Africa differ from Ford's only in style. The Administration has adopted former Secretary of State Kissinger's policy of seeking South African cooperation by encouraging the establishment of 'moderate' black governments in Namibia and Zimbabwe and making every effort to prevent deep-seated change in the exploitative political-economic system which dominates the area.

It is true that the Carter Administration persuaded Congress to repeal the Byrd Amendment, under which the United States permitted imports of chrome from Southern Rhodesia in violation of UN sanctions. The U.S., however, continues to import refined chrome from a Union Carbide Corporation plant in South Africa, and it remains difficult to determine the source of ore for this plant.

The only overt U.S. reaction—spurred by the rising resistance in South Africa which has shocked government and multinational corporate officials into realizing that *apartheid* cannot endure indefinitely—has been stronger verbal condemnation of white minority rule in South Africa. U.S. corporations have pledged to improve working conditions for their black employees, but given their resistance to affirmative action, backed by law in the U.S. itself, is it realistic to expect effective action to be taken in South Africa in violation of South Africa law? The Administration's verbal protests against *apartheid* will remain empty criticism unless reinforced by substantive action.

The Carter Administration has continued to encourage the expansion of U.S. business interests in South Africa. In November 1976, the South African *Financial Mail* asked future President Carter, in an interview that at his request[1] was not printed until after his election:

> Would you free up American investment through Export-Import Bank loans and otherwise encourage the increase in private American lending and corporate activity in South Africa?

He replied:

> Yes indeed. . . . Economic development, investment commitment and the use of economic leverage against what is, after all, a govern-

ment system of repression within South Africa, seems to me the only way to achieve racial justice there.

Since then, the Administration has reviewed its southern African policy and reaffirmed the unrealistic conclusion that U.S. corporate investment provides a lever for social change and majority rule in the region.

UN Ambassador Andrew Young has frequently reiterated this position. Young seems to believe—erroneously—that the civil-rights battle in the U.S. was won through the intervention of giant corporations. As he has explained,[2] he is working through the United Nations "to see if we can't begin to evolve business ethics and do some of the things internationally that we made business do in the South [of the United States]." He simply rejects the stance taken by the southern African liberation movements and the presidents of the neighboring frontline states: "I don't consider armed struggle at this point . . . a viable option."

Protests in the U.S. have focused on the way U.S. investments and bank loans have strengthened *apartheid* and the oppressive South African regime. Protesters have also noted that these investments and loans have undermined American employment.

The Carter Administration, like its predecessor, is making no serious attempt to encourage popular participation in policy-making on these issues. The government's Export-Import Bank has continued to insure and guarantee loans to finance U.S. exports to South Africa. U.S. firms receive tax credits for investments in South Africa, although in the last two years the rate of growth of such investments has slowed as South Africa's economy has been weakened in the grips of depression and because of the extent of popular resistance to the current minority regime.

U.S. banks have mobilized a third of the more than $9 billion in foreign funds borrowed by South Africa to finance oil and military imports as well as to offset the domestic effects of the capitalist world economic crisis. The banks have this year taken the lead in selling Krugerrands (one-ounce gold pieces stamped with the picture of the Afrikaner leader) in the United States. Sales of these coins could keep as much as a fifth of South Africa's annual gold production off the usual world markets. The South African regime hopes in this way to push world gold prices higher and reduce its need to borrow further.

The U.S. Administration's support for further investments and continued loans to South Africa, despite that country's blatantly undemocratic political-economic system, can be explained partly by the philosophy of the Trilateral Commission. Carter, Young, Secretary of State Cyrus Vance and nearly twenty other members of the Carter Administration participated in this Rockefeller-initiated international institution. Trilateral Commission reports argue, on the one hand, that the U.S., Europe and Japan "increasingly need the developing countries as sources of raw materials, as export markets and, most important of all, as constructive partners in the creation of a workable world order." The reports argue that advanced capitalist countries suffer from an "excess of democracy."[3] This suggests that South Africa's violation of the black majority's democratic rights may not really concern Carter *et al.* as much as they claim.

More fundamentally, the multiplication of U.S. multinationals' investments in South Africa in the late sixties and early seventies is a feature of the process of transformation of the international structure of production in the capitalist world since World War II. The emergence of socialism in a third of the world, despite internal disagreements and splits, narrowed the sphere for free-wheeling corporate exploitation. Governments' colonial umbrellas, such as those that protected European firms' expansion in Africa, are no longer viable options. Competition between giant multinationals, intensified recently by the re-emergence of a general economic crisis, has contributed to the production of ever more sophisticated—and consequently expensive—technology. Relatively labor-intensive industries are being transferred to low-wage areas. Formerly, within the U.S., such plants moved to the southern states; increasingly since World War II they have been transferred to "hospitable investment climates" created by oppressive governments in the Third World. The concentration and expansion of capital goods production in the center—especially in the U.S., West Germany and Japan—has led to increasing competition for markets in the Third World.

In developing countries that are viewed as relatively "unsafe," multinationals take advantage of the local governments' import-substitution policies to sell sophisticated technology for last-stage assembly and processing of imported parts and materials in tariff-protected markets. In these countries, they produce luxuries for small high-income groups, (televisions, private cars, refrigerators) as well as more broadly based mass-consumed goods, like cotton cloth, beer and cigarettes. Despite rising unemployment levels in underdeveloped countries, the new machines and equipment sold by the multinationals are highly capital intensive. Parts and materials must be imported. All this is expensive. Countries relying on such inappropriate foreign technologies rapidly accumulate foreign debts, becoming increasingly dependent on multinational corporations and banks.

In countries that the multinationals consider more "stable," the companies have built basic industrial production designed to enable them to penetrate and dominate the regional market. In South Africa, this has led to competitive expansion of investment in integrated industries like the automotive, those based on electrical machinery, chemicals, petroleum and nuclear power. Here, too, the multinationals maintain influence through direct investment and through control of technologically advanced machinery and equipment. The ever-rising costs, added to increased military expenditures, have led South Africa to accumulate one of the highest per-capita foreign debts.

In the 1970s, the largest U.S. banks began to lend more of the funds deposited by customers at home to overseas firms and governments like South Africa's. The banks increase their profits through higher interest rates and government guarantees provided by these overseas borrowers. Over half the income of the 12 largest U.S. banks is earned by their overseas branches and affiliates. Citicorp, with only half its assets abroad, earned more than 70 percent of its income.

The transformation of the capitalist world's production structure, reflected by U.S. multinational involvement in southern Africa, has direct implications for the people of the United States. The increased capital intensity and automation of basic industries in the industrial center and the transfer of more labor-intensive production overseas by U.S.-based multinationals has contributed to higher rates of unemployment in the U.S. itself. Only a few of the growing numbers of jobless have been absorbed by the accompanying shift of employment into distribution and services. This pattern is emerging in other capitalist-core industrial countries as well. The same U.S. banks that are expanding loans overseas, often to South Africa, are forcing state and city governments in the U.S. to agree to cut back on jobs, welfare programs and essential services like schools and hospitals.

Multinational bank loans, corporate loans and investments do not contribute to balanced, integrated development or higher living standards for the masses in Third-World countries. They do not, as a result, lay a foundation for growing international trade, improved job opportunities and increased real incomes for workers everywhere. On the contrary, investments and loans are concentrated in countries ruled by oppressive regimes which use state power backed by military might to coerce the majority of the populations to work for below-subsistence wages. South Africa is a leading example; Brazil is another.

This book, which outlines the role of U.S. multinational corporations in the context of oppressive white minority rule in South Africa, portrays only a small but illuminating part of a much larger picture. As Americans, we need to understand what is happening in that faraway land on the other side of the globe. It has immediate and direct implications for our own lives.

Ann and Neva Seidman,
Cambridge, Mass.
10 November, 1977

REFERENCES

PREFACE

1. *Financial Mail* (Johannesburg), Nov. 2, 1976.
2. *Africa Magazine,* No. 67, March 1977. In reality, the South African struggle is qualitatively different from the U.S. civil rights campaign. In South Africa, a white minority has built its entire status as owners of factories, mines and farms by using state power to coerce blacks into a low-cost working class. The issue is not simply majority rule, but an end to the entire exploitative state-capitalist system.
3. See R. N. Gardner, S. Okito and B.J. Udink, *A Turning Point In North-South Economic Relations,* Trilateral Commission Report No. 3, 1974; and R.J. Crozier, S.P. Huntington and J. Watanuki, *The Crisis of Democracy,* Report on the Governability of Democracies to the Trilateral Commission (New York University Press, 1975). In addition to President Carter, Young and Vance, other members of the Carter Administration who were on the Commission include Vice President Mondale, Secretary of Defense Brown, Arms Controller Warnke and Deputy CIA Director Bowie.

PART I

Introductory

Chapter I

United States 'Interests' in Southern Africa

In the welter of daily headlines, the average American probably did not attach much significance to the report that the United State Government in late 1974, joined Britain and France in vetoing a resolution which would have ousted South Africa from the United Nations. Nor was he likely to have been very concerned when the U.S. again joined Britain and France in the following year to veto UN proposals to take severe economic measures to compel South Africa to end its colonial rule over Namibia (the former German colony of South West Africa). To most Americans, Southern Africa, in the 1970s, like Vietnam in the early 1960s, seemed remote and relatively unimportant.

In reality, however, the U.S. Government's action reflected a growing official U.S. concern with events in Southern Africa. In 1969, the National Security Council appears to have adopted the second in a list of five alternative options presented in a secret memorandum [1] as the basis of U.S. foreign policy in Southern Africa. Option Number Two proposed to balance U.S. relations in the region by compensating for, rather than abandoning, 'tangible U.S. interests' in the white ruled states. Every available means was to be utilized to turn the sights of black states away from the total liberation of the continent. This, it was argued, would enable the U.S. to realize its perceived economic and strategic interests simultaneously both in the independent African states and in those still ruled by minority white regimes.

1

In the years following the National Security Council's consideration of Memorandum 39, the United States passed through a series of crises: the U.S.-supported governments in Vietnam, Cambodia and Laos collapsed. Watergate exposed corporate influence and corruption in the heart of Washington. Congressional investigations revealed U.S. involvement in the coup which ousted the elected Chilean Government. The oil producing countries united in OPEC to win a major share of the oil profits formerly captured by U.S. and British-based multinational corporations, and developing nations mounted pressures for a greater share in the profitable returns generated by exploitation of other forms of rich mineral wealth. The collapse of the Portuguese dictatorship threatened to change the balance of power in Europe. Assessment of these events by U.S. officialdom seems to have led to a sharpened focus on Africa, a vast continent with three times the land area of the United States, untold mineral and oil riches, and a significant market potential in its population of 350 to 400 million.

The situtation in Southern Africa had by no means remained static while changes elsewhere led to renewed U.S. interest in the region. The winds of change that had liberated over 40 African states in little more than a decade had swept southward with increasing force. The military successes of the guerilla movements in the former Portuguese colonies of Mozambique, Angola and Guinea-Bisseau were major factors contributing to the collapse of the Portuguese regime. For the South African Government, the fall of Portugal constituted the loss of a vital ally in the maintenance of the *status guo* in the region. It raised the question of whether South Africa could depend on the continued annual inflow of tens of thousands of migrant laborers from the former Portuguese territories to provide labour for the mines and threatened South Africa's expanding economic interests there. Even more serious, Mozambique, right on South Africa's border, had become, not only an example for the oppressed black population of South Africa, but also a potential conduit for South African guerilla fighters.

The South African Government's response to this new situation contained two primary thrusts: first, it sought to extend its diplomatic 'outward reach' in an effort to achieve its own version of 'detente' with its black neighbours to the north. Envoys were sent to all nations that had shown any signs of willingness to open dialogue with South Africa. Prime Minister Vorster, himself, flew to Ivory Coast for secret talks with President Houphouet-Boigny and Senegal's President Senghor. He repaid a visit President Banda of Malawi had made some years before to South Africa. He was invited to Liberia by President William Tolbert. Secret negotiations were initiated between Vorster and President Kaunda of Zambia. New York Times columnist Graham Hovey, who interviewed Vorster, explained:[2]

Mr Vorster's goal is clear: by cooperating with Mr Kaunda to promote a peaceful solution in Rhodesia, showing flexibility on the future of Namibia (South West Africa), bolstering economic ties with a black Government in Mozambique and offering help to needy African states, he hopes to get the world off South Africa's back on the apartheid issue.

The use of the term 'detente' inevitably invites comparison with the efforts of the United States and the Soviet Union to build detente to lessen the danger of a global war. In the official South African view, the term connotes a lessening of tensions generated by the struggles of the national liberation movements for an end to colonial and white minority rule in Southern Africa. Given this perspective, the official South African outward reach towards detente is clearly designed to undermine and, if possible, destroy those struggles. From the outset, Vorster has made it quite clear that he does not plan fundamental changes in the structure of South Africa's political economy. He has no intention of granting Africans the right to participate as citizens in the South Africa body politic: 'In white South Africa, he declared,[3] 'the whites will rule — and let there be no mistake about that'.

The second major thrust of the South African Government's strategy' was to accelerate its efforts to strengthen its ties with powerful Western nations in what it proclaimed as an 'anti-communist crusade'. The United States, because of its predominant world position, constituted a primary target.

From the South African viewpoint, the United States had, at the end of World War II, assumed the burden of empire from Great Britain. The South African historian, C. W. de Kiewiet, explained the implications of the new U.S. role in the framework of this perspective:[4]

In one sense the decline of Great Britain as a world power... had been precipitate... For the United States, as the dominant world power, the inheritance was not empire, but a vast region of instability, backwardness, and strategic exposure. The challenge for the United States was to fill the vacuum, to prevent its collapse into chaos, and to protect it against forcible entry...

Of the comprehensive and diversified American policy of

containment, South Africa was an important beneficiary... The efforts to promote stability, and to prevent chaos were implicitly exercised on its behalf as well. In spite of the rising tide of critical comment, the freedom to conduct its domestic affairs remained unchanged. South African success was based on the success of American foreign policy.

A number of events indicate that U.S. officials responded positively to South Africa's increasingly urgent overtures after the collapse of Portuguese colonialism. William Bowdler, formerly U.S. Ambassador to Guatemala when the U.S. officially endorsed an anti-insurgency programme there in which thousands of Guatemalans were killed, was appointed the new U.S. Ambassador to South Africa.[5] South African military men were invited to meet U.S. Joint Chiefs of Staff and other high-ranking U.S. officers to discuss strategy.[6] An article by a former CIA official, one of the organizers of the Bay of Pigs invasion of Cuba, argued that only South Africa could provide the kind of stable government the U.S. needed for its strategic :military interests in the area.[7] A ranking minority member of the House Armed Services Committee and five Republican colleagues, after an all-expenses-paid trip to South Africa, recommended an end to the U.S. arms embargo and a military alliance with the South African Government.

The above items were reported in the press. Reports of increased CIA activities in Southern Africa[8] gave rise to fears of additional clandestine activities. These fears were not set to rest by a former Deputy Director of the CIA in a signed article in the *New York Times* in February, 1975:[9]

The 'realists' of the 'national security establishment' argue that covert action ought to be taken in those relatively few cases in which world events can be turned in a direction more favorable to the United States by a crucial marginal boost from the C I A

He explicitly mentioned the post-coup Portuguese situtation (and subsequent events proved the CIA *had* intervened there to provide a 'crucial marginal boost'.[10]) The implications of his argument for Southern Africa were self-evident. In the fall of 1975, on-going Congressional investigations revealed that the CIA, under Democratic as well as Republican administration, had for more than a decade been deeply involved in supporting one and possibly two opposition groups in Angola. The aim was allegedly to lay the foundation for establishment of a governmnet sympathetic to U.S. 'interests' in that country.[11] In December, 1975, the U.S. Government admitted[12] that the CIA had covertly begun massive shipments of at least $60 million worth* of arms through Zaire and perhaps Zambia to the two groups, in opposition to the newly independent government established in Luanda, the Angolan capital, and recognized by increasing numbers of African states. The South African Government publicly announced [13] that it, too, had sent military equipment and soldiers to bolster the efforts of the two U.S. - supported   opposition groups to oust the new Angolan Government. Widespread fears were expressed, in both the U.S. press and the U.S. Congress, that further escalation might lead to a full-fledged, Vietnam-like situation, with the United States firmly committed to a working alliance with South Africa.

Yet the Angolan conflict was only one aspect of the complex struggle spreading throughout the southern third of the continent, a land area as big as that of the United States. The liberation movements of Namibia, Zimbabwe (Rhodesia) and South Africa had taken up arms to fight for the right to govern themselves. Growing U.S. involvement in the region carried with it the inevitable danger that sooner or later the United States might find itself once again embroiled on the wrong side of a people's war for freedom.

The aim of this book is not to detail the overt or covert maneuvers of the United States Government in the events in Southern Africa. Rather it is to explore the underlying and contradictory reality of the Southern African political economy and its growing ties with U.S. - based multinational corporations.   These constitute the foundation of the 'tangible U.S. interests' which the U.S. Government has seemed so reluctant to abandon in shaping its policies for dealing with the emergent liberation movements of Southern Africa.

A Model of Underdevelopment in Southern Africa

Analysis of the complex reality of Southern Africa may be facilitated by utilization of a theoretical model designed to expose the underlying causes of underdevelopment. This model was initially formulated to illuminate problems confronted by the typical newly independent country in sub-Saharan Africa. [14] As elaborated here, it incorporates additional features suggested by Osvaldo Sunkeld in his effort to explicate development of underdevelopment in Latin America. [15] It is a basis hypothesis of this book that this combination proves a useful guide to explain the way development in South Africa has fostered and shaped underdevelopment throughout the entire Southern

---

*Evidence indicated that the actual amount of weapons exceeded this dollar figure, which was written down to minimize U.S. intervention.

Chart 1:   MODEL of UNDERDEVELOPMENT

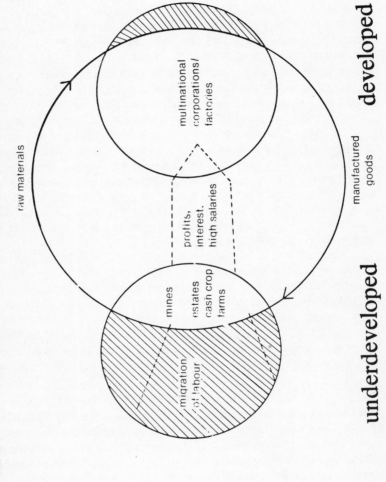

raw materials

multinational
corporations/
factories

profits,
interest,
high salaries

mines
estates
cash crop
farms

migration
of labour

manufactured
goods

developed

underdeveloped

African region. At the same time, it exposes the relationships between South Africa and the more developed nations of the west.

The model proposed may be depicted by a simple line drawing (Chart 1.1). The developed nations of Western Europe and the United States are shown as almost entirely and directly integrated into the capitalist world commercial system. Only a relatively small area (indicated by shading) remains underdeveloped, incorporated into the development process only marginally. It consists of the underemployed and, today, growing numbers of unemployed, whose impoverishment persists in the midst of the exponential growth of technology which has created the potential for the highest levels of living in history.

Less developed countries, like Africa, are, on the other hand only marginally incorporated into the world commercial system through so-called 'modern' export enclaves geared to production of raw materials for shipment to developed country factories to contribute to higher living standards there. This marginal involvement of the typical African state has not, as orthodox western economists predicted, stimulated a multiplier effect to spread development throughout the entire economy. On the contrary, the political and economic institutions imposed in the export enclave have fostered and sustained underdevelopment and external dependence on the developed nations.

The underlying explanation of 'underdevelopment' incorporated in the model is to be found in the manner in which entire regions have been shaped, historically, into extensive reserves of cheap labour for the foreign-owned mines and plantations, and, in some areas, African-owned cash crop farms,* which produce low cost raw materials for export. Almost all manufactured goods, especially capital goods for the raw materials-producing sectors and luxury items for the few who can afford them, have been imported. Pre-existing handicrafts industries have been stunted or destroyed by colonial restrictions and the import of mass produced goods. The bulk of the investible surpluses produced has been and continues to be shipped out of the country in the form of profits, interest and high salaries for the management of the foreign firms, trading companies and associated financial institutions which dominate the export enclave. Little has been left for investment in manufacturing and agricultural sectors to produce goods to meet the needs of the masses

---

*Primarily in West Africa, Uganda and Tanzania. Since independence, African-owned cash crop farms have been widely encouraged in Kenya, as well. African farmers in the Portuguese colonies were forced to produce cash crops for exports.

of the population. The entire political economy of the typical African economy has been shaped to be externally dependent on the sale of raw materials, the importation of manufactured goods, and the expertise and capital supplied by foreign firms which control the production and trade and siphon out the surpluses produced.

Post-independence strategies adopted by most African states have done little to alter this picture. African governments, accepting orthodox advice, have sought to build infrastructure and attract more foreign investment to build import-substitution industries. These have, for the most part, been relatively capital-intensive, last-stage assembly and processing plants. They produce a range of luxury goods for narrow high-income groups associated with export production, along with a few profitable mass-consumed items like beer, cigarettes and textiles. Increasingly, they package imported parts and materials produced by more basic industrial plants located in the developed countries. In effect, they ensure tariff-protected markets in the African nations for the multinational companies, which may, but do not necessarily, own shares in them. This pattern of 'industrialization' can only marginally alter the inherited pattern of external dependence suggested by the model.

It may seem at first inappropriate to use this model of underdevelopment to explain the events taking place in South Africa, the most industrialized nation in Africa. Official U.S. Government and United Nations documents separate South Africa from the rest of the continent. They place it in the category of developed nations because of its extensive industrial growth and high overall per capita income.

Closer scrutiny suggests, however, that the model does provide a useful heuristic guide for analyzing what is happening in Southern Africa taken as a whole. It helps to explain the underlying reasons why the South African regime imposes *apartheid* at home while at the same time seeking new ways to expand its ties with independent African regimes to the north.

It may be necessary to interpolate here a comment on the nature and role of this proposed model for analyzing southern African reality. The concept of a model, as here employed, is not one which seeks to encapsulate a static phenomenon. It does not attempt to picture some kind of equilibrium state, in the manner of models proposed by western orthodoxy. If it is to serve any function at all, it is as a guide for analyzing the dynamic, constantly changing phenomenon of the development of underdevelopment in southern Africa. The test of its utility is whether it is helpful in exposing the critical points at which contradictory tendencies give rise to and result from those changes which are taking place. In sum, the argument here advanced is that the proposed model is capable of contributing to the necessary understanding of the way the historical pattern of change has, over the last century, welded Southern Africa, in reality as well as for purposes of analysis, into what may justifiably be termed an 'underdeveloped' region. South Africa's advanced industrial sector, in this context, constitutes that marginal area within the larger region which is closely and directly meshed into the western commercial system. The foundation of South Africa's 'development' has been and continues to be the valuable mineral resources combined with the vast reservoir of low-cost labour provided by the systematic underdevelopment and impoverishment of the African populations, not only within its borders but also throughout the entire region.

The strategic geographical location of what has come to called 'South Africa' at the tip of the African continent, its rich agricultural and mineral resources, and its pleasant climate, early attracted foreign colonists. The production and export of minerals especially gold and diamonds, to the developed nations of the western world, made possible the accumulation of sufficient wealth by a handful of local mining finance houses to enable them to achieve a degree of financial independence from direct foreign control by the early 20th century They have, nevertheless, remained crucially enmeshed with foreign-based multinational corporations and financial interests. Foreign firms have always provided essential world market outlets for South African mineral wealth, the base of domestic capital accumulation. Increasingly, as more advanced, capital-intensive technologies have become essential, they have provided the source of technological know-how and the added foreign exchange needed to acquire them. Foreign firms have played a particularly critical role in facilitating the rapid expansion of manufacturing industry which has, in recent decades, made South Africa the most 'developed' nation on the continent.

South Africa's rapidly-growing commercial agriculture, mineral and manufacturing sectors have, however, never been hermetically sealed off from the underdevelopment by which it is surrounded. On the contrary, South Africa's particular distorted form of industrial growth could only have been achieved by the imposition of the conditions of underdevelopment which shape the impoverished lives of the masses of people within its borders and throughout the region. From the outset, the settlers and mine companies have depended on the imposition of laws and institutions which have forced Africans to provide a continuing supply of cheap labour. In South Africa itself,

Africans were forced off the best lands so that they could no longer adequately support themselves and their families. Throughout the region, in the colonial era, taxes, marketing systems and, in some cases, outright forced labour, gave Africans little choice but to trek to the mines and plantations to earn a little much-needed cash. Even after neighbouring countries have attained the trappings of political independence, the South African Government has, wherever possible, exerted pressures to elevate ruling elites to perpetuate a dependency relationship. This has not only ensured a continuing flow of migrant labour. It has also maintained the necessary markets and enabled South African-led consortiums to open profitable new mineral deposits to provide new sources of raw materials for South African manufacturing industries.

In short, South African agricultural and mineral wealth was a necessary but not sufficient condition for South Africa's industrial growth. The additional essential ingredient was the reservoir of low cost African labour. The African workers built the farms, the mines, the factories. The white settlers and foreign-based multinational firms, through which the regional economy was meshed into the world capitalist system, creamed off the surpluses.

The Purpose of This Book
The aim of this book is to try, within the framework of the overall contours suggested by the proposed model, to explain three phenomena which are critical to understanding what is happening in Southern Africa today and the implications of U.S. involvement there.

The first part seeks to examine the underlying characteristics of South Africa's political economy. These arise from and reflect the way the white ruling class, itself by no means monolithic, has over time alienated the masses of the African population from the land and forced them to provide the necessary labour force, first for the farms and the mines, and, more recently, for the manufacturing sectors. From the outset, the racist ideology of white supremacy, backed by repression and military force, was employed to justify the systematic imposition of this process of the development of underdevelopment.

The distorted form of South African 'development' has, on the one hand, led to the emergence of an increasing struggle by Africans for liberation. The Government has met African resistance by creating the myth of 'independent' Bantustans. At the same time, it has introduced still more repressive measures and built up its military strength.

On the other hand, South African industrial growth has increasingly become characterized by an inherent structural paradox. The Afrikaner Nationalist Party, which captured state power after World War II, systematically enforced the array of interventionist devices available to the state capitalist regime to foster rapid industrialization. It alternately coerced and enticed the mine companies to invest some of the capital accumulated by exploiting the African population, to build a modern, 'independent' industrial economy. As the manufacturing sector expanded, however, it inevitably began to confront the sharp market limitations imposed by the impoverishment of the masses of the African population. The underlying paradox of manufacturing growth in the midst of mass poverty has created an internal pressure, a source of internal instability, inexorably forcing the South African regime to seek to expand beyond its national borders.

Part II of this book is concerned with analyzing the historical roots and characteristics of this fundamental paradox.

The third part of this book examines the phenomenon of rapidly growing U.S.-based multinational corporate investment in South Africa, especially in the last decade. These constitute a major feature of the material U.S. 'interests' in Southern Africa cited by the U.S. Government's secret Memorandum 39. Their rapid increase reflects, in part, the changing relationships among the major western powers which dominate the world commercial system into which South Africa's 'developed economy' is intertwined.

In the decade of the 1960s, one African nation after another declared political independence from the British and French colonial empires which had ruled the continent for over half a century. The new states remained only partially tied into the trading and financial networks built up by the British and French firms during the decades of colonialism. U.S.-based multinational corporations and financial interests found it increasingly possible to enter new spheres of interest in Africa, from which they had previously been excluded by colonial policies. Apparently, however, they found white-ruled South Africa a more attractive base for their expanded activities on the continent.

Some of the largest U.S. firms had established a foothold in South Africa, although only marginally, long before World War II. British firms had remained South Africa's major foreign investor and trading partner throughout the quarter of a century following the end of the war. As Britain's own economy became weakened in the 1960s, U.S. corporate expansion became an increasingly significant feature of the South Africa economy. U.S.-based firms and financial interests, seeking new sources of mineral raw materials and areas of profitable investments, as well as markets for their expanded output of manufactured goods, began to multiply their investments and financial linkages there.

As in other former British colonies in Africa, U.S.–based firms have sometimes entered joint ventures with British concerns in South Africa, reflecting, in part, their growing penetration of the weakened British home economy. In other cases, they have made their own arrangements directly with South African Government and private mining and manufacturing interests.*

For the South African regime, U.S.–based multinational corporate involvement provides more than valuable capital and technological know-how. It also adds to the material base for extending official U.S. support for South African policies in the African and world political arena.

Part III seeks to expose the extent of this material base, the economic 'interests' which apparently lie behind what appears to be growing U.S. governmental support of the South African regime.

The fourth part of the book will outline the contradictory tendencies set into motion within the rest of Southern Africa as South Africa has extended its official policy of 'outward reach.' These tendencies vary from country to country, but reflect three underlying features.

First, the annual drain of labour, essential to the profitable expansion of South African mines and white-owned farms, has constituted a critical feature in the persistent and deepening pattern of the 'development of underdevelopment' characteristic of neighbouring countries.

Second, the expansion of South African-based mining and agricultural concerns has in no way fostered balanced national development in other nations in the region. On the contrary, it has warped their economies into a relationship of external dependency on the South African state capitalist structure, and through it into the western commercial system dominated by multinational corporate interests. The drain of profits, interest, and high salaries to South African and multinational firms has been a major feature in the persistent pattern of underdevelopment characteristic of the region.

Third, the need of South African manufacturing industries for

---

*Analysis of Latin American history after 'liberation' from outright European colonial rule in the 19th century exposes a parallel pattern of expanding US corporate involvement in that continent.

markets has led the South African Government to utilize a variety of techniques — from joint infrastructural projects and common markets to development loans and 'advice' — to open the doors of neighbouring countries to South African products. The resulting sales of South African manufactured goods in the neighbouring countries have hindered the construction of domestic industries which might have increased productive employment opportunities for the populations there.

The last chapter of Part IV is devoted to a more detailed examination of the complexities which have emerged in Zambia during the decade of political independence characterized by a declared struggle to escape from the dependency relationship inherited from the colonial era. In particular, the chapter focuses on the inadequacies of development strategies which left the national political economy dependent on the sale of copper, still mined and sold on an uncertain world market by South African-oriented multinational corporations. It exposes the way the rapid expansion of a bureaucratic-parastatal structure, built around the mines and the largest state-owned manufacturing holdings in independent sub-Saharan Africa, has fostered the emergence of a ruling elite linked to the multinational corporate world.

The fourth part of the book, in short, seeks to outline the implications of the contradictory tendencies that have continued to perpetuate the underdevelopment of the political economies throughout the Southern African region.

REFERENCES

CHAPTER ONE

1. E. Lockwood, 'National Security Study Memorandum 39 and the future of United States Policy Toward Southern Africa,' *Issue, A Quarterly Journal of Opinion*, published by the African Studies Association, Vol. IV, No. 3..Fall, 1974.
2. G. Hovey, *New York Times*, 1 April 1975.
3. G. Hovey, *New York Times*, 25 March 1975.
4. 'South Africa and the Walls of Troy', in *South Africa International*, Vol. V, No., 5, January 1975, pp. 116-7.
5. *Washington Notes on Africa*, (110 Maryland Ave., N.E., Washington, D.C. 20002) February, 1975.
6. Ibid.
7. W. Bissel, 'Hope Won't Make Cape Good', *Armed Forces Journal International*, November 1974.
8. *London Times*, 20 October 1974.
9. R.S. Cline, 'Erasing the 'C' in 'Covert': In omplete Se urity'. *New York Times*, 27 February 1975.
10. P. Geld, *New York Times*, 25 September 1975.
11. Ibid.
12. D. Binder, *New York Times*, 18 December 1975.
13. M.T. Kaufman, 'South Africa Impact in Angola Depicted', (dateline: Pretoria) *New York Times*, 24 December 1975.
14. A. Seidman, *Planning for Development in Sub-saharan Africa*, Dar es Salaam: Tanzania Publishing House, 1974), Chapter 1.
15. 'External Economic Relations and the Process of Development' (Chile: Facultad Latinoamerican de Ciencias Sociales, Santiago, mimeo, 1973).

PART II

The South African Sub-Centre

Chapter II

The South African Paradox

South Africa's population of over 24 million occupies a vast land area, some 471,000 square miles, almost as large as France, England, Italy and West Germany combined. Its extensive agricultural land and valuable mineral deposits have for decades provided foodstuffs and raw materials for peoples of Europe.

TABLE 2.1
POPULATION AND LAND AREA OF SOUTH AFRICA

Year	Area [000 sq. miles]	White	African	Coloured	Asian	Total
1960	471.5	3,088	10,928	1,509	477	15,944
1970		3,727	15,036	2,022	618	21,403
1974 (est.)		4,160	17,745	2,306	709	

SOURCE: *Quarterly Economic Review, Annual Supplement,* 1974; *South African Digest,* 8.11.74.

Yet the South African political economy is characterized by a paradox of rapid industrialization in the midst of mass poverty. Much economic theory would predict that, on the one hand, rising productivity and employment would lead to higher living standards, while, on the other, rapid industrialization could not take place unless the market simultaneously expands.

The explanation of this seeming paradox is to be found in the history of the evolving structure of South Africa's industrial ex-

15

pansion which has been fostered by and strengthens the oppressive racist regime. Concentration of industrial control and massive state participation have facilitated the mobilization of the investible surpluses necessary to industrialize. Heavy military expenditures and expanding export markets have, at least in the short run, filled the gap between growing production and the sharply limited internal demand. In the longer run, this paradox is a source of basic internal instability and pressure for expansion.

The High Level of Industrialization

The South African economy is, today, highly industrialized compared to most less developed countries. Its per capita income is over $1,120, the highest in Africa. It exceeds that of several European countries. The annual growth rate of the Gross Domestic Product has averaged 6 to 8 per cent over the last two decades, one of the highest in the Western world.

Manufacturing is the most important sector in the South African economy, contributing almost a fourth of the GDP. In the rest of Africa and Asia, in contrast, manufacturing characteristically accounts for less than fifteen per cent of GDP.[1] In South Africa, manufacturing's contribution exceeds that of the two primary sectors, mining and quarrying, and agriculture, forestry and fishing, combined.

TABLE 2.2
GDP BY KIND OF ECONOMIC ACTIVITY

	$m.	1966 %	$m.	1973 %
Business Enterprises:	$10,538	87.2	18,598	85.6
Agriculture, Fishing and Forestry	1,243	10.3	2,148	9.8
Mining and Quarrying	1,526	12.6	2,399	11.0.
Manufacturing	2,794	23.1	5,404	22.3
Electricity, Gas and Water	298	2.5	596	2.7
Construction (contractors)	484	4.0	1,025	4.7
Wholesale and retail trade, Catering and Accommodation	1,703	14.1	2,872	13.2
Transport, Storage and Communication	1,126	9.3	1,886	8.7
Finance, Insurance, Real Estate and Business Services	1,138	9.4	2,378	10.9
Community, Social and Personal Services	225	1.9	426	2.0
General Government	1,076	8.9	2,238	10.3
GDP at factor cost	12,088	100.0	21,733	100.0

NOTE: A rand, at the time of the preparation of these materials, was worth $1.49. In the fall of 1975, the rand was officially devalued to equal $1.14. Throughout this book, however, the rand is valued at $1.49.

SOURCE: South African Reserve Bank, *Quarterly Bulletin,* September 1974, No. 113.

The rapid manufacturing growth, which has taken place since 1946, is reflected in the shift of employment from the primary sectors into manufacturing, commerce and finance. The physical output, as well as the value of output of the manufacturing sector, doubled from 1966 to 1973.

TABLE 2.3

EMPLOYMENT BY SECTOR, 1946 AND 1970

Sector	1946				1970			
	Total	White	Africa	%	Total	White	African	%
Agriculture, Forestry and Fishing	1,547	168	1,268	37	2,239	99	2,814	28
Mining and Quarrying	498	54	441	12	767	63	605	8
Manufacturing	360	131	163	8	1,024	280	512	13
Electricity, Gas and Water	13	5	6	*	50	14	264	*
Construction	153	50	76	4	446	96	10	6
Commerce and Finance	249	140	71	6	906	419	349	11
Transport and Communications	207	123	69	5	338	164	140	4
Services	962	178	673	23	1,484	225	1,064	
Unspecified	232	39	137	6	732	38	624	9
Total Economically Active	4,221	888	2,905	100	7,986	1,497	5,605	100

SOURCE: South African Reserve Bank, *Quarterly Bulletin,* September 1974, No. 113.

The most rapid growth took place in heavy industry (excluding machinery) reflecting the increasing integration and potential self-generating capacity of the economy. It is estimated[2] that South Africa supplies 80 per cent of its own industrial plant. Heavy equipment is domestically manufactured for the steel, chemical, oil, plastics, sugar, cement, paper and brickmaking industries. South Africa manufactures hydraulic presses, coal loaders, conveyor systems, mechanized handling equipment, boiler and steam installations, automatic stokers for power stations, water treatments and sewage plants, and mining equipment.

South African industry manufactures relatively sophisticated equipment. A diffusion plant at Boksburg in the Transvaal is producing the first transistors to be manufactured in Africa for use in telecommunications.[3] By 1975, a factory had begun to produce complete tractors [4] (not merely assembly of imported parts as is the case in other African countries). South Africa has been self-sufficient in the production of railroad rolling stock since the 1960s. [5]

Capital investment has been increasing steadily. Annual gross domestic fixed capital multiplied from $423 million in 1945 to $7,016 million in 1973, about 24 per cent of the GDP. Investment in manufacturing increased to over 20 per cent of the total, while investment in the primary sectors, mining and agriculture, declined to about 10 per cent. The overall growth of the manufacturing sector's output has been characterized by the increased size of the average firm in terms of numbers of employees, average fixed capital, and average value of output per firm. The number of firms, on the other hand, has declined. This reflects the widespread introduction of high level modern technology, which increases the economic scale of operation of individual plants. At the same time, it has facilitated the increased oligopolistic control of industry.

TABLE 2.4

GROWTH IN SIZE AND AVERAGE NUMBERS OF EMPLOYEES

OF MANUFACTURING FIRMS IN SOUTH AFRICA, 1924-1968

Date	Number of Firms	Average Value of Net Output	Average Fixed Capital	Average No. of Employees	Average Amt. of Fixed Capital Per Employee
1924-5	6,009	$12,260	$14,900	19	$784
1938-9	8,614	$22,050	$20,900	28	$746
1954-5	13,725	$104,500	$93,900	48	$1,936
1967-8	13,142	$271,200	$256,300	80	$1956
% Increase 1924/5- 1967/8	119%	2102%	1620%	321%	309%

SOURCE: D. Hobart Houghton, *The South African Economy*, (Cape Town: Oxford University Press, 1973) Third Edition.

Specific new projects underway in the early 1970s included a $44 million paper mill complex near Durban to produce 25,000 tons of paper pulp and 34,000 tons of paper a year beginning in mid-76. A huge fertilizer plant was being built at Richards Bay, and a new 400,000 ton-a-year plant was brought on stream. A plant was opened to produce 163,000 tons of limestone ammonium nitrate annually. One company, Fedmis, planned to spend $94 million to build four nitric acid plants and an ammonia plant over a five-year period.[5]

The basic metals industry budgeted $1,087 million for capital expenditures in 1974, a figure seven times as large as that spent in the previous year. The metal fabrication and engineering sector alone expected to spend $240 million.[6] That one-year investment exceeds the total accumulated investment in the manufacturing sector of, for example, Tanzania.

Capital expenditure in civil engineering in 1973 reached about $1,490 million, almost double the 1970 figure. Profits had also risen appreciably.[7]

The rubber industry planned to spend at least $75 million over a five-year period to expand output of tyres and industrial products [8]

Profits in manufacturing industry in the last quarter of 1973 alone were $380 million, 50 per cent higher than in the same period in 1972. [9]

Low Wages

This major industrialization programme did not, as traditional economic theorists suggest, lead to rising living standards for the vast majority of the population. The incomes of the Africans who provided the labour to run the factories, the mines and the farms, remained a fraction of those of whites, barely enough for a barren subsistence.

The officially reported average wages of Africans in all sectors of the economy, including the public sector, remained below the Poverty Datum Line (PDL), the minimum income estimated as essential to survive in South Africa.* For the average African family of five to six members, this bare survival budget provides that almost three fourths of all income be spent on food — a significantly higher proportion than is spent by the average African family in independent African countries. [10]

---

*In one of the many ironies of the *apartheid* system, the University of Port Elizabeth set a lower PDL for Africans than for Asians or for whites. This was because the URP survey used Government nutritional data for the minimum food necessary. These date are differentiated by race. In other words, the African is supposed to need less food than an Indian or a white!

TABLE 2.5

THE ESTIMATED EXPENDITURE OF INCOME AT
THE POVERTY DATUM LINE IN SOUTH AFRICA, 1973
(in U.S. dollars)

	$	Percent of Total
Food	102.97	72.5
Clothing	12.91	9.1
Fuel and Light	3.74	2.6
Accommodation	2.80	2.0
Transport	7.61	5.4
PDL Excluding Tax	140.06	98.6
Tax	1.88	1.3
PDL Including Tax	142.94	100.0

SOURCE: Financial Mail, 4.5.73.

The South African *Financial Mail,* commenting on the PDL
Survey, observed:[11]

But even the minority of Africans whose wages are at the PDL
are living in pretty dire circumstances. For the PDL makes no
allowance for the purchase of things like furniture and
household utensils, doctors' and chemists' bills [or education
— for which Africans, though not whites, have to pay] and
many other items which any white household would consider
necessities.
It is generally conceded that if any kind of reasonable living
standard is to be reached, a family's income must be 150 per
cent of the PDL...

A document published in the early 1970s by the Cape Town
University Students Representative Council Wages Commission [12]
estimated the PDL at $104 a month for a family of six. Seventy-nine
per cent of the African wage workers did not earn that much.
Inflation has been pushing up living costs rapidly since then. In June
and July of 1974, consumer prices rose at an annual rate of 20 per
cent. Food prices rose at a rate of 43 per cent, [13] particularly affecting
the vast majority of Africans who spend most of their incomes on
food. The estimated PDL had risen to about $141 a month. Although
wages had also increased, largely as a result of many strikes in the
intervening three-year period, they had not nearly kept pace with
inflation. Overall, prices rose by 17 per cent in 1975.[14]

TABLE 2.6

AVERAGE MONTHLY WAGES, APRIL 1975

A. In U.S. Dollars.

Sector	WHITE 1974	WHITE 1975	Change	AFRICAN 1974	AFRICAN 1975	Change	COLOURED 1974	COLOURED 1975	Change
Mining	791	891	100	54	99	45	179	224	45
Manufacturing	636	729	93	121	147	26	161	186	25
Construction	612	703	91	113	142	29	223	270	47
SA Railways & Harbours	568	735	167	n.a.	n.a.		n.a.	n.a.	

B. As a % of White Wages:	AFRICAN 1974	AFRICAN 1975	COLOURED 1974	COLOURED 1975
Mining	6.8	11.1	22.6	25.1
Manufacturing	19.0	20.2	25.3	25.5
Construction	21.7	20.2	36.4	38.4

SOURCE: Cape Argus, 2 August 1975.

In manufacturing, cash earnings in 1975 averaged $729 a month for whites, but only $147 for blacks. Black wages, overall, averaged about 20.2 per cent of those of whites.

The wages on the gold mines are significantly lower than in manufacturing. This is partly because the workers are migrant contract labourers who sign up to work in a mine twelve to eighteen months at a time. They work sixty hours a week, without leave, away from their families the entire time. [15] About four out of five are immigrants from neighbouring countries. This renders it especially difficult for them to organize to demand better wages and working conditions. The result is an extremely high degree of control by mine owners, backed by their own police and security forces, and very low wages for African miners who do the work.*

The Chamber of Mines raised the wages of newly-recruited African miners to about $80 a month in the fall of 1975, specifically to attract more South Africans (as opposed to foreign migrant workers).[16] Surface workers' pay went up to $52 a month. The new black underground wages total slightly less than the latest increase in wage and benefits to white workers. The African underground workers, doing the most dangerous work, still earn less than two-thirds of the 1973 PDL. African surface workers get only a third of it.

*There has been much unrest on the mines, however, mostly traceable to low wages and unsafe working conditions.

Wages do not include the board and lodging provided by the mine owners. The lodging consists of barracks with tiered bunks made of concrete. The food is mostly maize porridge and costs under 6¢ a day per man.[17] Real wages on the mines in 1971 were actually considerably less than those paid a hundred years earlier. [18]

The gap between the wages of blacks and whites on the mines is worse than in any other sector of industry in the country, and it has been widening. The ratio was 9 to 1 in 1911, 11 to 1 in 1946, and over 20 to 1 in 1970.[19]

In one commercial sector, wages are even lower than on the gold mines. That is in agriculture. Black agricultural workers in South Africa are treated in many cases like slaves. Periodic exposes in the newspapers show the truly terrible conditions under which workers are live on the white farms, but no significant changes are made.

There are two million employees on farms in South Africa. Most are African. About 125,800 are Coloureds and Asians. Figures from the preliminary farm census of 1973 show an average wage for black farmworkers of about $17 per month. In the Transvaal, almost half the resident farmworkers get a sack of maize a month, a plot of land with a hut or two, water and firewood. Housing 'remains atrociously inadequate..:[20]

A World Council of Churches study, conducted in the late 1960s, reported [21] that farm labourers commonly worked 12 hour shifts, received no annual holiday, and could take time off only if another family member was available to replace them. The report added

The wage paid to a farm labourer in South Africa is but a small part of an entire system of humiliation, degradation and indignity which is a feature of his life. Reports of merciless beatings, of shooting and even killings by white farmers are frequent.

The South African Government has designed a complementary prison labour system to assure the white farmers of an adequate supply of workers despite these low wages. There are 22 farm jails in the country. An African arrested for any offence, however petty, may be sent off to work as a labourer on the farms, contracted by the state for six months or more, unpaid. His family is not told where he has been sent. At one point, the African National Congress staged a massive boycott of potatoes, because it had been discovered that prison workers on the potato farms of Bethal had been forced to dig potatoes with their bare hands.[22] Labourers are dressed in sacks, their passes taken so they cannot escape, and left to be 'disciplined' by the farmer as he pleases.

The result of low African wages is what might be expected: malnutrition, disease and death. In 1962, the South African Institute of Race Relations referred to findings that four out of five unskilled urban African workers showed 'signs of undernourishment'[2].[3]South Africa publishes no infancy mortality rates for Africans, but the Medical Officer of Health for Port Elizabeth reported in 1969 that a third of African babies die before their first birthday. In Johannesburg, estimates have reached as high as 600 out of a thousand.

The System of Apartheid

South African employers are able to pay these starvation wages in all sectors of the economy because of the rigorous maintenance of the system of apartheid. This system institutionalizes racial discrimination to keep African wages low, expecially on the farms and mines, while the average standard of living among the whites has been raised to among the highest in the world. There are two basic features of the system: job and living segregation of black workers from white, and the establishment of Bantustans and migrant labour.

Most blacks never even have an opportunity to prepare for 'white collar' jobs. Africans have to pay tuition in all schools, whereas whites receive their education free. Africans are restricted to the 'Bantu Education' system, specifically designed to educate workers for service in white-owned industry. While over half the whites are in 'white collar' jobs, only 5.4 per cent of the Africans can enter even the lower range of employment in this category. (See Table 2.7.)

This discriminatory pattern is extended to manufacturing jobs through the colour bar which explicitly reserves skilled and supervisory jobs for whites. This is reinforced by agreements between white workers and industrialists.

The distortion inherent in this pattern is illustrated by a survey of 1,106,000 industrial workers made by the South African Federated Chambers of Industry.

There were no African artisans or apprentices. Less than one per cent of the Africans were supervisors. Forty-three per cent were 'operators'. The rest were semi- and unskilled. By contrast, over a fourth of the whites were artisans, a quarter were operators, and almost six per cent were supervisors. There were no semi- or unskilled white workers. The biggest difference in incomes between blacks and whites is caused by this job segregation: 'The wage gap in the same or comparable jobs for blacks and whites is only [sic!] about 30 per cent of the white wage.' [24]

TABLE 2.7

JOB CLASSIFICATION, COMPOSITION OF WORKING POPULATION, 1970

Occupational Group	White 000s	%	Africans 000s	%	Coloureds 000s	%	Asian 000s	%	Total 000s	%
Professional and Technical	202	13.5	93	1.7	24	3.4	9	5.0	328	4.1
Administrative and Executive	69	4.6	3	*	1	0.1	2	1.1	75	0.9
Clerical Workers	419	27.9	96	1.7	37	5.3	26	14.4	578	7.2
Sales Workers	160	10.6	110	2.0	27	3.8	31	17.2	328	4.1
Sub-Total	850	56.7	302	5.4	89	12.7	68	37.8	1,309	16.4
Farmers, Fishermen, Lumbermen	97	6.5	2,051	36.6	124	17.6	6	3.3	2,278	28.5
Miners, Quarrymen, Transport and Communications, Production Workers, Artisans and Labourers	408	27.2	1,689	30.1	308	43.8	74	41.1	2,479	31.0
Service Workers	105	7.0	1,011	18.0	133	18.9	16	8.9	1,165	14.6
Not Stated	35	2.3	549	9.8	47	6.7	13	7.2	644	8.1
Total Economically Active	1,498	100.0	5,605	100.0	703	100.0	180	100.0	7,986	100.0

SOURCE: *South African Year Book, op. cit.*
*Negligible (under 0.1 per cent)

TABLE 2.8

JOB CLASSIFICATION

RESULTS OF A SURVEY OF 1,106,000 INDUSTRIAL WORKERS

BY THE FEDERATED CHAMBERS OF INDUSTRY

| | PER CENT OF JOB CATEGORY | | | |
	White	Coloured/ Asian	African	Total
Artisans/Apprentices	89.8	10.2	0	100.0
Supervisors	68.2	13.6	18.2	100.0
Operators	13.4	34.6	52.0	100.0
Semi-skilled	—	11.1	88.9	100.0
Others	59.3	16.6	24.1	100.0
Total	24.2	22.4	53.4	100.0

| | PER CENT OF OWN ETHNIC GROUP | | | |
	White White	Coloured/ Asian	African	Total
Artisans/Apprentices	26.1	3.2	0	7.0
Supervisors	5.6	1.2	0.1	2.0
Operators	24.3	67.7	42.6	43.8
Semi-skilled	—	14.5	48.6	29.2
Others	44.0	13.3	8.1	18.0
Total	100.0	100.0	100.0	100.0

SOURCE: S. Bisheuvel, 'Black Industrial Labour in South Africa', in *South African Journal of Economics*, Vol. 42, No. 3, March 1974.

*i.e. number in each job category as percentage of total employment in the relevant ethnic groups.

In short, black wages are held down by limiting the kinds of work blacks may do. The white workers get inflated wages, and unite with the employers to hold down African wages. In the mid-1970s, the employers, faced with a shortage of white skilled labour, began to change the job structure in order to permit blacks to enter a limited range of jobs formerly done by whites. With white union cooperation, they 'diluted' white jobs, that is divided them up into less skilled pieces, which Africans were then permitted to do for much lower wages.[25]

Bantustans ('Homelands')

The other main device for keeping down African wages is the migrant labour and Bantustan system. The apartheid regime has allocated less than 13 per cent of the entire national land for 'African homelands'. These areas include no major towns. Existing towns which would logically have been part of them were carefully excised out and reserved as part of the white areas. Large farms and major mining deposits have likewise been explicitly severed from Bantustan areas, leaving them oddly shaped and devoid of productive activity.

Africans constitute over 70 per cent of the population of South Africa, and provide over 77 per cent of the nation's workforce. Yet they are permitted to consider themselves 'citizens' of these fragmented areas, migrating to 'white areas' only to work for the cash they must earn to live. Africans may not stay in the white areas unless they have jobs. Even then, they are not allowed to own a home permanently, or, in most cases, to bring their families to live with them. Even if they have lived in a white area all their lives, they are not 'citizens' and may be deported to a 'homeland' they have never seen.

The apartheid system is enforced largely through pass laws. Every African adult must always carry a 'reference' book, or pass, which must be signed by an employer. If he is found without one by authorities, he is liable to criminal charges or deportation to the homelands. It doesn't matter whether he merely forgot the book, if he was leaving the house just for a few minutes. As might be expected, hundreds of thousands of Africans are prosecuted under these laws every year, an average of 1,370 every day in 1973 alone. [26]

The result of the Bantustan system is twofold: On the one hand, Africans must migrate to white areas for employment in the factories and mines or on the farms, but they are forced to leave their families behind in the 'homelands'. Despite their official status as 'homelands', only 46.5 per cent of the Africans lived in the Bantustans in 1970. That is, 6.9 million remained in the Bantustans while eight million were forced to leave to seek work in the white areas. [27]

On the other hand, the homelands themselves are desperately overcrowded and poor, incapable of providing an adequate livelihood even for those who remain there. In reality, they constitute little more than a vast reservoir for the reproduction of new generations of cheap labour for the white-owned factories, farms and mines. Conditions are what might be expected for the almost seven million people crowded onto eroded, fragmented land areas with no cities or industries. Population density in the Bantustans is twice that of South Africa overall. Income per capita is about one fifteenth of the rest of the country. The picture is one of vast rural slums. [28]

TABLE 2.9

BORDER AREAS AND HOMELANDS:

POPULATION, AREA, GDP, POPULATION DENSITY AND GDP PER CAPITA

(1965)

	Population [thousands]	Square miles	Population per square mile	GDP [Rm.]	GDP per capita [rands]
Tswana areas	439	12,679	34.62	16.0	36.45
South Sotho areas	12	182	65.93	0.5	41.66
North Sotholand	872	14,475	60.24	27.0	30.96
Swazi areas	50	600	83.33	2.0	40.00
Transkei and Ciskei	1,875	17,937	104.53	66.0	35.20
Zululand	1,334	12,183	109.50	40.0	29.98
Total 'Bantu' areas	4,582	58,056	78.92	151.5	33.06
Republic less 'Bantu' areas	13,285	413,989	32.09	7,175.0	540.08
Total	17,867	472,045	37.85	7,326.5	410.06

SOURCE: T. Bell, *Industrial Decentralization in South Africa* (Cape Town: Oxford University Press, 1973).

As early as 1932, the Native Economic Commission commented on the poverty of the land reserves. The overstocking of cattle, traditionally a mainstay of the African agricultural system, was already a problem.[29]

The basic Government document on Bantustans, the Tomlinson Commission Report published in 1956, found that thirty per cent of the Bantustans' land was 'badly eroded', and 44 per cent more was 'moderately eroded'.[30]

In 1972, it was reported that, in the Zulu areas of Natal.

If the factors of excessive slope and low rainfall alone are considered, about 70 per cent of the areas of the Bantustan reserves can be regarded as of poor quality and generally unsuited to cultivation. (see Table 2.10)

The Tomlinson Commission reported a per capita income of $71 a year in 1956 in the Bantustans. Of this 'about half' was remitted by migrant workers. This dependency is increasing. [31] A 1969 estimate gave the per capita income as $32 a year, of which $22 was in cash. Including remittances from outside, the figure is $78, which, given inflation, is considerably below the 1956 figure.[32] (See Table 2.11)

TABLE 2.10

AVERAGE YIELD OF MAIZE (KILOGRAMS PER HECTARE)

Year	White Farmers A	Africans in Bantustans B	B as per cent of A
1954/5	880	220	25.0
1955/6	922	146	15.8
1956/7	1 018	299	29.4
1957/8	848	212	25.0
1958/9	879	254	28.9
1959/60	911	212	23.3
1960/1	1.112	254	22.8
1961/2	1.229	187	15.2
1962/3	1.250	204	16.3
1963/4	847	180	21.2
1964/5	964	143	14.8
1965/6	1.085	194	17.9
1966/7	1.855	293	15.8
1967/8	954	159	16.7
1968/9	976	230	23.6
1969/70	1.186	230	19.4
1970/1	1.587	—	—

SOURCE: D. Houghton, The South African Economy (Cape Town: Oxford University Press, 1973).

TABLE 2.11

TRANSKEI — EARNINGS OF MIGRANT WORKERS
$ millions

	1960/61	1966/67	Increase
Gross Domestic Product	$59.7	$81.2	36.4%
Earnings of 'temporary migrants'	$66.2	$113.2	68.5%

SOURCE: T. R. Bell, Industrial Decentralization in South Africa: (Cape Town: Oxford University Press, 1973).

Surveys in the late 1960s and 1970s showed that almost 90 per cent of the households living in the Transkei and Ciskei were receiving incomes below the PDL. The average household income was barely more than a third of the PDL requirement.[33] In the Transkei, 60 to 70 per cent of the African children die from malnutrition before they are ten. In Vendaland, a 1962 report asserted that 'through lack of food, many people, mostly mothers and children, could eat only three times a week'. There is no reason to think there has been any improvement since then.

Father Cosmas Desmond, in his book, *The Discarded People*[34] vividly describes the consequences of the systematic impoverishment imposed on the Africans by Bantustanization:[34]

> Mr Botha, Minister of B.A.D., [the Bantu Administration Department] boasted at a meeting on 19 October that there was not one African in South Africa who was starving, and he added that the Nationalist Government would not let it happen. When one has seen death certificates with the cause óf death given simply as 'starvation', when one has seen hundreds of children in hospitals throughout the country too weak from starvation to stand, one is no longer able to feel anger at such claims — one feels an immense pity at the wilful blindness of these men in power.
>
> In Natal I told the people in one settlement what the Minister had said. They laughed. They were obviously starving. I asked if I could photograph some of them and they said, 'Take all of us, we are all starving. How could we be anything but starving in these conditions?' At another place, I met a woman of thirty-five who was admitted to hospital weighing 50 lbs. The nurses told me that she had been on the point of killing and eating her sixteen-month-old baby when she was admitted. In the same hospital I saw a fifteen-month-old baby weighing less than 10 lbs, and a child of five who weighed 20 lb. There were dozens of similar cases.

This is not happening in the Sahel, but in the most industrialized country in Africa, a country no longer included among the less developed nations by the United Nation's economists!

The Bantustans have another function, besides serving as a labour reserve. By requiring unemployed Africans to return to their 'homelands', the Government hopes to remove unemployed Africans and consequent unrest from the vulnerable cities where the whites live.

The degree of unemployment in the Bantustans in illustrated by the situation in the Transkei. The male population of working age is 355,000. In an area with no major industries or towns, only 105,000 of these people worked the land. The wage labour force thus came to 250,000. Only 41,000 could find jobs in the Transkei, mostly in government, commerce and domestic service. There were 155,400 migrant workers, mostly on the mines. Slightly over a quarter, 64,000 men, had no jobs at all. The MP for the Transkei constituency said:[35]

> You should have seen them outside the labour office in Umtata [the labour office organises contract labour]. They were not

there in hundreds but in thousands. I saw them myself, all clamouring to go out to work, because there was no work for them there.

As long as the new manufacturing industries were concentrated near the urban areas, Africans would be forced to migrate there to live in order to fulfil their function as labour. To avoid the danger of large concentrations of Africans so near the white centres, the Government initiated a programme of decentralization by encouraging firms to build new plants in the border areas near the Bantustans. They were not encouraged to invest inside the Bantustans, although the Tomlinson Report had specifically declared that investment there would be necessary to enable to homelands to become truly independent.*[36] (See Table 2.12).

The three Government agencies directed to try to facilitate industrialization in the Bantustans and the border areas (the Industrial Development Corporation, the Bantu Industrial Corporation and the Xhosa Development Corporation) have spent much more in developing the border areas than in the Bantustans directly.

The annual rate of investment in the Bantustans by both Government and private industry was estimated at 35 per cent of that in the border areas. In 1971, out of a total of $294 million spent by the Government as assistance to industries for decentralization, considerably over half, $194 million, was spent in 'white areas'.[37]

In the decade from 1963 to 1973, the Industrial Development Corporation spent $242 million to foster industrial development in or near the Bantustans. This created some 60,000 jobs, of which two thirds were for blacks. About 10 per cent of the sum was spent, however, to build housing for 'white key personnel'.[38] In 1974, the annual expenditure increased to $34 million. Of this 20 per cent was spent for white staff housing.[39]

The most important official measure designed to stimulate investment in the border areas was the abolition of minimum wages there. Corporations were able to take advantage of the desperation of the unemployed in the Bantustans to pay wages significantly below the national average. Wages in fifteen of the most important border areas of the Bantustans in 1974 ranged from $10.50 to $15 a week. (See Table 2.12).

---

*White entrepreneurs dominate the trade in the Bantustans[35] but they were not allowed to invest there until the mid-seventies.

TABLE 2.12

EMPLOYMENT IN THE BORDER AREAS AND HOMELANDS

Region	1959/60			1967/68			1969		
	No.	% of Border Areas & Homelands	% of Republic	No.	% of Border Areas & Homelands	% of Republic	No.	% of Border Areas & Homelands	% of Republic
Cape	18,788	25.8	3.03	29,867	25.4	3.02	33,635	25.6	3.07
Natal	39,181	53.7	6.33	63,609	54.1	6.43	68,657	52.3	6.27
Transvaal	14,994	20.6	2.42	24,101	20.5	2.44	28,926	22.1	2.64
Total Border Areas & Bantustans	72,963	100.00	11.79	117,577	100.0l	11.89	131,198	100.0	11.99
Republic of South Africa	619,111	—	100.00	988,969	—	100.00	1094,144	—	100.00

SOURCE: Compiled from unpublished information kindly made available by the Department of Statistics.

NOTES: 1. The economic Regions included in the provincial totals for 1959/60 are: Cape 16, 18—21; Natal 31—36, 39; Transvaal 46, 47, 51. The corresponding regions for 1967/8 and 1969/70 are: Cape 0504, 0602—0604, 0701; Natal 0902—0901; Transvaal 1101, 1104—1108.

2. Owing to difficulties in obtaining comparable data for all the years certain centres in the border areas and homelands such as Taungs and Warrenton in the nothern Cape, and all those in the Orange Free State, have been excluded from tne table. Since they are excluded for all years, however, the figures actually given are comparable. Inclusion of these centres in the 1959/60 figures raises the contribution of the border areas and homelands in this year from 11.79 to 12.2 per cent.

SOURCE: T. R. Bell, 'Some Aspects of Industrial Decentralization in South Africa', in *South Africa International*, Vol.5, No.1, July 1974.

TABLE 2.13

WAGES IN FIFTEEN PLACES DESIGNATED PRIORITY GROWTH POINTS BY

DECENTRALISATION BOARD (AVERAGE AFRICAN WAGE PER WEEK)

1974, in U.S. dollars

Transvaal:		Natal:		Cape:	
Brits	$13.40	Ladysmith	$11.92	Berlin-East London	$14.90
Pietersburg	8.90	Newcastle	13.40	Kimberley	12.13
Potgietersrus	9.69	Richards Bay	13.40	King William's Town	11.92
Rustenburg	11.98	Isithebe	10.43	Umtata	10.43
Phalaborwa	11.92			Butterworth	10.43
Babelegi	10.43				

SOURCE: Financial Mail, 30.3.74.

In the first ten years during which the 'decentralization' programme was in operation, some firms, attracted by low wages and other advantages, opened plants in the border areas. Although the absolute number of jobs there increased, the percentage of total national employment provided in those areas nevertheless shifted only marginally from 11.79 to 11.99 per cent.[4]

The unemployment prevalent in the Bantustans will not be relieved by programmes of this type, nor will any significant degree of industrialization take place there. The primary purpose of the Bantustans is to maintain a reserve army of labour, compelled to work for extremely low wages in the border and white areas, because the workers have no alternatives.

Increasing Resistance

The third essential and complementary feature of the apartheid system is the shaping of the entire governmental machinery to enforce oppressive laws designed to compel African compliance with it.

The Suppression of Communism and the Terrorism Acts label any attempt to change the *status quo* 'Communist' and impose heavy penalties. The Minister of Justice has the power to ban anyone he considers subversive. A person banned may not speak in public, see other banned people, attend gatherings or be published or quoted, and is confined to a stated area.

The '180-Day' Law permits imprisonment of any dissenter in solitary confinement on the order of the Minister of Justice for 180 days, to be renewed at his discretion. Under these laws, many African leaders and a handful of outspokenly progressive whites have been imprisoned: Nelson Mandela, Govan Mbeki, Walter Sisulu, Bram Fischer, and countless others. Their organizations have been outlawed. Hundreds of Africans have been banned, tortured, and murdered.

The law prohibits African unions from being recognized by the Government, as coloured and white unions are. Even unions with only a few African members are denied official recognition. African union organizers are harassed, jailed, banned and sometimes killed.

Nevertheless, several massive strike waves swept through the industrial and public service sectors in the 1970s. Hundreds of thousands of African workers participated. Many strikes involved thousands of workers at a time. Industrial unrest has become a feature of South African life.

As the South African *Cape Times* reported, at the end of 1972, '[T] his year has seen as much industrial unrest as last year — at a rough guess. More than 50,000 African workers have been involved in stoppages at an estimated 180 factories and organizations'. A Swedish team of investigators, following a thorough on-the-spot analysis, concluded the numbers of strikes involving African workers was far higher.

TABLE 2.14
WORK STOPPAGES, 1965-1973/4

Year	Number of Stoppages	Numbers of Employees Involved	
		Whites	Non-Whites
1965	84	2,688	3,540
1966	98	1,862	3,253
1967	76	657	2,874
1968	56	248	1,705
1969	78	207	4,232
1970	76	865	3,303
1971	69	255	4,196
1972	71	410	8,814
1973- June 1974[1]	246	—	75,843

[1] Information available only on African workers.

SOURCE: *Labour and Industrial Relations*, p. 16 (1965—72) and A *Survey of Race Relations in South Africa*, 1974, p. 325 (1973/74), compiled in *South Africa. Black Labour-Swedish Capital*, a Report by the LO/TCO Study Delegation to South Africa, 1975.

The South African Congress of Trade Unions, in a memorandum to the 1975 conference of the International Labour Organization,[41] reported that between September 1973 and March 1975, 131 black miners were killed in clashes on South Africa's gold, copper, coal and platinum mines, alone. They asserted that the so-called 'riots' and 'tribal clashes' on the mines were 'in reality an expression of the profound discontent of the African workforce and anger at their intolerable conditions'. In the second half of 1974, a total of 135 strikes involving African workers took place. Over the six months, July to December 1974, 52 people, 46 of them Africans, were shot dead by the police. Scores of trade unionists, black and white, who refused to collaborate with *apartheid* were placed under banning orders, prohibiting them from carrying on with their union work. The response of the Government has been to heighten repression and terrorism.

Even employers who might wish to recognize African unions have been forbidden to do so. To quote the South African *Sunday Times*.[42]

> Industrialists are being subjected to powerful pressures by the Government not to recognize Black trade unions and to sack Black workers who strike illegally.
> The pressures are being applied through the Department of Labour, the Security Police, and the Bureau of State Security (BOSS)... Mrs Harriet Bolton [a trade union leader] told me... Labour Department officials had urged employers to sack Black workers who strike illegally... Mrs Bolton said no fewer than 24 trade unionists in her union's buildings had been visited by Security Police or members of BOSS...
> The Minister of Labour, Mr Marais Viljoen, has warned employers to have no truck with Black unions... Mr Viljoen bluntly told employers that Black workers who went on strike illegally should be first warned, and then sacked, if they disregarded the warning... 'The Government is decidedly not prepared to recognize Black trade unions. This Government will not let itself be dictated to by outsiders or internal agitators.'

The Government has also tried more subtle measures. These involved setting up 'works' and 'liaison' committees. The aim of these 'reforms' has been analyzed by the South African Congress of Trade Unions (SACTU)[43]

> The Nationalist Minister for Labour, Viljoen, ordered the Wage Board to examine wage determinations and update wages, and a Bantu Labour Regulations Amendment Bill was

introduced... These 'labour reforms'... are designed to weaken the bargaining power of African workers. The establishment of thousands of works committees and liaison committees all over the country will fragment even further an already fragmented black labour force, thereby inhibiting the growth of trade unions and rendering unified strike action involving more than one factory almost impossible.

The Act entrenches the policy of treating African workers differently from workers of other racial groups.

The rapid growth of South Africa's manufacturing sectors in the post-World War II period has taken place in the context of a racist system which has compelled the African majority to provide labour at less than subsistence wages. Segregation, Bantustanization and migratory labour, enforced by governmental machinery at all levels, have forced Africans into a reservoir of unskilled labour from which there is no escape: their only choice is to work for the low wages paid or to starve.

There are the facts underlying the seeming paradox of rapid South African industrialization in the midst of mass impoverishment. How did this situation come into being?

REFERENCES

CHAPTER TWO

1. R.B. Sutcliffe, *Industry and Development* (London: Addison Wesley Publishing Company, 1971).
2. Da Gama Publishers (Pty) Ltd., *State of South Africa, Economic, Financial and Statistical Year Book for the Republic of South Africa* (Johannesburg: 1973).
3. Ibid.
4. *South African Digest*, 27 September 1974.
5. Da Gama Publications, *Industrial Profile of South Africa* (Johannesburg: H & G Dagbreek, 1966).
6. Rhodesian Farmer Publications, *Development Magazine* (Salisbury) September 1974.
7. Standard Bank Ltd., *Standard Bank Review*, October 1974.
8. *South Africa Digest*, 15 November 1974.
9. *Development Magazine*, March 1973.
10. Cf. Ann Seidman, *Comparative Development Strategies in East Africa*, (Nairobi: East Publishing House, 1972), p. 136
11. 4 May 1973.
12. Cape Town SRC, Wages Commission, 'Poverty, Our Concern, Our Responsibility', in UN Unit on Apartheid, Notes and Documents, No. 25/74.
13. *Standard Bank Review*, September 1974.
14. South African *Financial Mail*, September 1975.
15. See Francis Wilson, *Labour on the South African Gold Mines*, (Cape Town: Oxford University Press).
16. *Rand Daily Mail*, 29 May 1975.
17. Counter-Intelligence Services, *Consolidated Gold Fields Ltd., Anti-Report* (London: 1972).
18. Ibid.

19. F. Wilson, op. cit.
20. *Financial Mail,* 4 July 1975.
21. Counter Intelligence Services, *Business as Usual: International Banking in South Africa* (UK: 1974), p. 21.
22. Mary Benson, *The African Patriots* (Harmondsworth: Penguin Books).
23. R. First, S. Steele, C. Gurney, *The South African Connection* (London: Maurice Temple Smith, Ltd., 1972).
24. S. Bisheuvel, 'Black Industrial Labour in South Africa', in *South African Journal of Economics,* Vol. 42, N. 3, March 1974.
25. Cf. R.E. Braverman, in *African Communist,* 4th Quarter, 1974.
26. *Financial Mail,* 11 October 1974.
27. *South African Year Book,* op. cit.
28. Trevor Bell, *Industrial Decentralization in South Africa* (Cape Town: Oxford University Press, 1975).
29. Ibid.
30. International Defence and Aid for Southern Africa, *South Africa: The 'Bantu' Homelands,* by B. Rogers (London: 1972).
31. T. Bell, op. cit., Rogers, ibid.
32. *International Banking in South Africa,* op. cit.
33. Ibid.
34. Cf. Father Cosmas Desmond, *The Discarded People* (Harmondsowrth: Penguin Books, 1971).
35. International Defence and Aid, op. cit.
36. T. Bell, *Industrial Decentralisation in South Africa,* op. cit.
37. *Financial Mail,* March 30, 1973.
38. *South African Digest,* August 27, 1974.
39. T. Bell, op. cit., B. Rogers, op. cit.
40. T. Bell, 'Some Aspects of Industrial Decentralisation in South Africa', *South African International,* Vol. 5, No. 1, July 1974.
41. South African Congress of Trade Unions, *Memorandum Submitted by the South African Congress of Trade Unions to the 60th Session of the International Labour Organisation Held in Geneva, June 1975* (mimeo, 1975).
42. 3 March 1974.
43. SACTU, op. cit.

Chapter III

The Historical Roots

The peculiar historical conditions in which South African development took place shaped the emergence of a white South African capitalist class, increasing monopolization of industry, and eventually a virile state capitalism. The entire system was, from the outset, enmeshed into world capitalist commerce dominated by giant multinational firms. At the same time South Africa's nationalistic white rulers sought a degree of independence for their own expansionary enterprises.

This chapter examines the historical roots of the system, the emergence of the national white capitalist class, its international linkages, and its increasingly monopolistic control of industry. The next chapter will explore the reasons for and the nature of the state capitalism which enforced an oppressive racist political economic system on the working people, the African majority.

The Mining Finance Houses

South Africa's rich diamond deposits were first commerically exploited in the middle of the nineteenth century. The diamond mines, initially near or on the surface of the earth, were cheap and immensely profitable to operate. This attracted many poor white immigrants. From the outset, they used their influence with the colonial government to deny Africans the right to own mines. This, together with the hut tax which required Africans to abandon subsistence agriculture· and to work to earn cash, was the initial step in forcing Africans to

37

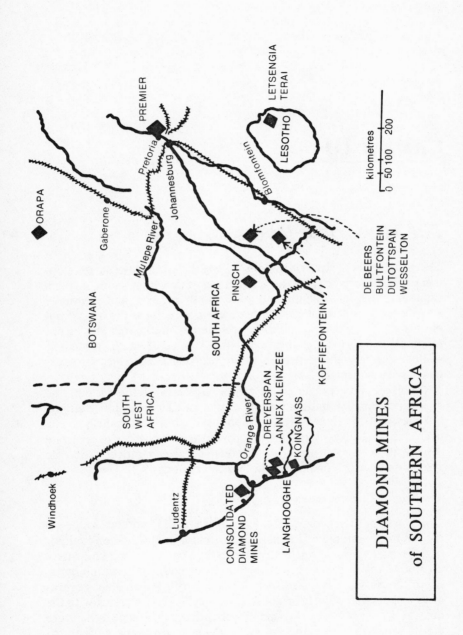

DIAMOND MINES
of SOUTHERN AFRICA

provide the necessary cheap labour to operate the mines at high rates of profit.[1]

As the surface diamond deposits were mined out, more capital-intensive methods were required to exploit those remaining. A handful of large, locally-based capitalist enterprises emerged with sufficient funds to purchase the needed technology. By 1887, the De Beers Company, headed by that swashbuckling adventurer, Cecil Rhodes, and the Kimberley Central Company run by Barney Barnato, dominated the field. The latter eventually emerged with De Beers.[2]

There was even then relatively little foreign capital in diamond mining. The mines were so profitable that the locally-based firms were able to finance themselves primarily from their own resources. It was estimated, just prior to World War II, that the total foreign capital invested in diamond mining was less than $50 million. The value of the diamonds sold had, by then, totalled almost $800 million.[3]

Unlike the diamond mines, the gold mines needed vast amounts of initial capital. But this was invested indirectly and remained under the control of local mining finance houses. Many of these were established. Over time however, as capital requirements grew, only a handful survived.[4]

TABLE 3.1

GOLD

	1970	1973	1974*
Net Gold Output (R millions)	837	1770	2,500
Contribution to GDP	5.7%	8.7%	8.9%
Government revenue from gold mining (income tax and lease payments)** (R millions)	117	456	750

SOURCE: Gerhard de Kock, 'Gold and the South African Economy — Some Recent Developments,' in South African Journal of Economics, Vol. 42,No. 3.

* Assuming an average price of $150 per ounce.
**Financial year.

As the South African Yearbook declares,[5] the gold mining industry is today 'controlled by seven major groups or financial houses'. These are Anglo American Corporation, Anglo Transvaal (Anglovaal), Rand Mines, General Mining and Finance Corporation (GM&FC), Johannesburg Consolidated Investments (Johnnies), Gold Fields of South African (GFSA, an associate of a British company, Consolidated Gold Fields), and Union Corporation, Ltd. Of the six major mining finance houses established before 1920, three were founded by South African diamond magnates (Rand

Mines-Beit; GFSA-Rhodes; Johnnies-Barnato); two were controlled by German banks; and one, Anglo American, was 'founded... with South African and an extra injection of British and American—capital' [6]

Most of the foreign capital available to the locally-controlled mining finance houses was provided in the form of indirect investment through the London Stock Exchange or the money markets in London, New York or continental Europe. As the South Africans themselves reinvested their profits into mining stocks, the relative proportion of local capital increased. [7] The percentage of mining dividends paid abroad steadily declined. In 1918, four out of every five dollars in profit was remitted abroad. By 1965 this had dropped to about one in four. In absolute terms, however, foreign shareholdings and remitted profits have increased as the mines have expanded. [8]

Not only are the mining finance houses large in terms of their extended investments in mining and other industries. They are so closely intertwined that to conceive of them as separate entitites would be entirely misleading. As the official South African Year Book observes, 'Cooperation between the individual groups is close, and directors are often exchanged'. [9]

A brief survey of the seven mining finance houses suggests the scope of their profitable operations in recent years, the amounts of surpluses they control for purposes of investment, and the degree of their influence in the overall South African economy.

Anglo American's Multinational Empire

Anglo American is by far the largest and most powerful of the South African mining finance houses. About 56 per cent of Anglo's shares are held by South African interests. A significant proportion of the rest are held in England but Anglo has close ties with the U.S. firm, Engelhard.(See pp.88 below).In 1974, Anglo's overal assets were estimated at over $7.4 billion. They equalled about 27 per cent of South Africa's total GDP. The parent company's own investments alone equalled $1.8 billion. The capital of the complex of mining, industrial and other kinds of companies administered within the group totalled over $5 billion more. Anglo produced 23 per cent of South Africa's coal and 25 per cent of its uranium. De Beers, the largest diamond mining company in the world and the largest company in South Africa, is a member of the Anglo-American group. Anglo owns about 30 per cent of De Beers. Anglo's Chairman, Harry Oppenheimer, is also chairman of De Beers. De Beers' mining subsidiary, alone, reported after-tax profits in 1973 of $372 million, more than double its 1972 returns. Anglo has, in recent years, become increasingly a part of the world network of multinational corporations. An outstanding example of this is Anglo's relationship with Charter Consolidated, a British group which acts as Anglo's agent in Britain, and with which Anglo has launched many ventures, both in South Africa and internationally. Charter owns 10 per cent of Anglo, and they are associates.

The estimated market value of Charter's total quoted and unquoted investments in 1973 were $778 million. About 11 per cent of these were in England, and almost half (45.9 per cent), were in South Africa. The remainder were scattered throughout Asia, Australia, North America, continental Europe and the rest of Africa. South Africa provided 44 per cent of Charter's investment income in 1973, followed by Zambia.

Anglo's partnership with Charter found expression partly in AAC of Canada Ltd., which was established in 1966 to consolidate most of Anglo, De Beers and Charter interests, including 'both direct and indirect investment in copper, zinc, cadmium, gold, silver, potash and uranium mining, chemical, crude oil and natural gas production and prospecting operations'. AAC Canada owns 34.75 per cent of Hudson Bay Mining and Smelting, 40 per cent of Francana Development Corporation and 10 per cent of Anglo Lake Mines Ltd.

Charter owns ten per cent of Rio Tinto Zinc. It also has interests worth over £250,000 (on 30 June 1974) but ten per cent or less of equity capital in: Falconbridge Nickel Mines of Canada; Alcan Aluminium; Union Corporation of South Africa; British Petroleum, 'Shell' Transport and Trading, Ultramar (which are all oil companies); Berelt Tin and Wolfram (Portugal); Atlantic Richfield, Exxon, Mobil Oil, Phillips Petroleum, Shell Oil, Standard Oil (Indiana); and Bethlehem Steel, among others.

Anglo-American owns 32 per cent common and 20 per cent convertible preferred stock of Engelhard Minerals and Chemicals Corporation (EMC), which markets ore and minerals, mines kaolin and other non-metallic minerals, and refines and manufactures precious metals for industry. EMC reported consolidated earnings of US $52.5 million in the year ended 31 December, 1973. [11] *

Another example is the Minerals and Resources Corporation Ltd, which is incorporated in Bermuda, and is a member of the Anglo

*For further discussion of this U.S. firm's linkage to Anglo, as well as its role in the U.S., see below, pp. 88 ff.

Chart 2: Structure of Anglo American Group and Its Major Associates

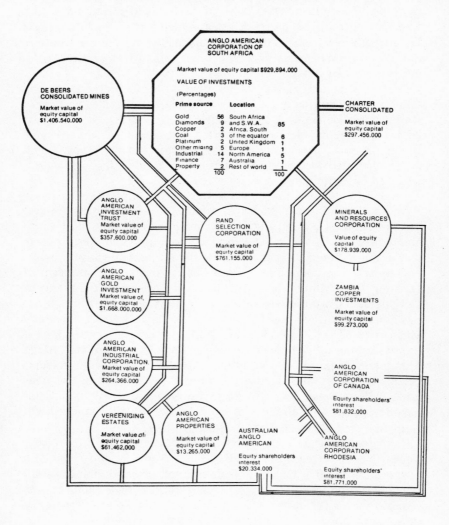

Source: Anglo American Corporation, *Annual Report, 1974.*

Group. Oppenheimer is also its chairman. This company owns 43 per cent of Trend Exploration Ltd., an unquoted U.S. company. Trend has 'a number of producing oil wells in North America and operates others... in Indonesia'. Taxed profits in 1974 were US $10 million.

Anglo is developing a gold mine in Australia through its subsidiary there. The mine is profitable only at the present high gold price. The mine's life should be only 28 months; it is to open within 18 months. Anglo is investing A$4.7 million.

De Beers has three subsidiaries in Ireland — De Beers Industrial Diamonds (Ireland) Ltd, Ultra High Pressure Units (Ireland) Ltd; and Industrial Grit Distributors (Shannon) Ltd.

Anglo is linked to other groups of international corporations through its directors. For example, Anglo's chairman, Oppenheimer, serves on the boards of Barclays Bank and the Canadian Imperial Bank of Commerce. G.C. Fletcher, a director of Anglo, Rand Mines, and GM&FC, is also on the boards of Rio Tinto Zinc, Société Nazionale Sviluppo Imprese Industrial, Société Financiere Louis le Grand; and Société Miniere de Martime. Dr. F.A. Zoellner, who is on the board of GM&FC, is advisor to the Dresdner Bank A/G.[12]

In short, the Anglo American Group is, in itself, a multinational corporation which, although based in South Africa, has investments in several continents through dozens of affiliates and subsidiaries. At the same time, it has direct links through its board of directors with some of the largest financial multinationals in the world.

The Other Giants

The second large mining finance house, Gold Fields of South Africa (GFSA) is even more closely intertwined with British interests than Anglo American. A British firm, Consolidated Gold Fields, holds almost half (49 per cent) of GFSA's shares. In 1974, over a fourth of Consolidated's profits of almost $100 million came from gold. Almost half were from South Africa.

GFSA, had investments of over $1 billion at market value in 1974, although its book value was barely more than a tenth of that amount. GFSA's consolidated profits for that year totalled $53 million, 145 per cent more than in 1973. The group operates seven gold mines and eight base metal and mineral operations, as well as various finance and property companies.

Gold Fields South Africa is an associate of Consolidated Gold Fields, a British company. GFSA's chairman is on the board of CGF, and CGF owns 49 per cent of GFSA. CGF has major holdings in 19 companies in Britain, 14 companies in Australia, Azcan Corporation in the US (85 per cent), and two companies in Canada.

The third big industrial group, the Union Corporation, held assets totalling $664 million in 1973, almost half again as much as those reported a decade earlier. It operates eight gold mines, along with a range of other activities. Reported after-tax profits were $41 million in 1973.

The Union Corporation acquired Bay Hall Trust in 1973, which gives it a direct interest of 30 per cent in Capital and Countries Property. This is a large real estate concern in England. Union Corporation also owns 30 per cent Minera Frisco SA, a Mexican mining firm; 14 per cent of British Acheson Electrodes; and $3\frac{1}{2}$ per cent of Hambros.

Johannesburg Consolidated Investments (Johnnies) is the fourth large group. Its net assets in 1973 were $588 million. Its reported after-tax profits were $23 million that year, up a third over the preceding year's.

TABLE 3.2
MINING FINANCE HOUSE INVESTMENTS BY AREA (%)
AND PRIME SOURCE

	Anglo* Amer	Union* Corp	Bar- low Rand	Con-** solid- ated Gold Mines	Johnnies**	Anglo* Vaal	Gen* Min
Year	1974	1974		1974	1973	1973	
Geographical							
SA & Namibia	81	93.7		49[b]			
Rest of Africa	6			26			
UK	1						
Europe	1	6.3		8			
North America	5			17[a]			
Australia	1						
Rest of World	1						
By Prime Source							
Gold	56	62.8		28	11.1	38	44
Diamonds	9	(d)			29.3		6
Copper	2	(d)		10	5.9		
Coal	3	(d)			4.8		6
Platinum	2	8.5		4	16.2		
Uranium		(d)					
Other Mining	5	5.5		9	3.0	27	(c)
Sub-Total	77	76.8		41	70.3	65	3
Industrial	14	10.0			24.7	31	6
Finance	7	11.5		35	5.0	4	41
Property	2	2.7					
Sub-Total	23	24.2		35	29.7	35	47

* Market of Directors Valuation of Investments
**Income from investments
a. Includes Asia
b. Includes all southern Africa
c. Under 'gold'
d. Under 'other mining'

SOURCE: Company Reports.

The total book value of the firth group, Anglovaal, is not quite $100 million. Its profits have averaged about 22 per cent over the last five years, totalling about $38 million before taxes in 1973: [12.]

The Barlow Rand Group, sixth of the big mining finance houses, had a turnover of about $875 million in 1974, and after-tax profits of over $55 million. The group was formed when a manufacturing conglomerate, Thomas Barlow and Sons, took over a mining finance house, Rand Mines, in 1971. Rand Mines had been directly linked with Anglo American's U.S. affiliate, Engelhard. (See below, p. 88).

General Mining and Finance Corporation, GenMin, or GM&FC, is the seventh group. It is in turn controlled by the Federale Mynbow Beperk Group, an Afrikaner group. GenMin held assets worth over $550 million in 1975. Its after-tax profit from subsidiaries alone was almost $27 million, while its income from investments was worth almost as much again.

The Interlinkages of the Mining Finance Houses

The giant mining finance houses are thoroughly intertwined at many levels and work closely together. Each group owns interests in many of the mines controlled by the others. For example, Anglovaal controls and operates five mines (there are over fifty), and has major interests in nine others. GM&FC has only one direct subsidiary gold mine, but administers or has portfolio investments in twenty five. Union Corporation admiinisters seven gold mines, but has major interests in eight others. This interlinkage extends to other kinds of mines and to manufacturing.

The largest platinum mine in the world, Rustenburg Platinum Mine, is 21 per cent owned by GFSA. Anglo has a major interest in both the parent company of the Rustenburg mine, the Union Platinum Mining Company Ltd and directly in GFSA. For its part,

CHART 3: Intercompany Linkages

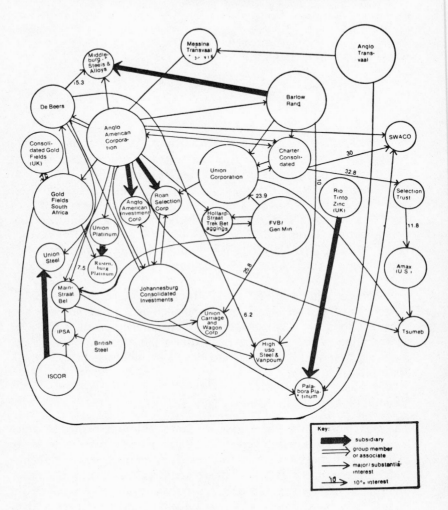

*Illustrates company linkages mentioned in text, only a few of the many which make up the network of corporate interests which dominate the South African political economy.

Source: Company reports..

GFSA has a 'substantial shareholding (but less than 10 per cent)' in De Beers Consolidated Mining Corporation, an Anglo associate, and also in Union Corporation. GenMin also takes part in the action: their share in Rustenburg (through Lydenburg Platinum Ltd and Waterval (Rustenburg) Platinum Mining Company Ltd) is 8.5 per cent. In addition, GenMin owns 29 per cent of Union Corporation.

Johnnies also has a 'major interest' in Lydenburg Platinum Ltd (as well as in two major Anglo subsidiaries — Anglo American Industrial Corporation Ltd and Rand Selection Corporation — and in De Beers.) This is not too surprising, for Anglo has substantial holdings in Johnnies. Johnnies and Anglovaal also both have major interests in Palabora Mining Company Ltd, an open pit copper mine managed by Rio Tinto Zinc. So do GFSA, Barlow Rand, and Union Corporation. Union Corporation has major interests in Charter Consolidated (Anglo's British Associate), and the Selection Corp., a member of the Anglo Group. Charter, in turn, has a major interest in Union Corporation. Barlow Rand has important interests in both Charter Consolidated and Union Corporation. Anglo American, in turn, has an interest in Barlow Rand.

Anglovaal and Anglo both have major interests in a coal mining company, The Messing (Transvaal) Development Company Ltd, which operates in Zimbabwe and South Africa.

Anglo has a considerable interest in GenMin through a company fromed by Anglo and Federale Mynbou, Hollardstraat-ses Beleggings (Eidendoms) Beperk. In turn, GenMin has shares in most of the major members of the Anglo Group. Among these are De Beers Consolidated Mines and the Anglo American Corporation itself. GenMin also has investments in Johnnies, GFSA, and Union Corporation Investments Ltd, a Union Corporation subsidiary.

The close links between Anglo and GM&FC are significant. Anglo's chairman, Oppenheimer, denies his associations with the Afrikaner Establishment, but the close relationship between his group and GM&FC shows that, where profitable transactions are involved, the gap is easily bridged.

The mining finance houses have, over the years, accumulated vast stores of profit. In the mid-1970s, however, when the world gold prices more than tripled, profits reached fantastic levels. In 1974, the profits of the gold mining companies soared to $2,340 million, almost two thirds of the companies' total income. The total wages bill, on the other hand, was only about 18 per cent of total mining company income. More than half of these wages were paid to whites, only slightly more than 10 per cent of the labour force. Non-whites, who constituted 88 per cent of the labour force, received only $302 million, less than eight per cent of the total company income. Their wages, in other words, were equal to only 12 per cent of total profits that year. [13]

The Mining Finance Houses and the South African Paradox

The mining finance houses dominate the South African economy. Their profits are huge and they have extensive international linkages. Since World War II, aided by extensive government measures, they have invested heavily in South African manufacturing industry.

The expansion of the mining finance houses, together with the peculiar circumstances of South African history, have contributed in several ways to shaping the paradoxical growth of manufacturing industry in the midst of the mass impoverishment of the black African population.

First, the mining finance houses combined with the white settler population to create the necessary conditions required to force Africans to provide cheap labour in all sectors of the economy. The gold mines, in particular, required a low cost labour force: [14]

> The [gold mining] industry was crucially dependent on huge amounts of cheap labour. South Africa's gold-bearing ore is so low-grade that the mines could never have been opened up if their labour force had to be paid 'European' rates. It is not just the rate of profit, but the very existence of the gold-mines... that has always depended on the exploitation, at below subsistence wage rates, of black labour.

The growth of mining in South Africa was accompanied by the rapid expansion of the white settler population. The initial white population consisted primarily of Afrikaners (Boers) whose forebears had come from Holland as farmers centuries earlier. New immigrants came, mainly from England, in hopes of getting rich quick by working on the mines. Today, Afrikaners constitute about two thirds of the white population. Many whites, especially the Afrikaners, were poor. They had evolved a peasant society in the 300 years they had been in South Africa. [15] Their farms, like the mines, were dependent on low-paid black labour. Without that labour, their primitive farming methods would have left them on a level no higher than that of African subsistence farmers. The white farmers used their political franchise to press for pass laws, and the whole repressive mechanism to force Africans to work for low wages. [16] This enabled the more powerful and wealthy among them to accumulate surpluses and ex-

CHART 4: Black Employment and Wages on South African Gold Mines

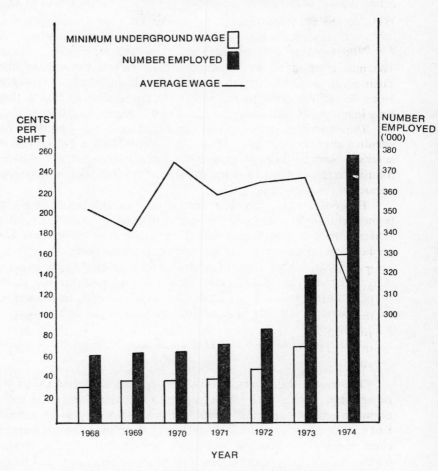

Source: *South African Journal of Economics*, Vol. 43, No. 1, March, 1970.

*South African cent = 1.5 United States cents

pand their farms. The small Afrikaner farmers who could not keep up were forced out of agriculture and entered the wage labour force in the cities. There, their lack of education and relevant skills hindered them from competing effectively against blacks. They too sought protection by law to preserve the more skilled, attractive jobs for themselves.

The Government, prodded by an electorate which excluded Africans, responded by institutionalizing racism through the imposition of the Colour Bar in all areas of social,political and economic life. Blacks were explicitly excluded from semi-skilled and skilled jobs on the mines, as well as on the farms and in manufacturing industry. The state corporations established in manufacturing reserved specific jobs for the whites only. [17] The Colour Bar had the effect of uniting white workers with the government and employers against the blacks, who were thus forced to work for less than subsistence wages in all sectors of the economy.

Secondly, gold played a crucial role in the development of manufacturing by financing the import of essential machinery, parts and materials. Before World War II, the manufacturing industry used 50 per cent of all raw materials imported. Its exports on the other hand provided only a tiny fraction, 2.5 per cent of the total exports. After the war, in 1946/7, raw materials imported for use in the manufacturing industry totalled $305 million while manufactured exports were worth only $105 million. This trade gap was made up by .gold exports.[18]

A director of Consolidated Gold Fields emphasized [19]

> The possession of an export article... with the attributes of gold, which all the world wants, is a great advantage to a young country. Gold as a final means of settling international indebtedness can enter through doors which import controls close to other commodities. And hence, from the establishment of the Union, South Africa could pay, without undue difficulty, for the capital goods it urgently needed to expand its total productiviy.

Third, the diamond and gold mines, together with the relatively large and better-paid white population,had, by the post-WorldWar II period, endowed South Africa with a larger market for sophisticated manufactured goods than existed in most other African countries. The average population of the independent African states of sub-Saharan Africa, excluding Nigeria, Ethiopia and Sudan, was about two million, less than half the four million whites in South Africa. The average per capita income of the typical African state was about $100, less than a tenth of the more than $1000 enjoyed by South African whites.

Finally, the accumulation of huge surpluses by the handful of giant mining finance houses enabled them to extend their domination to manufacturing. At first they invested in production of parts and materials required by the mines themselves. Over time, guided and assisted by government, they came to dominate every branch of manufacturing from breweries to steel-making.

Over the last several decades, as a result of their expansion into related fields, the mining finance houses have burgeoned into 'industrial groups'. Anglo American's Annual Report of 1973 describes the all-embracing character of these extended industrial empires:

> The term 'group' has a wider meaning in the South African mining industry than its statutory definition of a parent company and its subsidiaries... (The) parent house not only plays a role in the administration of companies that are not necessarily subsidiaries but provides them with a full range of administrative and technical services and is able, by virtue of its financial strength and standing, to assure them of capital for expansion and development.

As is the case with the mining enterprises, the affiliates of these groups represent the mixed interests of South African private and government, together with foreign, capital. They dominate the basic chemicals, metals, and engineering industry, the heart of the growing South African manufacturing complex.

One of the two most important chemical manufacturing companies in South Africa, for example, is African Explosives and Chemicals Industry (AE&CI) with assets of $1250 million at the end of 1973.[20] By 1973, AE&CI accounted for a fourth of the sales of chemicals and chemical products, and about ten per cent of fixed capital investment in chemicals in South Africa.[21] Its main products are explosives for the mines and chemical fertilizers. Harry Oppenheimer of Anglo is chairman of its board. AE&CI is owned 42.5 per cent by Anglo and 42.5 per cent by the giants British chemical firm, ICI. The remainder is owned by the South African public.

AE&CI is particularly important for the South African economy because of its heavy investment in Sasol berg. In this it cooperates with SASOL, the Government's chemicals corporation, using SASOL's basic chemicals output. (See below, pp. 63 ff.).

South Africa's chemicals industry initially developed in response to the stimulus from the mining sector. More recently, it has come to provide major fertilizer output for the agricultural sector as well.

AE&CI was formed from several smaller firms in the 1920s because the South African market was too small to support more than one major chemicals firm.[22]

The original participants were De Beers and Nobel Chemicals (a British firm) with capital of about $3 million. Nobel later merged with ICI. Originally the company produced only blasting explosives, detonators, some phosphatic fertilizers, and a few dips and sprays based on imported sulphur. There were three factories.

The company took over most small fertilizer importers.* They then invested in a plant, synthesizing ammonia from coal, $865,000— 'an enormous investment by 1930 standards.' Having a domestic source of ammonia 'would allow industrial expansion on a scale not dreamed of before'. [23] It made possible production of ammonium nitrate for blasting and nitrogenous fertilizers, among others.

AE&CI is now an important fertilizer producer. It is opening a new plant to produce limestone ammonium nitrate, and a 400,000 ton a year fertilizer plant in cooperation with another company, Fedmis. Triomf, a very large company in fertilizers, is 49 per cent owned by AE&CI, which supplies Triomf with locally manufactured urea, ammonia, and sulphuric acid. [24]

As in the case of the chemicals industry, the mining finance houses control that section of the basic metals industry which is not government-owned. They also have interests in the government's parastatals in that sector. Barlow Rand, for example, owns Middelburg Steel and Alloys. This company has four subsidiaries and supplied in 1970 over 18 per cent of the 'western world's' low-carbon ferro-chromium.[25] One of the subsidiaries is Southern Cross Steel, which operated the first stainless steel plant to be opened in South Africa (in 1967). Before Southern Cross opened, all stainless steel was imported. By the mid-1970s, it was producing about half the stainless steel consumed.[26] De Beers also has major interests in Southern Cross; Anglo has a large interest in Middelburg Steels and Alloys (as well as in Union Steel, a subsidiary of ISCOR, the Government Iron and Steel Corporation). Several of Anglo's directors are on the boards of Middelburg Steels and Alloys and Southern Cross Steel. [27]

Another conglomerate, Mainstraat Beleggings (1965) (Edms.) Bpk. was formed in 1965 by Anglo and the Federale Mynbou/General Mining Group (a member, with GM&CF, of the FVB Group)

* Among them was Rhodesia Fertilizer Company, 'with subsequent doubling of sales in that territory...'

primarily for investment in engineering and heavy industry. Its main interests are in Durban. Another company in which various groups have interests is Kohler Brothers (GenMin and Union Corporation).

The relatively smaller amount of capital required in light manufacturing industry has permitted the entry of more independent small firms than in the heavy industry. One needs only to look at the list of the mining finance houses subsidiaries, however, to realize that they dominate this field, as well. This is particularly true of Anglo American.

Harry Oppenheimer, Anglo's Chairman, likes to portray himself to the world as a liberal. He essentially runs the Progressive Party, the main white opposition to the Nationalists in power. He claims to oppose apartheid which, he asserts, [28]

is not just a policy of oppression but an attempt — in my opinion an attempt doomed to failure — to find an alternative to a policy of racial integration which is fair to both White and Black.

He insists that economic development will bring about the downfall of *apartheid:*

I have always thought that the rapid economic development of South Africa would in the long run prove to be incompatible with the government's racial policies...

He objects as strongly as any Nationalist to the effort to bring about the downfall of white minority rule by any form of international economic blockade:

How wrong-headed then are those who seek to help the Blacks by preventing the capital-inflow from abroad into South Africa, which is so necessary for their welfare.

Oppenheimer would be far more convincing if the many firms owned or controlled by his Group stopped provoking tribal fights among the workers on the mines, improved housing and paid better wages. What he does not recognize or more probably, what he is unwilling to admit, is that the entire system of *apartheid* has been intertwined with, and provided the foundation of, the peculiarly exploitative form of economic development which has fostered Anglo American's phenomenal growth.

Summary

The underlying explanation of the paradox of rapid industrial growth in the midst of mass impoverishment in South Africa lies in the peculiar historical circumstances which shaped the emergence of highly concentrated, intertwined mining finance houses headed by the Anglo-American Company. These, together with the Afrikaner agricultural interests, imposed the racist system of apartheid to ensure an adequate supply of cheap black labour, at the same time winning the political support of the majority of white workers by explicitly reserving for them the better jobs and higher incomes.

On the one hand, the creation of a relatively high income group among the whites, barely a fifth of the population, at the expense of the vast majority of blacks, provided a small initial market for locally-based industry. On the other hand, the accumulation of vast surpluses by the mining finance houses provided part of the necessary funds for financing the industry, simultaneously ensuring that they would dominate the resulting manufacturing growth.

The historically-shaped conditions laid a partial foundation for South African's mushrooming manufacturing industry after World War II. On this foundation, an alliance of white mining and agricultural interests, built a state capitalist regime which, despite surface conflicts and disagreements, stimulated and protected the emerging domestic manufacturing industries. This will be the topic of the next chapter.

REFERENCES

CHAPTER THREE

1. Cf. H.J. and R.E. Simons, *Colour and Class in South Africa,* 1850 – 1950 (Harmondsworth: Penguin Books, 1968).
2. R. First, C. Gurney, J. Steele, *The South African Connection* (London: Maurice Temple Smith Ltd, 1972).
3. Ibid.
4. Counter Intelligence Service, *Consolidated Gold Fields Anti-Report* (London: 1972).
5. Da Gama Publishers, *State of South Africa* (Johannesburg, 1973).
6. *South African Connection.* op. cit.
7. Ibid.
8. Ibid.
9. Da Gama Publishers, op. cit.
10. All information on mining finance houses is from the annual report of the company under discussion unless otherwise stated.
11. *Financial Mail,* 11 October 1974.
12. Consolidated Publishers, *Who's Who of Southern Africa* (Johannesburg, 1971).
13. *South African Journal of Economics,* June 1975, Vol. 43, No. 2.
14. *South African Connection,* op. cit. See also D. Hobart Houghton, *The South African Economy* (Cape Town: Oxford University Press, 1974) 3rd edition.
15. C.f Report of the Carnegie Commission on the Poor White Problem (Pretoria).

16. Ibid.
17. *South African Year Book,* H.J. and R.E. Simons, op. cit.
18. Houghton, op. cit.
19. W.J. Busschau, quoted in *CGF Anti-Report,* op. cit.
20. African Explosives and Chemicals Industry, *Annual Report, 1973.*
21. Da Gama Publishers, op. cit; Republic of South Africa, Department of Statistics, *Bulletin of Statistics,* Quarter ended June, 1973, Vol. 8.
22. AE & CI, op. cit.
23. Ibid.
24. Ibid.
25. Barlow Rand, *Annual Report, 1974.*
26. Da Gama Publishers, op. cit.
27. Combined Publishers (Pty.) Ltd., *Who's Who of Southern Africa.* Johannesburg, 1971.
28. "The Social Responsibility in Business", *Optima,* published by the Anglo American Corporation, De Beers and Charter Consolidated, Vol. 25, No. 1. October 1975.

Chapter IV

State Capitalism:
The Political-Economic Underpinning

South African Fascism

Over time, the white settlers in South Africa, particularly the more wealthy and powerful Afrikaner elements, succeeded in welding the majority of whites behind a powerful political movement built around the chauvinist ideology of white supremacy and centered in the Nationalist Party. They argued that South Africa should reduce its dependence on foreign capital by strengthening their national economic position, especially through the development of an increasingly integrated manufacturing base. Once they had captured state power shortly after World War II, the Nationalists declared this to be one of their primary objectives.

Because the mining finance houses had accumulated vast surpluses, South Africa was historically not confronted, as are most less developed nations, with a capital shortage. Since many of the companies were locally based, there was less of a problem of capital outflow. By the end of World War II, however, the economies of scale imposed by the modern technology available for manufacturing required not only vast amounts of capital, but also large markets capable of absorbing their output. Despite the high incomes of the white population, South Africa's market remained relatively small. From the outset, therefore, it was not sufficiently profitable for private entrepreneurs, domestic or foreign, to invest in manufacturing without extensive state support. Achievement of the Nationalists' goal of industrialization required extensive Government intervention. In this, the Government provided a willing partner to the mining finance houses as well as foreign interests, directly, by investing in industry itself, and indirectly, through import controls and tax incentives. In this respect, South Africa provides a classic example of state capitalism.

The South African Government provided the necessary protection for new industries. It directly financed and obtained the necessary technology for some of the critical basic industries in close cooperation with South African and foreign firms.

The Government introduced planning procedures typical of a state capitalist regime. It set targets in the *Economic Development Programme* for annual increases in production by sector. Increasingly, it emphasized the growth of basic, as opposed to consumer goods, industries. In 1973 it targeted a 9.5 per cent increase for basic steel products, 8.5 per cent for motor vehicles, 8.2 per cent for coal mining, 7.9 per cent for electrical machinery and 7.6 per cent for basic industrial chemicals. In contrast, clothing and mining (including gold), were to grow only 4.3 per cent. Although these targets were not all reached[1], they indicated the Government's expectations.

TABLE 4.1
ECONOMIC DEVELOPMENT PROGRAM OUTPUT TARGETS
(AVERAGE ANNUAL INCREASE, 1972 - 77, PER CENT)

Basic Steel Products	9.5
Motor Vehicles	8.5
Coal Mining	8.2
Electrical Machinery	7.9
Basic Industrial Chemicals	7.6
Paper and Paper Products	7.6
Transport Equipment (except motor vehicles)	7.4
Non-Electrical Machinery	7.0
Textiles	6.8
Clothing	4.3
All Mining, Including Gold	4.3
Overall Growth Rate	5.5

SOURCE: Economist Intelligence Unit Ltd., *Quarterly Economic Review Annual Supplement* 1974 (U.K.: 1974).

Import Controls

The Government has utilized the usual set of tools available to a state capitalist regime in an effort to stimulate the private sector to achieve the targets. One of the most important among these has been the exercise of import controls.

South African imports have been categorized into three classes. The first class comprises goods which need no import licenses at all (9 per cent of total imports); the second class needs a general license within a given quota (80 per cent of imports); the third class needs a special permit (8 per cent of imports).[2] This system, starting in 1949, has gradually evolved, changing to the extent that the planned targets have been achieved.[3] In the 1950s, favorable treatment was afforded to the import of capital goods and raw materials needed by the infant manufacturing sector. At the same time, certain consumption goods regarded as non-essential (such as foodstuffs, clothing and luxury items) were prohibited, providing a stimulus to the local production of them, as well as saving foreign exchange. The rapid transformation of the South African economy during the 1960s was facilitated by a commercial policy that assured substantial protection to the domestic manufacturing industry for an expanding range of goods and preferences for the import of required capital goods and materials.

By the early 1970s, this policy had evolved to stimulate basic industries, as contrasted to simply light consumer items. The percentage of the weight of cars, for example, to be locally produced was increased from 50 to 66 per cent.[4] Mere assembly was to be discouraged by taxation. The excise duty on cars which were not two-thirds locally made was raised from 15 to 20 cents per pound. Most manufacturers have, therefore, complied.

The same procedure has been applied to television sets, which are just being introduced (broadcasting started in January 1976). The import of complete sets is not allowed. The import of 240,000 sets (rather less than half of expected demand) in 'semi-knocked down form' was permitted before the end of 1975 to meet the initial demand. After that, all but 'special imported components, including colour tubes' are to be locally produced. Six local manufacturers have franchises already.[5]

How much of the industrialization resulting from import controls has been simply import substitution, and how much new industrial growth has expanded domestic markets and production, is difficult to ascertain. By the mid-seventies, South Africa did have a considerable amount of heavy industry, especially associated with production of mining equipment and transport facilities. At the same time, although consumer goods imports have declined the economy has become increasingly dependent on the import of capital and capital goods imports.[6] Machinery and equipment are the most important category of imports, excluding oil, for which no figures are given.[7] South Africa still has almost chronic balance of payments deficit. This remained true even when gold exports were included, although the rapid increase in gold prices in the 1970s became a significant off-setting factor.[8]

Merchandise imports in 1967 were worth $2893 million in 1967. Six years later, in 1973, they had almost doubled to $5,279 million. The trade gap widened in 1974, largely because of the oil boycott of South Africa declared in 1973. In the second quarter of 1974, imports were $8,516 million at a seasonally adjusted annual rate (exports were $5,003 million); in 1973 for the equivalent period they were $4,753 million (exports: $3,495 million).   The Economist reported that while oil prices contributed to the rise, imports of commodities and equipment also rose sharply. Steel imports were particularly heavy.[9]

Imports, excluding oil, were expected to maintain an annual growth rate of around 60 per cent for the rest of 1974 at least.

Direct State Investment

The second major technique by which Government has contributed to the expansion of the manufacturing sector has been through direct investment. Government's share in fixed investment in recent years has been almost half of all investment in the entire economy. Rather than decreasing as the manufacturing sector has grown, government investment has actually more than doubled since 1967. It has also increased as a per cent of total investment. Government investment in manufacturing alone in 1973 was almost seven times what it had been in 1967. This suggests that the growth of the South African economy in recent years has largely been by direct Government investment. Without this massive direct Government participation, it is highly unlikely that the South African manufacturing sector could have attained its much-vaunted high rate of growth.

Table 4.2 shows the latest available breakdown of investment between the private and public sector in detail.

The Government in South Africa, as elsewhere in former British territories in Africa, invests in manufacturing through parastatals (public corporations). The Government's overall holding company is

*These figures are merchandise imports and exports, which exclude gold. As gold is South Africa's largest export, that does make an important difference. Even with gold, however, the balance of payments is shaky. One authority writes that in 1969, it began to emerge as a real cause for concern... (Since 1970) exports actually declined in absolute terms, while imports began to rise at a high rate, resulting in a gap which became too large to be filled by gold and capital imports.'[10]

Table 4.2

GROSS FIXED DOMESTIC INVESTMENT IN SOUTH AFRICA

	1968 $m.	%	1971 $m.	%	1974 $m.	%
Gross Domestic Fixed Investment	3,486	100.0	5,632	100.0	8,738	100.0
By Public Authorities	1,199	34.4	1.984	35.2	2,787	31.9
By Public Corporations	381	10.9	533	9.5	1,193	13.7
Sub-Total	1,580	45.3	2,518	44.7	3,981	45.6
By Private Business Enterprises	1,905	54.7	3,114	55.3	4,757	54.4
In Manufacturing	588	16.9	1,004	17.8	1,814	20.8
By Private Business Enterprises	515	14.8	815	14.5	1,278	14.6
By Public Institutions	73	2.1	189	3.4	536	6.1
Investment by Public Institutions as % of total in Manufacturing		12.4		18.8		29.6

SOURCE: South African Reserve Bank, *Quarterly Bulletin*, September 1975, No. 117.

the Industrial Corporation of South Africa Ltd. This controls the Iron and Steel Corporation (ISCOR), SASOL (whose main factory is an oil-from-coal plant), and FOSKOR, which produces phosphates. A fourth company, the Industrial Development Corporation, is mostly involved in diverse manufacturing.

ISCOR. The most important of these state corporations, ISCOR, by 1973 was producing almost three fourths (72.2 per cent) of the steel consumed in South Africa, up from 68.4 per cent in 1972.[11] Almost a fourth (22.5 per cent) was produced by other South African companies. Only a little over five per cent was imported. (9.5 per cent was imported in 1972).

ISCOR produced 4 million tons of steel in 1973 at a net profit (before taxes) of $5.8 million. Its assets had increased by about a third to $1,604 million between 1972 and 1973, alone, an indication of the corporation's rapid expansion rate.[12] It should be noted that the profit rate of such a state corporation is arbitrarily determined by the prices it charges its customers. By holding its prices and profits low, (in this case it appears to be less than 0.4 per cent), a state corporation may subsidize private firms utilizing its output. Thus the Government waived dividends worth about \$13.2 million last year, so as 'to keep the domestic sales price of steel to a minimum'.[14]

ISCOR was founded in 1928. It was 'financed by the Government after private companies had shown little interest in this project, which was considered to be in the national interest'. Its first steel was produced in 1934.[15] Government owns 57 per cent of shares; the rest is held by the public. Four of the seven directors are appointed by Government, the rest by the other shareholders.[16] Its most rapid growth, however, occurred in the post-World War II period.

By the 1970s, it operated two large steel works, one in Pretoria, one in Vanderbijlpark. A new one at Newcastle, which it bought from Amcor in 1970, came into production in 1974. ISCOR is South Africa's only producer of tinplate, and works iron mines, dolomite quarries, coal mines, and tin and zinc mines. The iron mines are mostly at Thabazimbi in the Transvaal and Sishen; the colliery is in Natal, and the tin and zinc mines are in Namibia.[17]

ISCOR has been able to take advantage of the latest technological innovations as a result of its relatively late entry onto the world commercial scene. It has four LD basic oxygen furnaces in operation at the Vanderbijlpark and Newcastle works for steel production, among the first oxygen furnaces to be built in the world. The present LD plant at Vanderbijlpark cost \$59 million. When the third furnace is commissioned, it will be possible to produce about three million tons a year.[18]

ISCOR brought a hot strip mill on stream, with an annual capacity of two million tons, in late 1974. A new 900 tons-a-year cold rolling mill began production in mid-1974, reducing overall steel imports by 220,000 tons of hot and 240,000 tons of cold rolled sheets. The continuing expansion of the economy was, however, expected to require that total steel imports would increase to 770,000 tons, as compared with only 211,000 tons in 1973. Prices of imports are 70 to 150 per cent above prices of local steel,[19] partly because of tariffs and partly because the Government subsidizes ISCOR.

ISCOR plans to more than double its capacity in the ten year period ending in 1983. Its proposed new investments will total about \$3,725 million, including normal expansion of mine and quarry activities. Production is expected to rise from 4 million tons to somewhat over 10 million tons of raw steel.[20] To achieve this goal, the Government has agreed to increase its capital contribution by about \$240 million, which it will pay ISCOR at a rate of about \$30 million a year.[21]

Chart 5. Some of the Parastatals Established by the South African Government

SOUTH AFRICAN GOVERNMENT

CSIR — Technological research

Land and Agricultural Bank → Aid to white farmers

SASOL — oil from coal plants building another = 1,500 million various chemical plants

I.D.C. — Miscellaneous subsidiaries, including:
Dabama Textiles
So. West Africa Water & Electricity Corp (SWAWEK)
ALUSAP (tinsmelting)
FOSKOR (phosphates)
SAPEKOE (tea estates)
SAFMARINE (shipping)
Export finance
investments in Bantustans

ISCOR — Union Steel and other subsidiaries including:
50% Carbon Diamond Industries (tungsten, carbide metals & tools used by Iscor group)
Incor Zinc (Pty) Ltd
Ferrous Scrap Distributors
Durban Navigation Collieries
Various employee services & media for sales & distribution, including London office
UIS tin mine in Namibia

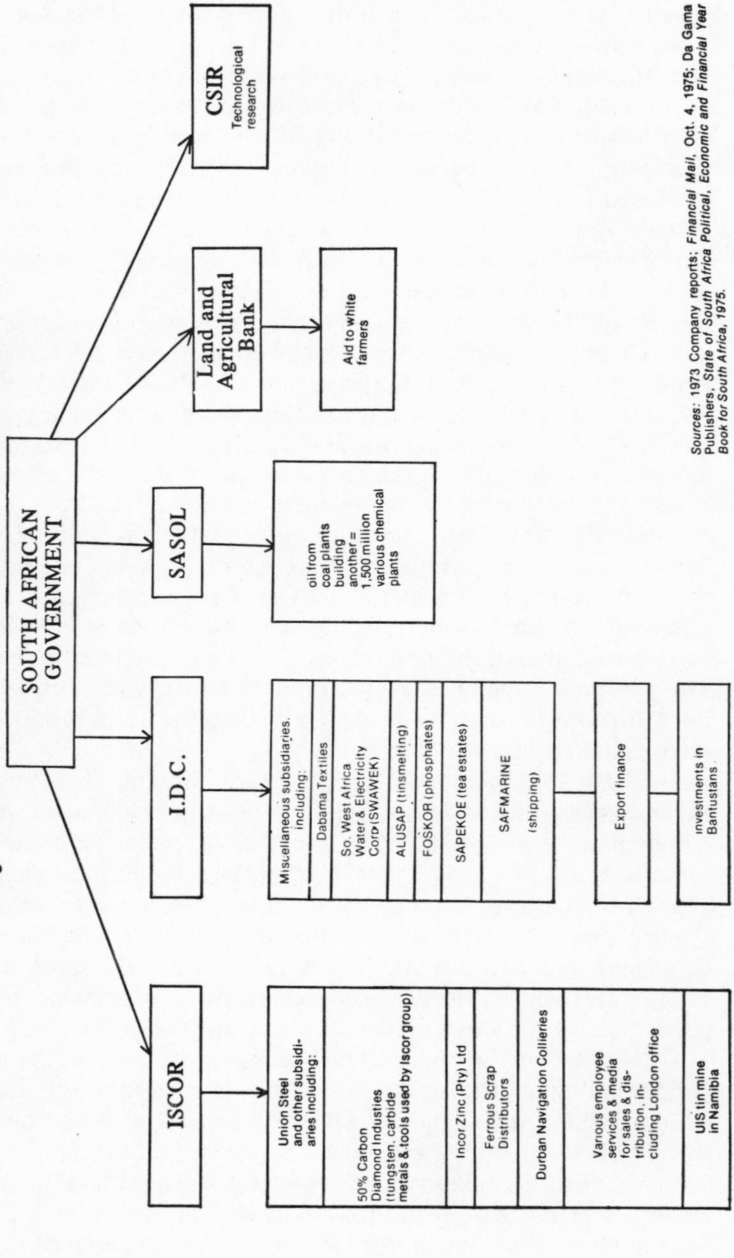

Sources: 1973 Company reports: *Financial Mail,* Oct. 4, 1975; Da Gama Publishers, *State of South Africa Political, Economic and Financial Year Book for South Africa, 1975.*

In addition, ISCOR is spending $58 million on a programme to make South Africa self-sufficient in coke. The programme includes the production of coke, coke oven gas, and by-products, to feed the extended iron and steel works. It is to be completed by 1977.[22]

ISCOR is instrumental in a Government plan to build a $1,600 million[23] plant in Saldanha Bay to produce three million tons a year of steel semis. It will employ 1,300 whites and 2,300 blacks. The ore is to come from Sishen. The plant will use two blast furnaces, three LD converters, three continuous casting plants, and one billet mill to roll continuously-cast blooms into billets. The project involves building an 853-kilometre railway from Sishen to Saldanha, and an increase in Sishen's output from three million tons to 15 million tons. It is to be operational by 1977. Most of production will be for export.*

AMCOR, another ISCOR subsidiary, was formed in 1937 and is centered in Kookfontein. It supplies the entire South African market for ferro-alloys, and exports them 'on a world-wide basis' . It also produces graphite electrodes for the South African market, fertilisers, phosphoric acid and sodium phosphates. It is adding new furnaces to its Kookfontein and Witbank works to meet local and export demand.[24]

A third major subsidiary is the Union Steel Corporation (USCO). This company, started in 1919, is the oldest steel company in South Africa. It is based in Vereeniging. It has two major works. The Vaal works produces most commercial quality steels and castings; the Klip works produces special steels and forgings. USCO is the largest producer of hollow drill steel in the world. In addition, it has various engineering subsidiaries. USCO's fixed assets in 1973 were worth about $80 million. It employs over 6,000 people.[25]

SASOL. Another important parastatal is SASOL (South African Coal, Oil and Gas Corporation). SASOL is particularly critical for South Africa in view of its efforts to become independent of the world oil producing countries. Using the most up-to-date technology, obtained in part from U.S.- based multinational firms, it operates the largest oil-from-coal plant in the world. By 1973, it was already producing 12 per cent of the country's oil requirements, about 250,000 to 285,000 barrels a day. About eighty per cent of South Africa's energy needs are directly satisfied by coal, so that its overall petroleum requirements are relatively lower than for most developed countries. The coal-from-oil process is rather expensive, so that the Government continues to encourage oil exploration. SASOL also produce products

---

*As part of its expansion programme, ISCOR is buying a $7 million computer from the U.S.

normally derived from crude oil, as well as other synthetic chemical compounds.[26]

SASOL was established in 1950. It was financed by private and state capital through the Industrial Development Corporation. The plant, located in a town named Sasolburg, came on stream in 1955. It expanded to convert imported naptha into ethylene for the plastics industry. In 1956, it opened a fertiliser plant capable of supplying almost half the country's nitrogenous fertiliser needs. SASOL also owns 50 per cent of a new oil refinery being built near Sasolburg. At present, two hydrocarbon synthesis processes are being used, one of American and one of German design.[27]

South Africa plans to build 'a second SASOL', ten times the size of the present complex, based on coalfields in the Transvaal. The $1,500 million project should be completed in six years. It will produce petrol, diesel, and petroleum products. South African Senator Horwood asserted it is the largest single industrial undertaking ever started in South Africa. Capital is to be obtained from the Strategic Oil Fund (which will mean raising taxes), export credit finance, and 'monies voted by Parliament'. The 'new' SASOL is South Africa's response to the oil boycott.[28]

As a basic chemicals plant, SASOL is intricately intertwined with and stimulates the rest of South Africa's manufacturing sector. It cooperates closely with private companies. As the South African yearbook declares [29]

It has always been SASOL's policy to stimulate, as far as possible, secondary manufacturing industries based on its products. The result has been the establishment of a number of industries in the close vicinity. This giant chemical complex includes factories for the production of compound fertilizers, poly-ethylene, PVC, cyanide, arctons, synthetic rubber and raw materials for the manufacture of soft detergent.

IDC. Of all the South African parastatals, the Industrial Development Corporation (IDC) has the most generalized functions. In several respects it was a forerunner and prototype of the development corporations which the British colonial government established elsewhere in Africa. It was founded in 1940 [30]

...to facilitate, promote, guide and assist in the financing of new industries and industrial undertakings and schemes for the expansion, better organisation and modernisation of, and the more efficient carrying out of, operations in existing industries and industrial undertakings...

The Corporation's initial capital was about $15 million. By 1970, its assets had multiplied almost 40 times to $563 million, almost two times the total assets of the independent Government of Zambia's industrial development corporation, even after that government took over 51 per cent of the major industrial firms. Its after-tax profits were about $12 million, a relatively low rate of return, which was justified by its role in facilitating new projects in critical sectors of the economy. It had participated in 1,250 industrial ventures, 'financing their expansion and growth to an extent of R 850 million ($1,266 million)'[31] Four years later, its after-tax profits had almost doubled to $23 million.[32]

The IDC was the basic impetus for the growth of South Africa's textiles industry in its early days. By 1970, the IDC subsidiary, the Da Gama Textile Company, held four textile companies. Two of these were to have expanded capacity 45 per cent by 1977.[33]

Since 1956, IDC has concentrated on export promotion as an essential prerequisite for the continuing expansion of South Africa's manufacturing sector. It has been designated to play an important role in the decentralization programme, promoting the location of new industries in the border areas near the Bantustans, described above (pp.30–32).

Safmarine. As part of its emphasis on export promotion, IDC has built up Safmarine, now one of its most important subsidiaries. Safmarine owns 37 vessels. These include two passenger liners, 18 cargo liners, two supertankers, and three tankers. It operates 31 chartered vessels. Its pre-tax profits in 1974 were about $28 million, more than triple their 1970 level.[34] It is introducing the most modern shipping technology by building up a fleet of container vessels. It borrowed about $220 million from a consortium of French banks, headed by Banque de l'Indochine, to buy four 50,000 ton celluar container ships.[35]

Soeker. In its role of promoting critical new projects, IDC joined Sasol to form Soeker, an oil-prospecting firm, to contribute to South Africa's efforts to reduce its dependence on oil-producing nations. Soeker was reported to have achieved some success in 1974:[36]

...international experts are confident that South Africa could find commercially viable pockets of oil.

The IDC more than doubled Soeker's financing from $11 million in 1974 to $30 million in 1975, because of the oil boycott.[37] Soeker also has a subsidiary, Swakor, which operates in Namibia, granting oil prospecting licences there. Swakor, too, is financed by the South African Government.

FOSKOR. In a third area, IDC established FOSKOR in 1951 to produce phosphates. Its initial capital of $1.5 million was multiplied to over $45 million by 1970. Prior to its entrance into production, South Africa had to import all its phosphates. By 1973, production of crude phosphate had risen to two million metric tons. FOSKOR planned to spend almost $60 million to increase production by over a third by 1976.[38]

ESCOM. Public utilities have always been state-owned and operated in South Africa, as they have in most other former British colonies. By the 1970s, ESCOM, the state-owned Electricity and Supply Commission, was supplying about four fifths of the electricity consumed in South Africa. It operated 19 steam power stations. It began construction of the largest coal-fired power station in the world, Matla, to be commissioned in 1978. Matla's ultimate capacity was to be 3,600 MW, with six generators. ESCOM is buying three 600 MW turbo generators from the British firm, Babock and Wilson, for $144 million. These were to be manufactured locally in part.[39]

ESCOM also began planning to build a nuclear power station near Cape Town, utilizing its own national, rich uranium reserves. It obtained the necessary technology for the reactor from United States companies (see below, p.93). Production was expected to be 1000 MW, at a cost of some $600 to $700 million. The first reactor was to be completed by 1982, the second a year or two later. The second reactor was to increase capacity to 2,000 MW, with the ultimate capacity expected to be over 10,000 MW.[40]

The South.African Railways and Harbours Corporation. The second major state-owned public utility corporation is the South African Railways and Harbours Corporation, which has built the most extensive railroad network in Africa. It has continued to expand its operations in the 1970s. It plans improvement in its marshalling yards along the Reef and Pretoria, as well as renovation of its rolling stock, at a cost of about $450 million.[41]

Other Government Intervention.   The South African Government had long extended its participation in the economy to the provision of credit to white farmers. It created the state-run Land and Agricultural Bank of South Africa in 1912 to advance funds to (white) farmers, cooperatives, agricultural societies and companies, and Government agricultural regulatory boards.[42] The bank is responsible directly to the Parliament through the Minister of Finance.

The Government makes a major contribution to the advancement and adaptation of technology in South Africa. It runs the Council for Scientific and Industrial Research (CSIR), with an annual budget of $10 million, and an initial capital outlay of $15 million. The scientific staff is 600; the technical administration, a thousand.[43] They are important in developing South Africa's military technology, besides more peaceful industrial development.[44]

Growing Government Debt

The Government's expanding investment in South Africa's industrial sectors has by no means been costless. It has been financed largely through increasing Government indebtedness. This more than doubled in the decade from 1965 to 1974 to over $1,500 million, equal to about 25 per cent of South Africa's total current Government budget in the latter year. About 95 per cent of these funds were borrowed domestically, which has contributed to the mounting inflationary pressures pushing prices up throughout the South African economy. In 1975, the Government planned to borrow another $1,700 million, of which an increasing share, 20 per cent, was to be borrowed abroad.

TABLE 4.3
THE INCREASING GOVERNMENT DEBT,
1965-1974

	1965 $mn	%	1969 $mn	%	1973 $mn	%	July, 1974 $mn	%	% Increase 1965-1974
Domestic	4,726	95.4	7,440	97.9	10,647	95.2	10,856	94.6	130%
Foreign	229	4.6	158	2.1	538	4.8	632	5.4	171%
TOTAL	4,956	100.0	7,596	100.0	11,184	100.0	11,479	100.0	132%

SOURCE: South African Reserve Bank, *Quarterly Review*, September 1974, (Pretoria: Government Printers.)

Government-Mining Finance Houses-Foreign Firm Linkages

In intervening in the critical sectors of the South African economy, the parastatals have cooperated closely both with the domestic mining finance houses and with foreign-based multinational corporations. The mining finance houses have provided some of the inputs and part of the necessary domestic finance. Their firms are often among the main purchasers of the parastatal output. The foreign firms, on the other hand, provide much needed up-to-date technology and additional finance, including essential foreign exchange. There are innumerable examples of the close community of interest created through this interlinkage. Only a few will be cited here.

Anglo American owns 15 per cent and British Steel owns 35 per cent of the International Pipe and Steel Investments (IPSA), the major ISCOR subsidiary in which ISCOR itself directly owns 50 per cent through its holding company, Metkor.

Alusaf, the aluminium smelter in Richards Bay, is a major state-private project owned jointly by the Industrial Development Corporation; the Swiss Aluminium Ltd, the Industrial Finance Corporation of South Africa; Alcan, the South African affiliate of the enormous multinational aluminum corporation; and the mining-finance house, Rand Mines. The plant processes imported bauxite, saving South Africa an estimated $20 million annually in foreign exchange. The total capital invested was about $90 million. The plant employs 300 whites and 500 blacks. [45]

Sentrachem, another parastatal, which together with Anglo's affiliate, AE&CI, controls four fifths of the South African market for chemicals, is 60 per cent owned by Central Chemical Investments. This latter holding company is jointly owned by BP Chemicals, and the Industrial Development Corporation. [46]

The Palabora Mining Company is linked with the ISCOR subsidiary, the Union Steel Company (USCO). Palabora supplies the crude copper part of which USCO processes into wire, and part of which it markets abroad. [47]

The leading shareholders in the Sarusa Development Corporation, along with the Industrial Development Corporation, are GM&FC, Sanlam and Volkskaas. The last two companies are Afrikaans-owned, and close to the Government. Sarusa, in turn, owns 40 per cent of Saruhar (Pty) Ltd., a fishing company. [48]

An underlying objective condition of this tight interlinkage of Government and private interests is, of course, their close technological-cum-economic relationship. To whom could ESCOM turn for coal for its new power stations if not to the big mining companies? GM&FC is investing about $60 million in a new colliery to supply the 9.6 million tons of coal required annually by ESCOM's giant new coal fired power plant. Anglo opened a colliery in 1968 to supply coal to ESCOM's Arnot power station, setting up the Anglo Power Collieries (Pty) Ltd., which then proceeded to open another mine to supply the Kriel power station when it was constructed. This is a profitable contract for Anglo's subsidiary, which sold 1.7 million tons of coal in 1973 at an after-tax profit of about $365 million, an amount which was expected to increase after renegotiations with ESCOM.

To cement this technical-economic-financial sphere of coordination, the Government-run parastatals share directors with the private companies. For example, the chairman of the FVB group, Dr P.E. Rousseau, is on the boards of FOSKOR, SASOL and Safmarine, and is a governor of the South African Reserve Bank. J. Ogilvie-Thompson, a director of Anglo, is also a director of Union Steel, as well as Johnnies, Rand Mines and AE&CI. E.P. Gush, a director of Anglo, Johnnies and GM&CF, is a director of USCO. C.G.F. Human, a director of GM&CF, and also of the West German firm, Siemens, is on the board of ISCOR. [49]

There are many more examples. Shared directorships form a network tying all the mining finance houses closely with the state-parastatal machinery.

Summary

South Africa came late to the industrial scene. The backbone of its prior economic growth had been exploitation of low-cost African labour to mine its rich mineral wealth by a handful of powerful mining finance houses. Despite the significant investible surpluses accumulated by the mining companies and its relatively large population, the impoverishment of the masses of the Africans narrowly limited its potential domestic market for manufactured goods. The Nationalist Party's 'solution' to this seeming paradox was for the Government to intervene, directly through its own investments, and indirectly through such devices as import controls, to create a hothouse environment for manufacturing production. In the process the Government parastatals involved in the growing manufacturing sector became increasingly intertwined with the oligopolistic mining finance houses as well as foreign multinationals.

The peculiar brand of state capitalism that emerged, however, had no pretence of welfare about it. The Africans were to provide the labour, the whites to benefit from the riches produced. In fundamental respects, the resulting system constituted fascism of a classic type. Georgi Dmitrov described fascism as 'the open terrorist dictatorship of the most reactionary, most chauvinistic, and most imperialist elements' of monopoly capitalism. [50] He was talking about fascist Italy and Nazi Germany, but it applies equally to the present system in South Africa. State and monopoly capital (in the form of the mining finance houses) are inextricable linked. As an 'open terrorist dictatorship' South Africa is unsurpassed.

REFERENCES

CHAPTER FOUR

1. The Economic Intellegence Unit Ltd., *Quarterly Economic Review,* Annual Supplement 1974 (London: 1974).
2. Da Gama Publishers (Pty) Ltd., State of South Africa, *Economic Financial and Statistical Year Book for the Republic of South Africa* (Johannesburg, 1973).
3. Ibid.
4. Ibid: also, D.H. Houghton, *The South African Economy,* (Cape Town: Oxford University Press, 1973).
5. *Financial Mail,* 17 November 1975.
6. Sean Gervasi, *Industrialisation, Foreign Capital and Forced Labour in South Africa* (New York: UN Unit on Apartheid, 1970).
7. *Financial Mail,* 23 May 1975.
8. Cf. Republic of South Africa, *Monthly Abstract of Trade Statistics,* (Pretoria: Government Printers); South African Reserve Bank, *Quarterly Review* (Pretoria: Government Printers).
9. Economic Intelligence Unite, Ltd., *Quarterly Economic* Review; Southern Africa. March 1974.
10. H.J.J. Reynder, 'Export Status and Strategy', *South African Journal of Economics,* Vol. 43, No. 1. March 1975
11. Da Gama Publishers, op. cit.
12. Iron and Steel Corporation of South Africa, *Annual Report* 1973.
13. Sachs, *Patterns of Public Sector in Underdeveloped Economics,* (Bombay: Asia Publishing House, 1964).
14. ISCOR *Annual Report,* 1974.
15. Da Gama Publishers, op. cit.
16. D. Hobert Houghton, *The South African Economy* (Cape Town: Oxford University Press, 1973), Third Edition.
17. ISCOR. op. cit.; Da Gama Publishers, op. cit.
18. *South African Digest,* 1 November 1974.
19. *Quarterly Economic Review,* op. cit., March 1974.
20. ISCOR. op. cit.
21. Standard Bank Ltd., *Standard Bank Review,* October 1974.
22. Rhodesian Farmers Publications, *Development Magazine* (Salisbury) August 1974.
23. *South African Digest,* 20 September 1974, & 4 April 1975.
24. *South African Digest,* 20 September 1974.
25. Da Gama Publishers, op. cit.
26. Ibid. *Quarterly Economic Review. Annual Supplement,* op. cit.
27. Da Gama Publishers, op. cit.
28. *South African Digest,* 13 December 1974.
29. Da Gama Publishers, op. cit.
30. The IDC of South Africa Ltd., 1940-1970, *Thirty Years on...* (Johannesburg: Hortors Printers, 1971).
31. Ibid.
32. Ibid; *Financial Mail,* 11 October 1974.
33. *Financial Mail.* ibid.
34. Ibid.
35. Ibid; IDC. op. cit.
36. *South African Digest,* 18 April 1975
37. *Johannesburg Star,* 27 July 1974.
38. Da Gama Publishers, op. cit.; Standard Bank Ltd. *Standard Review,* July 1974; *Financial Mail.* 11 October 1974.
39. African Research Bulletin, Vol. No. 10; *Financial Mail,* 11 October 1974.
40. *African Research Bulletin,* Vol. 11, No. 2
41. Ibid., Vol. 11.
42. Da Gama Publishers, op. cit.
43. Ibid.
44. Ibid.
45. Ibid.

46. *Financial Mail,* 18 October 1974; R. First, C. Gurney, J. Steele, *South African Connection* (London: Maurice Temple Smith, 1972*).*
47. United Steel Corporation, *Annual Report* 1973.
48. United Nations General Assembly, "Report of the UN Council for Namibia". *Official Records, 28th Session,* Supp. No. 24 (A/9024).
49. Consolidated Publishers, *Who's Who in Southern Africa* (Johannesburg: 1974).
50. G. Dimitroff, *The United Front: The Struggle against Fascism and War* (New York: International Publishers, 1938).

PART III

Penetration by U.S.-Based Multinationals

Chapter V

The Growing Involvement of
United States Corporate Interests

In the peculiar historical circumstances in which they have emerged, the mining finance houses, backed by the racist South African Government, attained a degree of political-economic independence from international capital needed to develop an extensive manufacturing sector significantly larger than that of any other African economy. It is apparent, nevertheless, that the oligopolistic companies and financial interests dominating South Africa remain extensively enmeshed into the multinational corporate world, dependent upon it for both finance and advanced technologies.

Until recently British companies and banks continued to provide the primary thrust of foreign capital on the South African stage. In the last decade and a half, however, outright British colonial rule, along with that of the French, Belgian, and, most recently, the Portuguese, has collapsed as one African state after another has asserted political independence. In this context, U.S.-based multinationals have begun to expand their ties, trade and investment, sometimes in consortiums with other foreign firms, in some cases in partnership with local government and/or private interests, in some cases alone.

By far the most important area of outright U.S. investment in the African continent is South Africa. The rapid growth of U.S. investment there, which has critical implications for the American people, as well as for Africa, will be analyzed in this part.

72

Option Two — Memo 39

Confronted by mounting opposition from African liberation movements, unable to rely on traditional British ties and support because of the impact of the monetary and commercial crisis on Britain's own political and economic climate, the oppressive South African regime has turned more and more to the United States for support. The United States Government, while still officially voicing abhorrence of *apartheid,* has been by no means unreceptive to South African blandishments. Secret memorandum number 39, prepared by the U.S. National Security Council in 1969 under the direction of Secretary of State Henry Kissinger, defined the alleged U.S. 'interests' in the region which, in view of subsequent events, appear to have been critical in shaping U.S. policy:[1]

> Our interests in the region are important but not vital. Our investments, primarily in South Africa, total about $1 billion[*] and our trade yields a highly favorable balance of payments advantage. This geographically important area has major ship repair and logistic facilities which can be useful in our defense forces. An important NASA space tracking station is located in South Africa...

Option No. Two of that memorandum, which events of the ensuing years indicate was adopted as policy, was based on the premise that

> The whites are here to stay and the only way that constructive change can come about is through them. There is no hope for the blacks to gain the political rights they seek through violence, which will only lead to chaos and increased opportunities for the communists. We can, by selective relaxation of our stance toward the white regimes, encourage some modification of their current racial and colonial policies, and through more substantial economic assistance to the black states (a total of about $5 million annually in technical assistance to the black states) help draw the two groups together and exert some influence in both for peaceful change. Our tangible interests form a basis for our contacts in the region, and these can be maintained at an acceptable policitical cost.

The study frankly admits that

> The current thrust of South African domestic policy does not involve any basic change in the racial segregation system...

*Note that this figure is larger than indicated for that year by official public reports of U.S. investment used throughout this paper, suggesting the possibility that the scope of U.S. investment may today in reality be significantly more than official data given below indicates, too.

There is virtually no evidence that change might be forth-coming in these South African policies as a result of an approach on our part.

The 'interests' which have fostered this supportive attitude towards South Africa, although 'not vital', involve some of the most powerful multinational corporations based in the United States. Their stake in the South African political economy has grown rapidly in the years since the National Security Council's secret memorandum was written. They have made a major contribution in bolstering the efforts of that country's racist regime to become a strategic economic, political and military base in the vast African continent.

U.S. sales to South Africa continued to grow in the 1970s at the very time when African states and the United Nations were calling for intensified political and economic action to end the racist regime's rule. By 1974, the U.S. had already become South Africa's third largest supplier, after West Germany and Britain, providing 16.6 per cent of South Africa's total imports. U.S. exports to South Africa continued to grow at a rate of almost 25 per cent in the first four months of 1975. They were expected to be worth $1.4 billion for the year, more than double the 1972 figure. [2]

This rapid expansion of U.S. trade both reflected and facilitated the expansion of U.S. investment in South Africa, especially in the manufacturing sector.

The U.S. Place in Overall Foreign Investment in South Africa

Official South African statistics show that all foreign investment has roughly tripled since the mid-1950s to almost `12 billion. About two thirds of this is direct long-term investment which gives foreign multinational corporate direct control over their business in South Africa.

U.S.-based multinationals have, however, expanded their investments in South Africa more rapidly than any others. They provided about a fifth of all foreign direct investment, second only to British firms, in 1972. Official South African data probably understates the role of U.S. multinational corporations in South Africa, however. As will be shown below, a significant share of U.S. investments are made through U.S.-controlled British affiliates or subsidiaries, as well as through other Western European firms.

Closer examination of the foreign investments in South Africa by area indicates that British firms still provide about over half of all direct long-term private investment, and only somewhat less of the direct short-term investment.

U.S. multinational corporations are predominantly committed for the long term in South Africa. Their investments make up 20 per cent of all the total foreign long-term direct investments. U.S. capital constitutes only about 10 per cent of total foreign non-direct investment. Western European-based multinationals, in contrast, provided only a tenth of the long-term foreign direct investment, and about a fourth of the short-term direct investment. Western European capital is far more significant in non-direct investment which does not provide them with outright control than in direct investment. It provided over 40 per cent of all foreign capital in the non-direct category in 1972. This suggests that European multinational firms and banking consortiums are more important in providing finance without as much direct control as U.S.-based multinationals exert in South Africa.

British-based multinational banking interests provided most (about 80 per cent) of the direct foreign central government and banking sector capital available to South Africa. Western Europe provided an important amount of short-term capital in this sector. It is perhaps most significant, however, that the International Monetary Fund was still, in 1972, providing almost 60 per cent of all short-term non-direct investment funds available to South Africa from the central government and banking sector. It reflects the supportive role played *vis á vis* South Africa by this official financial institution, controlled by the Western developed nations. In particular, the IMF provided a critical source of funds to offset South Africa's chronic balance of payments deficits.

It is also significant that, at the very time that South Africa was seeking to attract foreign investors, South African firms were expanding their investments in other countries. South African investment outside of South Africa itself totalled over $4 billion in 1972, equal to a third of all foreign capital invested in South Africa. It was more than twice as large as the officially reported total of U.S. investment in South Africa. This suggests that while the South African Government sought to attract foreign firms to contribute capital, technology, and, hopefully, political support for its domestic economy, oligopolistic mining finance houses were seeking new sources of profitable investment elsewhere. The implications of this are discussed more fully in Chapter 11.

The Expansion of U.S. Investments

South African Government and business circles have gone out of their way to attract U.S. investment in recent years. As was observed in

Fortune Magazine a few years ago, South Africa appeared to be a good business prospect to American firms:[3]

> The Republic of South Africa has always been regarded by foreign investors as a gold mine, one of those rare and refreshing places where profits are great and problems small. Capital is not threatened by political instability or nationalization. Labour is cheap, the market booming, the currency hard and convertible.

The United States Government, despite its declared official disapproval of *apartheid,* has actually facilitated U.S. investment in South Africa. George F. Kennan, U.S. author and statesman, has spelled out the rationale lying behind the U.S. Government's acquiescence to the exploitative South African system:[4]

> The wage disparities, as between Whites and Blacks, are of course, excessive and onerous and deserve prompt correction. But one must not forget that there are severe limits to the pace at which this correction could safely be effected. A sudden and complete removal of these disparities would unquestionably undermine the competitive viability of great sections of the South Africans' mining and industrial establishment, which now give employment to hundreds of thousands of black Africans, and would in many instances force the closing of the enterprises, with consequences disastrous to black African living standards.

This kind of rationalization is considered sufficient to justify U.S. efforts to encourage expanded private U.S. investment in South Africa. A study for the U.S. Department of Commerce, designed to attract potential investors to South Africa, asserts [5]

> The United States Mission in South Africa, and particularly the economic and commercial officers assigned to the Embassy at Pretoria and consular establishments at Johannesburg, Durban, Cape Town and Port Elizabeth, consider the rendering of assistance to present and potential U.S. investors to be a vital part of its task in the country, and indeed, this commands a considerable portion of the officers' attention.

Official U.S. data shows that United States investments in South Africa doubled in the five years after the National Security Council outlined U.S. political, economic and strategic interests in that country. By 1973, it totalled about $1,240 million, about a fifth of all reported foreign investment there, second only to that of the British. It jumped another 17 per cent to $1457 million in 1974, suggesting continued U.S. investor confidence in South Africa, despite the collapse of its Portuguese ally.

Although the kind of detailed data reported for 1974 (see Table 5.1 below) is not yet available for subsequent years, the estimated expenditures of majority-owned affiliates of U.S. companies for additional property, plant and equipment in South Africa indicate that U.S. investments there have continued to grow at an increasing rate.

TABLE 5.1

ESTIMATED EXPENDITURE OF MAJORITY-OWNED AFFILIATES OF UNITED STATES COMPANIES FOR ADDITIONAL PROPERTY, PLANT AND EQUIPMENT IN SOUTH AFRICA, 1973-1975

(In millions of US dollars)

Year	Total	Mining & Smelting	Petro- leum	Manufac- turing	Trade	Other
1973	200	10	D	81	28	D
1974	233	9	D	124	16	D
1975	241	20	D	127	18	D

NOTE D = suppressed to avoid disclosure of data of individual reporters.

SOURCE: U.S. Department of Commerce, Survey of Current Business, March 1975, Table 2C, pp. 22-23.

Added together, the 1974-75 estimated expenditures would have resulted in an almost 40 per cent increase in U.S. corporate investment in South Africa.

It should be re-emphasized that official U.S. data used throughout this chapter does not represent the full picture of U.S. involvement in South Africa. The expenditures data, for example, relate only to direct investments of majority-owned affiliates of U.S. firms. Expenditures of firms in which U.S. investment constitutes less than half are excluded. Furthermore, U.S. investment has increased in recent years in British firms, the traditional primary source of foreign capital in South Africa, ·as well as in other European-based multinationals.* There can be little doubt that U.S.-influenced or

*U.S. investments in Europe doubled from 1968 to 1973, totalling $37 billion. In the latter year, U.S. investment in England constituted almost a third of this amount. By 1974, U.S. firms owned about 50 per cent of the British auto industry, 40 percent of its computer industry, and 20 per cent of its pharmaceutical industry.[7]

controlled investment in South Africa is significantly greater than these official figures show.

Although officially-reported direct U.S. investment in South Africa constitutes less than two per cent of all U.S. overseas investment, the flow of U.S. dollars to that country plays a crucial role that cannot be measured in purely quantitative terms. On the one hand, they strengthen the influence and interest of U.S.-based multinationals in shaping the exploitative South African political economy. On the other, they contribute the capital, managerial skills and technology South Africa requires to build up its industrial base and expand its neo-colonial role in relation to its politically independent neighbours.

Almost four hundred U.S. companies are reported to have invested in South Africa to date. Many, if not most, are interlinked through ties among their U.S.-based parent companies and banking interests.

Thirteen of the largest of these U.S.-based multinationals play a crucial role in South Africa. Twelve of them alone supplied over three quarters of the U.S. capital invested there in 1972. The data as to the investment of the 'thirteenth giant, Union Carbide, is not available' [7]

These thirteen firms play a powerful role in the United States political economy, itself, as well as in South Africa. Between them, they own about 25 per cent of the assets of all U.S. industrial corporations. The produce about a fourth of the manufactured value added in the U.S. itself. [8]

These giant U.S. multinationals are closely intertwined with each other, as well as with most of the other U.S. companies which have invested in South Africa, through their boards of directors and banking ties. Most are grouped around the Rockefeller or Morgan interests. Although it has been argued [9] that these two groups may come into conflict, especially in the arena of the U.S. political economy, in Southern Africa they appear to have joined together at numerous points to expand their highly profitable business. These firms have, furthermore, sufficient contacts in high U.S. governmental circles to exercise significant influence in shaping official policy towards South Africa.* (See Appendix to Part III).

---

*Recent reports have exposed the fact that some United States firms with investments in South Africa have built up huge political 'slush funds', totalling millions of dollars, in secret numbered accounts in Switzerland, or in the accounts of subsidiaries' headquarters in remote places like the Bahamas.[10] Whether and to what extent these funds have been utilized to promote company objectives in South Africa has not been revealed.

Table 5.2

Estimated investments of thirteen large
U.S. Corporations in South Africa in 1972

Name of Firm	U.S. Owner(s)	Approx. Investment ($000,000)	% of Reported Total U.S. Investment in SA [a]	Rank Among U.S. Firms[b]
Caterpillar (Africa) and Barlow Caterpillar	Caterpillar	6.4	0.7	34
Chrysler South Africa	Chrysler	45.0	5.0	4
Firestone South Africa	Firestone	25 – 30[c]	3.0	37
Ford (South Africa)	Ford	80 – 100	11.0	3
South African General Electric	GE	55	6.1	5
General Motors South Africa	GM	125	14.1	1
Goodyear South Africa	Goodyear	15	1.7	14
IBM (South Africa)	IBM	8.4[d]	1.0	8
Standard Telephone & Cables (plus other companies)	ITT	50 – 70	7.8	9
3M South Africa	3M	12[c]	1.3	50
Mobil Oil Southern Africa, Mobil Refining Co., SA	Mobil	87[d]	9.7	7
Caltex Oil (South Africa)	Texaco and Std. Oil of California	103	11.4	6
Chrome Corporation (South Africa)	Union Carbide	n.a.	n.a.	28

NOTES: Total U.S. investment calculated at U.S. $900 million.
[a] I.e. Rank among U.S. firms in *Fortune's* list of largest U.S. firms.

[b] Estimated by CIS from available data.
[c] Figure from source other than company.

[d] SOURCE: *Church Investments, Corporations and Southern Africa*, p. 33.

Table 5.4 shows that U.S. investments have grown rapidly in the major sectors of the South African economy, and indicates their average rates of profit compared to the investments and returns in the rest of Africa.

This data, it should be noted, is based on questionnaires submitted regularly by the Department of Commerce to a sample of U.S. corporations with foreign investments. It is neither fully comprehensive, nor necessarily a completely accurate assessment of the

TABLE 5.3 U.S. INVESTMENTS IN SOUTH AFRICA

A. U.S. INVESTMENT IN SOUTH AFRICA COMPARED TO THE REST OF AFRICA
(in millions U.S. dollars)

	U.S. Investment in South Africa				U.S. Investment in Africa, outside South Africa			
	1968	1970	1973	1974	1968	1970	1973	1974
All Industries								
Book value at year end	692	864	1,240	1,457	981	2,612	2,830	2,223
Net capital outflows	5	44	80	153	303	319	-427	-364
Reinvested earnings*	26	52	148	136	45	105	177	220
Earnings	120	141	234	263	551	704	618	1,010
Balance of payments income to US	74	78	80	117	509	602	446	793
Mining and Smelting								
Book value at year end	78	90	158	(D)	309	350	397	442
Reinvested earnings*	-7	-2	8	8	9	27	15	(D)
Earnings	31	39	36	37	38	58	33	(D)
Petroleum								
Book value at year end	147	172	274	(D)	1,567	1,916	2,002	1,340
Reinvested earnings*	**	**	**	(D)	15	52	145	174
Earnings	**	**	**	(D)	501	594	548	915
Manufacturing								
Book value at year end	332	438	558	624	68	100	143	
Reinvested earnings*	16	30	61	67	4	7	-1	
Earnings	37	58	93	96	5	10	4	
Finance and Insurance*								
Book value at year end	*	*	*	37	*	*	*	54
Reinvested earnings*				-1				3
Earnings				4				6
Trade*								
Book value at year end	134	163	251	156	185	245	286	73
Reinvested earnings*	17	24	79	9	16	19	18	9
Earnings	52	44	105	18	6	42	33	14
Other*								
Book value at year end				51				113
Reinvested earnings*				(D)				1
Earnings				(D)				(D)

BV   RE*   E

BV   RE*   E

TABLE 5.3

B. U.S. INVESTMENT IN SOUTH AFRICA COMPARED TO THE REST OF AFRICA AND AS A PERCENTAGE OF OVERALL U.S. INVESTMENT ABROAD

	1968	1970	1973	1974
As % of U.S. Investment in Africa:	25.8	24.8	30.5	39.6
in mining and smelting	20.1	20.4	28.4	(D)
in petroleum	9.3	8.2	12.0	(D)
in manufacturing	83.0	81.4	79.6	79.6
in other				31.1***
in finance and insurance				41.1***
in trade				68.1***
As % of all U.S. Overseas investment:	1.1	1.1	1.15	1.2
in mining and smelting	1.5	1.5	2.1	(D)
in petroleum	0.7	0.7	0.9	(D)
in manufacturing	1.2	1.3	1.2	1.2
in other	0.3	0.2	0.3	2.5***
in finance and insurance				0.3***
in trade				1.4***
U.S. firms' profits in South Africa as % of U.S. profits in total Africa:	17.8	16.6	27.8	20.7
in mining and smelting	44.9	40.2	52.1	(D)
in mining manufacturing	88.0	85.2	95.8	90.1
in other	89.6	51.1	76.0	(D) ***
in finance and insurance				40.0***
in trade				56.2***
Rate of profit of U.S. investments in South Africa	17.3	16.3	18.8	18.1
in mining and smelting	39.7	43.3	22.8	(D)
in manufacturing	11.1	13.2	16.6	15.4
in other	38.8	27.0	41.8	(D)***
in finance and insurance				29.7***
in trade				11.5***
Rate of profit of US firms in rest of Africa	27.8	26.9	21.8	45.4
in petroleum	35.3	31.0	27.4	68.3
in mining and smelting	12.3	16.6	8.3	(D)
in manufacturing	7.3	10.0	2.8	6.2
in other	3.2	17.1	11.4	(D)***
in finance and insurance				11.3***
in trade				19.2***

NOTES: *'Reinvested earnings' represents US owners share in reinvested earnings of foreign corporations.

**Combined in other industries.

***Until 1974, finance and trade were included in 'other', as indicated. In 1974, they were separated out. The basis of calculation also appears to have been changed. So the results are not entirely comparable.

(D) Suppressed by source to avoid identification of specific companies.

SOURCE: US Department of Commerce, *Survey of Current Business.* October, 1971; October, 1969; August, 1974.

objective situation. [11] It seems unlikely, given the increasingly critical scrutiny of U.S. companies' investments in South Africa by shareholders** and public interest groups in the United States, that the companies have been completely candid about their South African holdings.*

Summary

A handful of the biggest firms in the U.S. have provided over three fourths of United States investments there. They are linked with each other, as well as with most of the nearly 400 other U.S. companies which have invested in South Africa, through their boards of directors. Their integration into the South African economy has been facilitated by their relationships with the two giant Rockefeller banks, which have greatly expanded their business in the area in the last fifteen years, particularly since the Sharpeville massacre. Their directors have extensive contacts with important U.S. Government circles.

Together, these firms comprised the growing 'economic' interest which, even when it was smaller, apparently helped to convince the U.S. National Security Council that the U.S. Government should maintain cordial relations with the South African Government in 1969. Today, their interest is far larger.

All but one of the remaining chapters of Part III aim to analyze in more detail the composition and role of U.S. multinational investment in South Africa's mines, manufacturing, oil and finance. They will indicate, too, the linkages of the largest of these firms to critical positions in the U.S. Government which enable them to exert extensive influence on critical policy-making agencies. The final chapter seeks to summarize the scanty evidence available relating to U.S. governmental efforts to influence the South African workers' reponse to U.S. investment in South Africa.

**The Council of Churches has played a major role in exposing the exploitative activities of these firms, and encouraging their members who hold stock to speak out at stockholders' meetings.

*This may also explain the increasingly frequent use of (D) in the Chamber of Commerce tables, especially for 1974, and after, indicating suppression of data to avoid identifying individual companies.

REFERENCES

CHAPTER FIVE

1. National Security Council Interdepartmental Group for Africa, *Study in Response to National Security Study Memorandum 39: Southern Africa.* AF/NSC—IG 69-August 15, 1969.
2. *Cape Argus,* 15.8.75.
3. J. Blashill, 'The Proper Role of US Corporations in South Africa', *Fortune,* July 1972, p. 49.
4. 'Hazardous Courses in Southern Africa', in *Foreign Affairs,* published by the Council on Foreign Relations, January 1971, Vol. 49, No. 2.
5. Cited in I. Mackler, *Pattern for Profit in Southern Africa,* (New York: Atheneum, 1975), p. 55, fn. 25.
6. Mackler, *op. cit.,* p. 79.
7. Corporate Information Centre, *Church Investments, Corporations and Southern Africa,* p. 64.
8. U.S. Bureau of Census, *Annual Survey of Manufacturing,* 1970.
9. V. Perlo, *The Empire of High Finance* (New York: International Publishers, 1956), pp. 136–139.
10. E.g., M.C. Jensen, 'How 3M Got Tangled Up in Politics', *New York Times,* March 9, 1975. See also reports in 1975 and 1976 of Gulf's involvement in politics.
11. Cf. Peggy Musgrave, 'Tax Preferences to Foreign Investment,Report to the Joint Economic Committee, Congress of the United States', *The Economics of Federal Subsidy Programmes,* Part 2, pp. 185-91.

Chapter VI

U.S. Investment in South African 'Strategic' Minerals

Key U.S. agencies concerned with strategic mineral resources have, in the last decade, increasingly stressed the advantage of expanding U.S. investment in South Africa to provide 'secure' sources of strategic minerals.[1] In 1970, the U.S. Congress established a National Commission on Materials Policy to formulate a national policy for 'national and international materials requirements, priorities and objectives, both current and future, including economic projections.'[2] The Commission's first report asserted that South Africa and Rhodesia were among the very few countries where U.S. firms could expect to continue to mine for strategic minerals. Its recommendations reflected its concern with securing investments abroad against possible expropriation, as well as reducing U.S. dependence on foreign sources of supply. In this context it concluded:[3]

> The list of historically politically stable nations where companies can expect to obtain suitable concessions for both explorations and mining as in the last 75 years is not long: principally Canada, Australia, South Africa and Rhodesia.

The United States does obtain some critical raw materials from Southern Africa through the activities of U.S. firms there. These include chromium (essential for making stainless steel); platinum, used in telephone and telegraph instruments, relays, aircraft magnetoes, vehicle and boat engines; asbestos, used for insulation,

TABLE 6.1

EXTENT OF U.S. DEPENDENCE ON SOUTH AFRICA FOR STRATEGIC MINERALS: KNOWN RESERVES; SOUTH AFRICAN PRODUCTION AS PER CENT OF WESTERN WORLD PRODUCTION; U.S. IMPORTS AS PER CENT OF TOTAL U.S. CONSUMPTION; IMPORTS FROM SOUTH AFRICA AS PER CENT OF TOTAL U.S. IMPORTS, 1974

Strategic Mineral	Known Reserves[a] as % of World Reserves in: SA	US	US Imports as % of Total US Consumption	US Imports from SA as % of all US imports (1972)	SA production as % of Western World's output	US Firms involved in South African Production
Chromium	65%	none[b]	100%	low carbon ferrochrome: 33% [c] high carbon ferrochrome: 42%	32%	Allied Chemical Corp. (through controlling interest in Montrose Exploration SA); Union Carbide Corp (through Chrome Corp. SA); Eastern Stainless Steel (through Southern Cross Stainless Steel, owned in partnership with Rand Mines (d)
Platinum	64%	4.8%	99%	18% (1972) 40% (1974) In 1974, SA became the 2nd largest source because it processed more of its output for direct sale (previously sold through UK)	85%	Rustenburg Mines, for which Rand Mines d is negotiating control.
Asbestos	6.2%	4.1%	over 85%	36%	13%	
Antimony[e]	6.9%	4.1%	85%	59%	31%	
Manganese	33%	none[f]	100%	36%	33%	

Strategic Mineral	Known Reserves[a] as % of World Reserves in: SA		U.S. Imports as % of Total US Consumption	US Imports from SA as % of all US imports [1972]	SA production as % of Western World's output	US Firms Involved in South African Production
Gold	61%	9.2%	60—80% of new ore	Most imports from Canada (49%), Switzerland (33%), USSR (9%); rest from 23 countries.	83%	Rand Mines[d] has controlling interest in six gold mines. Anglo American controls extensive mining interests.
Uranium	21%	29%[h]	Information not available	18% of all imported concentrates.[i]	14%	Anglo American produces about 22% of SA output; Rand Mines controls three uranium mines.

NOTES:

[a] Known reserves refer to those which have been proven to exist and which are exploitable at a given cost level; excluded are reserves which may cost too much to exploit with available technology or which may exist but are unknown.

[b] In 1974, 900,000 tons of low-grade chromite were commercially produced and used, indicating the possibility that the U.S. has reserves which have not been previously considered.

[c] The U.S. buys 10—20 per cent of its requirements from Rhodesia under the Byrd Amendment, which exempts the US from its commitment to the UN boycott of Rhodesia, despite the US agreement to it. In 1974, the US purchased 5 per cent of its low carbon ferrochrome imports and 6 per cent of its high carbon ferrochrome imports from Rhodesia. Rhodesia produced about 11 percent of the Western World output.

[d] Engelhard, an American, was chairman of Rand Mines' Board before his death.

[e] Other metals may be substituted for a number of its uses. Expansion of US production depends in part on solving costs of environmental protection.

[f] US has reserves which may be exploited at great cost, though improved technology might reduce the cost later; extensive deposits of manganese nodules are known to exist on the ocean floor beyond the continental shelf which require new technology to exploit, as well as resolution of complex legal problems as to ownership.

[g] Includes Namibian output.

[h] Much larger reserves are available at prices higher than $10 per lb.

[i] The US permits American firms exploiting overseas deposits a 22 per cent depletion allowance. As of 1977, the US will gradually permit domestic use of imported enriched uranium, previously prohibited; after 1983, there will be no restriction on use of imported enriched uranium.

SOURCES: US Department of Interior, US bureau of Mines, *Commodity Data Summaries*, 1974; Donald A. obst and Walden P. Pratt, eds., *US Minerals Resources*, Geological Survey Professional Paper 820, (US Govt. Printing Office, Washington, 1973); and US Dept. of Interior, *Mineral Yearbook*, Volume I (Government Printing Office, 1974).

textiles, plastics, vehicle and airplane production; antimony, used in lead, plastics, ceramics and glass; manganese, essential in stainless steel, metallurgical and chemical productions; gold, which is still key to the world monetary system; and uranium, which is the primary ingredient of nuclear projects for both peaceful and military use.

It should be emphasized, however, that in the metals business, reserves are discovered and mines established partly because of accidents of history as well as their relative profitability. Expansion of U.S. purchases of strategic metals from South Africa has taken place in large part becauseU.S.firms have built up their contacts with South African mining houses which have been in the business of mineral production over a prolonged period of time. South Africa, because of the early and profitable mineral discoveries and extensive settler population, has been far more extensively surveyed geologically than the rest of Africa. In 1958, just before African governments began to attain independence, only about 10 per cent of the continent had been surveyed.[4] In recent years, new deposits of a wide range of valuable minerals have been discovered, as the new African governments have begun to invest in the necessary systematic exploration.

The African governments have sought to obtain a greater share of the wealth produced by their mines by a variety of devices, including better wages for their employees, higher taxes, and, in the late 1960s and 1970s, government acquisition of shares, as well as some forms of participation in management and marketing. The South African Government, in contrast, uses its state police power to herd African miners into camps and to keep them at work during the life of their contract, while the companies are given a free hand to maximize their profits. U.S. firms have apparently preferred to expand their investments in this environment.

As a result, although U.S. investment has continued to grow in independent African countries in absolute terms, it has grown much more rapidly in relative terms in South Africa. U.S. investment in South African mines and smelters doubled from about $78 million to $158 million in the few short years from 1968 to 1973, rising from 20 to 28 per cent of all U.S. investment in this sector in Africa. The resulting rate of profit of U.S. mining firms in South Africa in 1973 was, on the average, almost three times that of U.S. mining firms in the rest of Africa. In 1974, the data on U.S. investment in South Africa was suppressed by the U.S. Dept. of Commerce to avoid disclosure of data relating to individual firms.

A relatively few U.S. firms are deeply involved in the business of mining and smelting in Southern Africa. They exert significant influence in South Africa as well as in the United States. They have typically participated in joint ventures with the powerful South African mining finance houses. They are so intertwined with the mining finance houses that it is sometimes difficult to determine whether the U.S. or South African firms are dominant. At the same time, key members of their boards provide direct links with the U.S. Government, where they are able to perpetuate the illusion that the U.S. does have strategic interests in South Africa.

U.S. firms contribute capital and some management to the South African mining finance houses. More importantly, perhaps, they provide the most up-to-date technologies where these are warranted to maximize profits from the low-paid African migrant workers. As discussed below,(p.138) about four-fifths*of the miners are brought on contract from neighbouring countries. They are forced to live in crowded dormitories, sleeping on concrete bunks, in fenced-in mine compounds. Their wages are among the lowest in South Africa, averaging about a twentieth of what a typical U.S. mine worker earns. Recently, the increased difficulty in recruiting labour for the mines through the very low wage contract system, especially with the independence of Mozambique and Angola, has led to significantly increased efforts to substitute capital-intensive technologies for cheap labour. This policy has been strengthened as a result of the growing unrest in the mines, in which over a hundred miners have been killed since 1973 for making increasingly militant demands for better wages and working conditions. U.S. firms are in a position to suppy South African mines the most advance technologies in the world, as well as some of the capital needed to finance them, to reduce dependence on African labour.

The Engelhard Connection

The U.S. firm most intimately entwined with South African mining finance interests is Engelhard Minerals and Chemicals Corporation, the world's largest refiner and fabricator of precious metals. As a result of a complex series of stock transactions from 1969 to 1972, the Anglo-American Group, built around the biggest mining finance house in South Africa, came to own about 30 per cent of the common stock and 20 per cent of the preferred stock of Engelhard Chemicals and Minerals. [5] Engelhard family interests own about 11 per cent of the common and 7 per cent of the preferred stock of the company. G.W.H. Reilly, who came up through the ranks of the Anglo-American Corporation to become President and Chairman of its

*fn: Since Mozambique's independence, the number of foreign miners has dropped to half.

board of directors, also sits on the board of Engelhard Minerals and Chemicals Company.

Charles Engelhard, himself, while he was alive, was a moving spirit in efforts to expand U.S. economic as well as political ties with South Africa. As Chairman of the big finance holding company, Engelhard Hanovia, he was in a position to contribute effectively to this goal. His adulation of the South African regime's policies was summed up in his comments on Vorster's selection as Prime Minister of that country in 1966:[6]

> The policy of South Africa as expressed by the new Prime Minister is as much in the interests of South Africa as anything I can think of or suggest. I am not a South African, but there is nothing I would do better or differently.

Engelhard backed his verbal support with concrete actions. Two years before Sharpeville, he founded the American-South African Investment Corporation to attract capital to the Republic at a time of great economic and psychological need for the white minority government. After the Sharpeville massacre, South Africa faced a serious loss of foreign confidence and a capital outflow. Engelhard arranged a $35 million loan with the United States banking interests. He sat on the board of the Witwatersrand Native Labour Association and the Native Recruiting Agency, two official agencies which brought Africans from Mozambique and Rhodesia to work at below-subsistence wages in the South African mines.

The Engelhard company's continuing ties with the U.S. Government[7] undoubtedly facilitate efforts to obtain governmental support for its activities in South Africa. Engelhard himself was a close friend of both Presidents Kennedy and Johnson. He contributed generously to the Democratic Party. He represented the United States at the independence celebrations in Gabon, the coronation of the Pope in 1963, the first anniversary of Algeria's independence, and at Zambia's independence ceremonies in 1964.

After Engelhard died in 1971, J. G. Harlan, previously a U.S. Government official, became a key member of the Engelhard Board of Directors. Harlan's former government status put him in a position to contribute significantly to the favourable presentation of the South African regime's potential contribution to U.S. interests. He served in the Treasury Department from 1937 to 1948, when he became in-volved in the U.S. Foreign Aid Programme in which he participated until 1958. In that year he became Deputy Commissioner to the Defense Materials Service, where he remained until he became

Commissioner of Property Management and Disposal Services from 1966 to 1969. He then became Vice-President of the Engelhard Minerals and Chemicals Corporation. In 1971, he became Senior Vice-President and President of the Engelhard Industries Division in Newark. Harlan has also served as a representative on the President's Committee on the Economic Impact of Defense and Disarmament, as Project Manager of the President's Special Task Force on Use of Surplus Property; and as a member of the Industrial Study Board to study the effects of government policies on regional economic levels. All these posts served to consolidate his relationships with top-ranking US Government personnel dealing with the precious metals which Engelhard Company processes and markets. They also undoubtedly facilitate continuing efforts to convince U.S. officials to strengthen America's reliance on South African 'strategic' materials. In this respect, Harlan's efforts are undoubtedly strengthened by the extensive ties with the U.S. Government of another Engelhard Board member, J. T. Connor, who also sits on the board of the powerful Chase Manhattan Bank.

The Copper Companies

American Metal Climax (AMAX)* has long been involved in Southern Africa, and has participated with Anglo-American in several projects in neighbouring African countries. It had, through a subsidiary, acquired ownership of about half of Zambia's vast copper mines prior to that country's independence. The other half belonged to Anglo-American.

AMAX and Anglo-American have invested jointly in the newly discovered Botswana copper-nickel mine at Selebi-Pikwe. The companies required the Botswana Government to acquiesce to sending the crude copper-nickel matte to AMAX's refinery in the United States, before shipping it on to Metallgessellschaft (with which AMAX has ties) in West Germany.[8] AMAX, together with Newmont, owns a majority of shares in the highly profitable Tsumeb Copper mines in Namibia.**

---

*AMAX was 126th on Fortune's 1973 list of the 200 largest U.S. firms in terms of sales, and 75th in terms of its nearly $2 billion in assets.

**Both AMAX and Newmont are violating United Nations efforts to end foreign investment in Namibia as long as South Africa illegally maintains its rule there. Frank Coolbaugh, formerly Chairman of the Board and Chief Executive Officer of AMAX, is a director of Tsumeb.

W.A.M. Burden, a member of the AMAX board, provides direct contacts with agencies concerned with military and international affairs. Burden served as director of the National Aviation Corporation (1939-41); as Vice-President of Defense Supplies Corporation (1941-42); Assistant Secretary of Commerce in Charge of Air, and as a member of the National Advisory Committee for Aeronautics (1942-47). He became a special assistant for Research and Development to the Secretary of the Air Force (1950-52). He was Ambassador to Belgium for 1959-61, and is Chairman of the Institute for Defense Analysis and a Director of the Council on Foreign Relations.

Newmont, another U.S. firm with world-wide mining and finance interests,** is deeply involved in Southern Africa. It owns over half of the O'okiep Copper Company with mines there and in Namibia, and almost a third of the Tsumeb mine in Namibia. Newmont's Vice-President worked for eight years, from 1947 to 1955, as General Manager of Rhodesia Corporation and Falcon Mines. One of Newmont's South African subsidiaries, the Palabora Mining Company, produces copper, magnetite, vermiculite and sulphuric acid. Its 1973 sales totalled $110 million; it employed about 3,070 workers.

In 1974, the Tsumeb and O'okiep companies announced plans to build an electrolytic copper refinery, costing over $40 million in Cape Town, South Africa, to treat all the blister-copper output of the two companies' smelters. In January 1975, it was reported that they had decided not to build the refinery. The Johannesburg *Financial Mail* speculated that this might be because AMAX sought to be 'divested of its SWA projects'.[9] This reinforced a two-year-old rumour that AMAX wanted to pull out of Namibia, a desire that might well have been strengthened by the threat of United Nations seizure of cargoes after 30 May 1975.* AMAX and Newmont both faced stockholder questions on these issues in their May 1975 meetings.[10]

A Newmont Vice-President explained bluntly why his company continued to invest in South Africa: 'We know the people and the Government and we back our conviction with our reputation and our dollars.' He boasted that American firms could make an average

---

**Among other interests, Newmont owns 10 per cent of the shares and its Chairman sits on the Board of the Southern Peru Copper Corporation, which exploits Peru's most profitable open pit mines in Southern Peru.

*The United States Government joined France and Britain to veto this proposal, however, and AMAX remains as involved in Namibia as ever.

profit of 27 per cent on investment in South Africa, over double the profit from comparable investments in the United States.

The Chrome Issue

The U.S. firm, Union Carbide, has extensive mining interests in South Africa and Rhodesia. It produces 20 per cent of South Africa's chrome, as well as owning a large chrome mine in Rhodesia. It also has had close ties with high U.S. governmental circles. Kenneth Rush, who was with Union Carbide from 1937 to 1969, winding up as executive vice-president in 1961-66 and president from 1966-69, became U.S. Ambassador to Germany (1969-72). Deputy Secretary of Defense (1972-3) and Deputy Secretary of State (1973-4).

Union Carbide exercised its powerful Congressional lobby in the early 1970s to get the Byrd Amendment passed and to prevent subsequent efforts to defeat it. As a result, the United States has continued to import chrome from Rhodesia, in violation of the U.S. Government's official declaration of support for the United Nations decisions to boycott that country.*

Among the other U.S. firms which have investments in South African minerals, are some of the biggest household names in America. Alcan Aluminum of South Africa** has joined with Union Steel Corporation in a $16 million plant at Richards Bay. Kaiser Aluminum has built the largest productive aluminum hot line in South Africa. King Resources of Denver controls the country's only titanium mine, situated in a border area near East London. U.S. Steel has constructed a $16 million ferrochrome smelting plant in the Sekhukhuniland border area in the Eastern Transvaal. With Newmont Mining and two South African companies, Anglovaal and De Beers, it is prospecting for copper and precious stones in Botswana and Namibia. Other strategic materials which the United States imports from Southern Africa include corundum, lithium and amosite asbestos.

Uranium and Nuclear Technology

The U.S.-based multinational mining corporations' connections with South Africa's mining groups is by no means a one-way street. The U.S. firms, together with the U.S. governmental agencies over which they appear to have a significant influence, have made major contributions to South Africa's technological advance. This contribution

---

*See pp. 212ff below, for the facts regarding Rhodesian chrome.
**Linked with Alcoa through its affiliate Alcan of Canada.

has been particularly critical in an area which has dangerous military implications: the production of nuclear power. An agreement was worked out in the early 1970s for ESCOM, South Africa's electricity utility, to purchase nuclear enrichment services from the U.S. Atomic Energy Commission for its nuclear power station at Duipefontein. The U.S. Atomic Energy Commission (AEC) has one of the few facilities in the world for enriching uranium into the tiny pellets that go into the reactor core. It will provide ESCOM with enrichment services up to 2000 MW and reprocess the burnt fuels. The South African *Financial Mail* claims[11] that the AEC contract was part of a U.S. effort to guarantee South African sources of uranium oxide to power American nuclear plants.

A Massachusetts firm, the Foxboro Corporation, has gone further by providing the technology necessary for South Africa to operate its own unique new process for producing enriched uranium itself.[12] The initial reactor which made that development possible was provided by the United States under Atoms for Peace Program about a decade ago. The American Allis-Chalmers corporation helped construct the South African facility, and the South African technicians were trained at Oak Ridge, Tennessee, Atomic Energy Labs managed by the U.S. Government in the U.S. South Africa declares that its new method is competitive with the U.S. process because it takes less initial capital investment. It reportedly hopes to export large quantities of enriched uranium fuel for nuclear power plants around the world.

By the mid-1970s, the U.S. Nuclear Corporation was reported to have already sent nearly 100 pounds of highly enriched uranium to South Africa, allegedly for research use. The danger is, of course, that the entire nuclear development programme could be used for nuclear weapons. Even this initial amount of material, which is concentrated well above the level required for nuclear weapons, is reportedly sufficient for the production of seven small atomic bombs.

U.S. Congressman Les Aspin objected to continuing U.S. nuclear assistance to South Africa because of these dangerous military implications:[13]

> With a plentiful supply of natural uranium and its own separation plant, South Africa can produce all the weapons grade uranium it wants. This capability strengthens South Africa's position militarily, diplomatically, and economically. When the inevitable showdown comes in southern Africa, Pretoria can threaten ultimate disaster unless it gets its way.

Summary

Official U.S. agencies have supported the expansion of U.S.-based multinational investment in South Africa's minerals, allegedly because of their 'strategic' value to the United States. Their potential 'strategic' value to the U.S. appears to be grossly overstated, an illusion which may be fostered by the close ties of top company personnel with the U.S. agencies involved. The fact is that U.S. mining firms investing is South African minerals reap an exceptionally high rate of profit made possible by the exploitation of black African contract labour. Closely meshed in with South Africa's mining finance houses, they not only provide essential capital to finance the mining sector's growth, but also critical technology to enable that sector to survive if the low cost labour supply is cut off by the African liberation movement in surrounding countries. More than that: U.S. firms, apparently in violation of United Nations agreements to which the U.S. Government is an official signatory, have contributed the essential technology and materials for the production of nuclear weapons from South Africa's uranium, a dangerous addition to the South African military machine in its dealings with the independent states of Africa and the world.

REFERENCES
CHAPTER SIX

1. A. Geddicks. 'Raw Material Strategies of Multinational Copper Companies Based in the United States', in A. Seidman, ed., *Natural Resources and National Welfare: The Case of Copper* (New York: Praeger, 1975), pp. 92-108. Mackler, op. cit., footnotes, pp. 43-4.
2. National Commission on Materials Policy, *Report*, 1970, cited in Geddicks, op. cit., p. 93.
3. Ibid.
4. United Nations. *Economic Survey of Africa Since 1950.*
5. Moody's Industrials, 1974, and Engelhard Minerals and Chemicals Corporation, *Report to the Securities and Exchange Commission*, 1971, pp. 1-6.
6. Cited in R. First, J. Steele, and C. Gurney, *The South African Connection Western Investment in Apartheid* (New York: Harper and Row, 1972), p. 132.
7. All information relating to memberships of boards of directors is from Dunn and Bradstreet. *Reference Book of Corporate Management*, 1974/75 (New York: Dunn and Bradstreet Inc., 1974); Standard and Poore, *Register of Corporations, Directors and Executives*, 1975 (New York: Standard and Poore Corp., 1974), Vol. II; and *Who is Who in Finance and Industry* (Chicago; Marquis Who's Who. Inc., 1973).
8. C. Uskewokunze, "The Legal Framework of Copper Production in Zambia', with comment by A. Alaxander, and R. Silitshena, 'Mining and Development Strategy in Botswana', in A. Seidman, ed., *Natural Resources and National Welfare: The Case of Copper* (New York: Praeger Special Studies, 1976).
9. *Financial Mail*, 31 January 1975.
10. *Southern Africa*, May 1975, p. 13.
11. *Financial Mail*, 29 November 1974.
12. *New York Times*, 24 April 1975.
13. Ibid.

Chapter VII

U.S. Contribution to South African Manufacturing Growth

Direct investments by U.S.-based multinationals in South Africa's burgeoning manufacturing sector have multiplied so rapidly in recent years that they have grown to be about four times greater in dollar terms than those in mining. This appears to reflect, in part, the critical role U.S. firms are playing in modernizing South African technology in all sectors. The U.S.-based multinationals also apparently view the racist South African regime as providing a stable and profitable framework for expanding their foothold in the vast potential African market. The estimated expenditures by U.S. majority-owned firms on property, plant and equipment manufacturing in 1974 and 1975 constituted over half those made in all South African industry in those years, and far exceeded those made by U.S. firms in the rest of Africa.

Some of the biggest U.S. manufacturing firms have been established in South Africa since the turn of the century, but by far the most rapid increase has taken place coincident with the efforts of South Africa's Nationalist Government to spur industrialization in recent years. Today, South Africa ranks fourteenth among all countries in the world in terms of U.S. investment in manufacturing. She follows after the major developed countries of the European Common Market, Japan, and Australia, and the largest Latin American countries, Mexico, Brazil, Argentina, and Venezuela.[1] In terms of U.S. manufacturing investment, South Africa far outranks all the independent nations of Africa, despite their strenuous efforts to attract U.S. capital to build much-needed factories. About four out of every five U.S. dollars invested in African manufacturing are in South Africa.

There appear to be several reasons for the rapid expansion of U.S. investment in South African manufacturing industry. The relatively high incomes of the four million whites, comparable to those in the U.S., provide a fairly large concentrated local market for the sophisticated kinds of goods which U.S. multinationals wish to sell by establishing processing plants. At the same time, the top management of the multinationals perceive a community of interest with the South African Government and business groups in their efforts to expand trading ties northward on the continent. Instead of risking their capital by direct investment in what they consider to be 'unstable' African-governed countries, they hope to gain a foothold through what they perceive as a business-like, rapidly growing economy run by people very much like themselves. The wages of African manufacturing workers are only between a tenth and a sixth of what they would be in factories owned by the same companies in the United States. It has been estimated, furthermore, that the effective tax rate paid by U.S. firms in South Africa is only about 22 per cent of net income.[2]

All in all, these factors assure U.S. manufacturing firms a very profitable business in South Africa. Officially, they reported an average profit rate of about 16 per cent in 1973, compared to 2.8 per cent for the rest of Africa. The South African rate declined to a little over 15 per cent in 1974, despite the growing world recession and rising oil prices.

The rate of profit in manufacturing in the rest of Africa was not reported in 1974, but U.S. manufacturing firms still reaped 90 per cent of their profit in Africa from South Africa. The averages for both South Africa and the rest of the continent are probably understated. There is widespread evidence in Latin America that companies overprice imported machinery, parts and materials to avoid paying local taxes.[3] There is no reason to believe that U.S. firms operate significantly differently in Africa. In any case, the average rate officially reported in South Africa considerably exceeds the average of about 11 per cent reported for manufacturing in the United States.

Whether any individual U.S. firms have had second thoughts since the collapse of Portuguese rule in Mozambique and Angola is not yet clear. The evidence does show a continued rapid expansion of U.S. investment in South Africa. South Africa is still making every effort to create an investment climate attractive to U.S. investors. The well-publicized abolition of a few of the more blatant features of 'petty apartheid' in the mid-1970s was designed to create an illusion of reform which the firms could report to critical shareholders back home. These changes in no way fundamentally altered the political economic structure which had rendered their investment in South Africa so profitable.

U.S. firms' contribution to South African manufacturing is not only far greater in dollar terms than in the rest of Africa. It has, especially in recent years, come to play a far more critical role in helping to build an integrated, increasingly self-sufficient national economy. In most independent African states, U.S. manufacturing firms have for the most part built only last-stage assembly and processing plants which continue to import parts and materials, as well as machinery and equipment, from their U.S.-based factories.[4] In effect, what they gain this way is a foothold in the tariff-protected markets of those countries for a limited local investment. In South Africa, in contrast, U.S. firms have begun to establish backwards linkages between their manufacturing investments and the rest of the economy. To illustrate, almost all of U.S. investment in the manufacture of machines in Africa is concentrated in South Africa (96.8 per cent in 1974). In this way, U.S. firms are contributing to building an increasingly advanced technological foundation for South Africa's industrial sector, already the largest in Africa. At the same time, they have as a result become more and more involved in South Africa's structure of exploitation.

Automobile Companies

In 1974 the U.S. Department of Commerce suppressed the data on expanding investments in the transport industry to avoid identifying individual companies. The fact is that the three largest automobile manufacturing firms in the United States, three of the top four biggest corporations in the U.S. itself, have come to play a crucial role in the South African economy in recent years. They compete for Government contracts to sell vehicles to the army and police. Two were first established in South Africa after World War I; the third became established there in the late 1950s, when the African countries further north were nearing political independence. Together, these three firms produce up to half of the motor vehicles sold in South Africa, including cars, trucks, and tractors. In the 1960s, the South African Government sought to strengthen its economy following the world outcry against the Sharpeville massacre. The U.S. auto companies further expanded their local production in accord with the requirement that over half the components of vehicles, by weight, must be locally produced. They also began to export vehicles built there to other countries, helping to improve South Africa's balance of payments.

General Motors [5] first erected an assembly plant in South Africa in 1926. GM South Africa has an assembly plant and manufacturing plant in Port Elizabeth, and an engine manufacturing plant just outside that city. It produces several GM models, and manufactures components such as radiators, engines, batteries, spark plugs, springs and sheet metal parts locally. GM's 'Ranger' is an all-South African-made model, sold not only in South Africa but outside the country as well.

In 1972, GM South Africa employed 4,797 workers, about half white, about 40 per cent Coloured, and 22 per cent African. The latter are almost all in unskilled or at most semiskilled categories. Hourly rates for Africans and Coloureds started at about 65 (U.S.) cents an hour, and rose at maximum to about $1.35 an hour. Almost all the Africans and a majority of the Coloureds were classified in the lower skilled, lower paid categories.

GM's South African operations alone constitute those of a large firm, although they produce only four per cent of GM's world-wide output. In 1971, GM South Africa's sales totalled 35,700 vehicles, equal in dollar terms to the sales of the 563rd U.S. firm listed by *Fortune* magazine among the 1,000 largest U.S. industrial corporations.

The biggest company in the world, GM has extensive contacts with the U.S. Government, as well as banking interests and other companies investing in South Africa. [6] One of its present board members served as U.S. Secretary of Commerce from 1965 to 1967. Several former board members have moved into U.S. and international posts, including McNamara, now head of the World Bank, and formerly U.S. Secretary of Defense during the Vietnam War. Directors of banks and financial concerns sitting on GM's board represent the National Bank of Detroit, the First National Bank of Chicago, Metropolitan Life Insurance Company, First Wisconscin Trust Company, the Mellon Bank, and the Morgan Guaranty Trust, besides Chase Manhattan. GM Board members also serve as links with many other firms investing in South Africa, including Proctor and Gamble, Eastman Kodak, Dupont, Pepsi Company, U.S. Steel, 3M (Minnesota Mining and Manufacturing) and the Owens Corning Fiberglass Corporation.

Ford, the second largest auto company in the U.S. also has extensive production operations in South Africa. Ford established its first plant there in 1923, as a subsidiary of its Canadian subsidiary. It expanded especially rapidly in the 1960s. It now owns administrative offices, assembly plants for cars, vans, tractors and trucks, an engine plant, and a parts and service depot. It sells 15 to 20 per cent of the cars and commercial vehicles in South Africa. It sold over 48,000 vehicles in 1971 alone. It employs almost four thousand workers, two thirds of whom are Coloured, and about 8 per cent African. In 1972, almost 90 per cent of the Africans and two thirds of the Coloureds were in job categories receiving less than 84 cents an hour.

Chrysler, the third largest U.S. auto manufacturer, established its first plant in South Africa in 1958 outside Cape Town. In 1967, it opened a new plant on the edge of the Tswana Bantustan, undoubtedly to take advantage of the 'large, readily available source of unskilled labour'.[7] In 1972, the original plant was closed down entirely. That year, at the newer plant, Chrysler employed about 2,000 workers, slightly over half African and Coloured, to produce 24,500 vehicles. The availability of a reservoir of African labour in the nearby Bantustan made it possible to increase the proportion of low-paid Africans on staff, reducing wage bills significantly. The average African wage was about $110 a month.

Electrical Equipment

General Electric, the biggest electrical firm in the United States, ranking fifth among all U.S. industrial corporations, has long maintained ties with South Africa, where it began operations in 1898. Today it holds its concerns there through its London-based affiliate, so that they are not officially counted among U.S. investments in South Africa. South Africa GE (SAGE) manufactures and sells a wide range of household appliances and housewares (refrigerators, freezers, washers and dryers, irons, percolators, electric kettles), industrial controls, capacitators, locomotives, and so forth. It also markets imported items, both for the consumer market and the growing industrial sectors. In 1973, its sales totalled $4.5 billion. It was one of the five companies chosen by the South African Government to manufacture television receiving sets. SAGE has built railroad locomotives for the South African Government, as well as for the Portuguese in Angola and Mozambique, under Government Export-Import Bank credit guarantees. It produced control relay panel for the Cabora Bassa Dam in Mozambique, at that time viewed as a key to continued Portuguese-South African rule in the region. It reportedly planned to compete to help build South Africa's first nuclear reactor.

In 1972, about half of SAGE's 1500 workers were African. Their wages ranged from $73 a month to $213 a month, with the bulk of them earning the lower rates. Eight per cent of the workers were Coloureds, starting at $63 (female) and $118 (male), and rising to an average of $193 a month. Whites making up about 42 per cent of the workers, received $186 a month for unskilled work, rising to $502 for artisans, the category in which most whites were working.

Westinghouse ranks fourteenth among all U.S. industrial firms, and, together with General Electric, dominates the U.S. electrical industry. It has two known subsidiaries in South Africa. One, Wabco, employs about 300 workers to produce and sell earthmoving equipment. A second Westinghouse subsidiary employs 450 workers, and sells about $14 million worth of railway signalling equipment annually.

International Telephone and Telegraph (ITT), ranking ninth among the largest firms in the United States, has extensive investments in South Africa. ITT's own role in supporting political regimes favourable to its activities, especially in Latin America, has been extensively documented. In South Africa, its subsidiaries include:

Standard Telephone and Cables [STC], one of South Africa's largest electrical manufacturing concerns. STC produces a wide range of technologically complex electrical equipment. Because it supplies communications equipment for the police and Simonstown Naval Base, as well as the South African Post Office, many employees must have security clearances. It also recruits engineers to operate the Simonstown base equipment. Apparently, neither ITT nor the U.S. Government views this as violating the UN embargo on arms to South Africa, signed by the United States. STC employs about 1,000 Africans, 1,500 Coloureds, 900 Asians, and 2,500 whites. The average African wage in 1972 was $125 a month, compared to $546 for whites. African Telephone and Cables, an STC subsidiary, manufactures electric wire and telephone cable. Another subsidiary, Miller's Electrical Line, is a wholesale distributor of industrial and general electrical installation material, cables, switch-gear, motors, domestic appliances and hardware and switchboards.

ITT Supersonic Africa, initially a marketing agent for ITT's Rhodesian subsidiary, *Supersonic Radio Manufacturing Company,* now manufactures radio equipment in the Pietersburg 'border area' in South Africa, taking advantage of the low wages paid to Africans there. Both ITT and Supersonic have maintained their ties with the Supersonic Radio Manufacturing Company of Rhodesia, which makes portable and automobile radios, record players, stereo players and television sets at Bulawayo. It continues to sell them throughout South Africa and Namibia, despite the United Nations economic boycott of Rhodesia for which the U.S. Government voted.

The South Atlantic Cable Company played a major role in construction of the Cape Town-Luanda link.

ITT's Speedwriting and Houghton Commercial Colleges are Johannesburg secretarial schools, open only to white students. ITT's *Avis* is the leader in the South African auto rental business, and has eleven offices, including one in Namibia. It also operates in Zimbabwe. ITT's *Master Directories* prepares the 'yellow pages' of the telephone books.

ITT interests also extend to other Southern African countries through its giant subsidiary, International Standard Electric Corporation (ISEC). In 1970, ISEC invested $15 million in Grupo Olivia, which owns four metallurgical and metal mechanical companies in Mozambique. Its Standard Electric (SARL) Portugal at that time reported plans to invest $36 million, not only in Portugal but also in its African colonies. ITT's Sheraton built a hotel in Luanda, the Angolan capital. An ITT subsidiary assembles television sets in Zambia from parts and materials imported, in all likelihood, from South Africa and perhaps Rhodesia.

ITT's contacts through interlocking directorships with other US firms investing in South Africa include Raytheon, Grace Lines, and Chase Manhattan Bank. E.R. Black, the ITT director who sits on Chase's Board, was formerly President of the World Bank.

A wide variety of U.S. manufacturing firms are included among the nearly four hundred U.S. companies with investments in South Africa. It is impossible to discuss them all in detail here. A few more may be merely mentioned to indicate something of the scope of their activities. As in the auto and electrical business, the more significant of them have interlocking directorships and/or banking connections in common. Not a few are pyramided structures, with subsidiaries which hold subsidiaries operating in South Africa.[8]

Data Processing

The International Business Machines Corporation of South Africa is a subsidiary of the sixth largest firm in the United States of the same name. It has contributed to South Africa the advanced technology for computerized data processing and systems management. It produces a wide range of data processing systems, electrical typewriters, and dictating equipment. It runs several data service centres. It employs about 2,600 workers throughout the country, and sells about $1.2 billion worth of goods a year.

Other U.S. firms in the South African data processing and computer business include Computer Services of Los Angeles; Collins Radio Company of Cedar Rapids, Iowa; Control Data Company of Minneapolis; Cutler Hammer International of Milwaukee; the National Cash Register Company of Dayton, Ohio; and Otis Elevator of New York.

Rubber

Several of the largest manufacturing firms in the United States have contributed to specific aspects of South Africa's basic industrial sector. Two of the biggest U.S. rubber firms have developed an extensive business in the production and sale of rubber products which are essential to the transport industry, as well as to industry in general. The Goodyear Tire and Rubber Company, the nineteenth largest firm in the U.S., has a South African subsidiary which employs about 2,500 workers and manufactures and sells about $45 million worth of tires, tubes, rubber hoses and belts annually.

The Firestone Rubber Company, another of the three big firms which dominate the rubber industry in the United States, also owns a South African subsidiary which employs about 2,000 workers and sells roughly the same amount of tires and tubes.

Agricultural Machinery and Equipment

A number of U.S. firms have expanded local assembly and sale of agricultural equipment and machinery for South Africa's wealthy white agricultural sector. International Harvester, the twenty-second largest industrial company in the United States, has established a South Africa subsidiary which employs about 800 workers. It produces and sells about $35 million worth of motor trucks, farm tractors, and implements and light industrial equipment each year. The U.S.-owned J.I. Case Company, a much smaller company, employs only about thirty workers in South Africa, selling about $1.5

million worth of agricultural tractors and implements as well as construction equipment.

Allis-Chalmers, 146th in Fortune's Directory of the 500 largest U.S. industrial corporations, not only produces agricultural machinery and electrical equipment in South Africa, but, as noted above (p.93), also sells nuclear reactors there. United States Industries, through its South African subsidiary, Big Dutchman, sells automated poultry, pig and cattle feeding subsidiaries. Deere and Company produces farm and industrial equipment. Caterpillar Tractor Company sells parts for earthmoving equipment. The Champion Spark Plug Company produces and sells spark plugs for general use in transport equipment.

Mining Machinery

Two U.S. firms are engaged in providing the latest technology for the South African mining industry. The South Africa affiliate of the Joy Manufacturing Company of Pittsburgh produces coal and hard rock mining machinery and equipment, core drills, diamond crowns and dust collection equipment. It employs about 750 workers. The Mine Safety Appliances Company of Pittsburgh employs about 525 workers in South Africa, producing and selling mining and industrial safety equipment. A number of medium-sized U.S. firms import parts, and produce several other types of industrial inputs in South Africa itself. The Timken Roller Bearing Company's South African subsidiary empoys about 190 workers, and sells about $5.5 million worth of output annually. The McKinnon Chain Company of South Africa, owned by Columbus McKinnon Corporation of New York, employs about 500 workers, and sells about $4.5 million worth of chains and chain accessories. The H.H. Robertson Company, owned by the Pittsburgh company of that name, employs about 590 workers in South Africa, producing specialized steel building materials. Its annual sales total about $20 million. The Masonite Corporation of Chicago has a South African subsidiary which produces and sells hardboard, insulation and masonite. It employs 1,010 workers, and sells about $10 million worth of products a year.

Chemicals

The South African Government has taken steps to ensure that its own parastatal, together with domestic private industry, dominates the industrial chemicals field. Nevertheless, the Industrial Chemical

Products Company of South Africa, a subsidiary of Amchem Products of Pennsylvania, does employ eighty workers, and sells about $3 million worth of industrial chemicals a year. A number of other U.S. firms are engaged in importing and last-stage processing of pharmaceuticals and related products for the high income white consumer market. These firms are relatively small compared to the giant multinationals in basic industry in the United States, and likewise are less significant in their size of output and employment in South Africa itself. They are, nevertheless, multinationals. As the chairman of Abbott Laboratories, a $145 million-a-year pharmaceutical company with plants in twenty-two countries, explained back in the early 1960s: 'We are no longer just a U.S. company with interests abroad. Abbott is a world enterprise, and many major fundamental decisions must be made on a global basis.' [9] With this perspective, Abbott and several other U.S. companies have imported the necessary equipment to last-stage process and sell a wide range of pharmaceutical products in South Africa.

The South African operations of Colgate Palmolive, which ranks 67th among the largest U.S. industrial corporations, are probably the most extensive of U.S. enterprises in this category. Colgate-Palmolive's South African subsidiary employs about 650 workers and manufactures and sells toiletries, soaps and detergents. It also holds controlling shares in two other U.S. firms: the Kendall Company, which in turn has another South African subsidiary, and employs sixty people to produce and sell surgical dressings and elastic goods; and Helena Rubenstein, which has a South African subsidiary producing cosmetics. Lakeside Laboratories, a third subsidiary of Colgate-Palmolive, is affiliated with Lakeside Laboratories of Milwaukee.

Other U.S. firms in this category include the Parke, Davis Laboratories, which employs about 175 workers in South Africa, and sells about $4 million worth a year. Lilly Laboratories of South Africa, held by Eli Lilly of Indianapolis, employs 116 workers, and sells about $6 million worth of pharmaceutical and agricultural products. Schrang Ltd, a subsidiary of the New Jersey Schering Corporation, employs 140 workers and sells $3 million worth of pharmaceutical and photographic materials in South Africa. The Philadelphia firm of Smith, Kline and French Laboratories owns two South African subsidiaries: one by the same name, and another called A.S. Ruffel. They produce veterinary and nutritional products, as well as pharmaceuticals. They employ about 100 persons, and sell about $1.5 million worth of produce a year. Wyeth Laboratories of South Africa, a subsidiary of Wyeth International of Philadelphia, employs about 160 workers and sells about $4.5 million worth annually.

The South African subsidiary of the American Home Products Corporation of New York, Whitehall Products, employs about 65 workers, and produces $2.5 million worth of pharmaceutical, toilet, and household products a year. C.D. Searle of South Africa, a subsidiary of the Chicago Company, employs twenty people selling about $2.2 million worth of pharmaceutical preparations.

Miscellaneous

While it is not possible to give details of all the U.S. firms with direct investments in South Africa a few additional well-known names might be added to suggest the extent of penetration by U.S. firms into South Africa's manufacturing sector. Cheeseborough-Pond of New York produces and sells cosmetics. Coca-cola licenses the production of soft drinks in South Africa. The Macmillan Book Company sells books there. Eastman-Kodak sells photographic goods. The Borden Company sells milk and chemical products. The Gillette Company produces razor blades and men's toiletries and cosmetics. The Singer Company of South Africa employs about 100 workers, and produces about $3 million worth of sewing machines annually.

Summary

Four out of five dollars of U.S. investment in African manufacturing industry are today in South African factories. In the context of the laws restricting black African unions and coercing Africans to work for less than subsistence wages, this investment has been very profitable for the U.S.-based multinationals involved. The rapid expansion of U.S. investment in South Africa's manufacturing sector has, at the same time, contributed to building and re-tooling all sectors of South Africa's economy.

This expanding U.S. investment in South African manufacturing has potentially far-reaching consequences: On the one hand, it has given giant U.S.-based multinationals a growing stake in maintaining the present system in South Africa itself. Along with the large U.S. mining firms involved there, they have extensive linkages with the U.S. Government which enables them to influence U.S. governmental policy to protect and continue their profitable business.

On the other hand, as the South African manufacturing growth· outpaces the narrow national market, the U.S. firms with investments there will undoubtedly seek ways to expand their sales. There is little evidence that they are planning to raise wages to broaden the internal market. It appears more probable that they will seek to exert pressures to facilitate export sales elsewhere on the continent. This may take the form of encouraging negotiations by U.S. as well as South African officials to persuade African governments to open the doors to South African manufactured goods.

REFERENCES

CHAPTER SEVEN

1. U.S. Department of Commerce, *Survey of Current Business,* Part II, August 1974, p. 18.
2. P. Musgrave, 'Tax Preferences to Foreign Investment, Report to the Joint Economic Committee, Congress of the United States', *The Economics of Federal Subsidy Programs,* Part 2, pp. 185-91.
3. Cf. L. Turner, *Multinational Corporations and the Third World,* (London: Allen Lane, 1973), Ch. 3.
4. Eg. A. Seidman, 'The Distorted Growth of Import Substitution Industry: The Zambian Case', *The Journal of Modern African Studies,* Vol.12, No.4, 1974, pp. 601-31.
5. Corporate Information Centre, *Church Investments, Corporations and Southern Africa.* (New York, 1972).
6. All information relating to memberships of boards of directors is from Dunn and Bradstreet, *Reference Book of Corporate Management,* 1974/5 (New York: Dunn and Bradstreet, Inc., 1974); Standard and Poore, *Register of Corporations, Directors and Executives,* 1975 (New York: Standard and Poore Corp., 1974), Vol.II; and *Who is Who in Finance Industry* (Chicago: Marquis Who's Who, Inc., 1973).
7. Corporate Information Centre, op. cit.
8. List of American firms, subsidiaries and affiliates, Republic of South Africa. Issued by the American Consulate General, Johannesburg, assisted by the American Consulates General at Cape Town and Durban, 1970. Information on sales and employment, unless otherwise noted, is from Dunn and Bradstreet, *Principal International Businesses,* 1974, and *World Wide Marketing Directors,* 99 Church Street, New York, New York. The ranking for firms among U.S. industrial corporations is from *The Fortune Directory of the 500 Largest Industrial Corporations,* New York, 1974.
9. Mackler, op. cit. p. 23.

Chapter VIII

U.S. Oil Companies in South Africa

The South African economy is, in one respect, particularly vulnerable to outside pressure: that is, oil. South Africa itself does not have any known extensive oil deposits. If nations opposing *apartheid* could effectively impose a blockade on oil imports, they could seriously dislocate South Africa's modern industrial economy.

U.S. firms have played an important role in helping the South Africa regime to overcome this danger. In the first place, since South Africa has vast coal mines, it has been able to reduce its dependence on oil to a lower level 'than any other developed country'. Its electrical utilities and many other plants, which might normally have utilized oil, burn coal instead. The state corporation, Sasol, has built one oil-from-coal-plant, and plans to build another ten times as large, to cost an estimated $1.5 billion. Sasol purchased a major share of the necessary technology from United States oil firms. The basic construction has been contracted by the Fluor Corporation of Los Angeles for about $1 billion.

More recently, U.S. firms, as pointed out above (pp. 93) helped the South African electrical utility, ESCOM, to build plants using nuclear power, another important substitute for oil.

Despite the lack of known oil reserves in South Africa itself, moreover, U.S. oil companies have doubled their investments there in recent years. By 1973, U.S. investments in petroleum in South Africa added up to 12 per cent of all U.S. petroleum investment in Africa.

Next to manufacturing, petroleum has become, in dollar terms, the second most important sector of U.S. investment in South Africa. Here again, official U.S. data conceals the specific amounts the companies have spent since 1973 on property, plant and equipment to 'avoid disclosure of data of individual reporters'.

Oil exploration around the Periphery

The biggest U.S.-based multinational oil firms have almost all been involved in recent years in exploring for oil throughout the peripheral areas of Southern Africa. In this they have received every encouragement from South African officials seeking to achieve at least regional independence from outside oil sources. The oil companies' concessions extend all the way around the shores of the southern third of the continent.

Gulf successfully struck oil in 1966 in Cabinda, a pocket of Angolan territory surrounded by Zaire. The Cabinda operation, considered by officials as 'one of the major growth areas of the Corporation', may be the fourth largest producer in Africa. Caltex has made discoveries in northern Angola.[2] Oil was undoubtedly one of the factors causing South Africa to intervene militarily in Angola following that country's declaration of independence from Portugal.

Natural gas has been discovered in Namibia, and is undoubtedly a contributing factor to South Africa's desire to maintain its domination over the region. Although U.S. oil companies are reported to have withdrawn from exploration activities in Namibia, under strong pressure from the UN Commission on Namibia, they have already helped South Africa to solve its oil problem by contributing to this valuable discovery.

Oil Refining and Distribution

The growth of U.S. oil business in South Africa itself, despite its lack of known oil resources, reflects the companies' expansion of refining capacity and distribution of oil and oil products throughout the region. In this way they, like their counterparts in mining and manufacturing, are contributing to building up the technological foundation of South Africa's industrial complex. At the same time, they are strengthening South Africa's central position in the southern region by giving it control over the refining and sale of oil products in less developed peripheral countries.

Mobil has boasted of its aid to the South African regime. It published a back-cover color advertisement in a special issue of the

South African *Financial Mail* in 1971, boasting that: 'Everyone is conscious of South Africa's need for its own supply of crude oil—and Mobil is doing something about it'.[3]

Mobil began operations in South Africa in 1897. One Mobil subsidiary operates a refinery in Durban. Another handles marketing. Mobil also holds a 25 per cent interest in a petroleum prospecting license for certain offshore areas, in partnership with Compagnie Francaise des Petroles, British Petroleum, and Shell. The company has presently purchased a 32.9 per cent interest in South African Oil Refinery (Pty) Ltd, which will operate a lubricating-oil refinery in Durban. Mobil is a leading supplier of fuels and lubricants to the oil rigs and drilling ships. It also provides expertise to South Africa for oil exploration technology, 'helping the Government exploration company, SOEKOR, to become almost completely independent of overseas consultants'.

Mobil officials declared in 1972:[4]

Mobil's position is that pulling out of South Africa would not be in the best interests of non-whites there nor in the interests of our shareholders.

What is needed... is not disinvestment but greater investment. Over the long term, only economic growth can create additional jobs, more job mobility, and greater opportunities for human advancement... With further economic growth, more and better jobs will become available for non-whites.

But from 1962 to 1970, Mobil only trained four Africans and 22 Asians and Coloureds for relatively higher skilled jobs, compared with 992 whites. The fifteen Africans enrolled in training in 1971-72 were all learning heavy-vehicle driving. The average African monthly wage in 1972 was $148 ($137 without a Christmas bonus).

Caltex Oil, a subsidiary jointly owned by Texaco and Standard Oil of California* was established in South Africa in 1911. It now operates a 43,000–barrel a day oil refinery in Cape Town, and markets a full range of petroleum products, mostly of local manufacture, throughout the Republic. Standard (California)'s own Chevron subsidiary companies, along with Texaco's Regent Company subsidiaries, own several concessions in South Africa and Namibia. Texaco markets petroleum products in Angola. Caltex has equity interests in two Rhodesian marketing and refining companies. A

---

* These rank respectively as the third and fifth largest firms in the United States. While U.S. anti-trust laws deny them the right to combine in the U.S., they receive official U.S. blessing for overseas combinations such as this.

November 1967, United Nations document[5] declared that Caltex had expanded its storage facilities to help the illegal white Rhodesian Government to prepare for. international embargos, although company officials have denied involvement.[6]

Caltex has about 2,000 employees, about a third of them African, Coloured, and Asian, in South Africa. The average African wage in 1972 was reported as $139 a month; the minimum was $111. Even this relatively high starting wage was below the Poverty Datum Line.[7]

Several other oil firms have established subsidiaries in South Africa in the oil business. Some have extended into sidelines. Hunt Oil's subsidiary, the Placid Oil Company of South Africa, is exploring for oil. Esso Standard of South Africa, a subsidiary of Standard Oil's 100-per-cent owned affiliate of Geneva, Switzerland, is in the petroleum and chemical business. Ashland Oil and Refining Company's South African subsidiary, Valvoline Oil Company, is producing lubricants and rust preventives. Atlantic Richfield's ARCO South Africa is exploring for oil. Getty Oil has a South Africa subsidiary, Tidal, which is mining diamonds.

Summary

U.S. oil companies have made significant, if officially obscured, contributions to South Africa's efforts to reduce its dependence on outside oil suppliers. They have provided the necessary technology to reduce direct dependence on oil in South Africa. They have explored for oil and gas throughout the southern region, and, where they found it, shipped it out in crude form. They have erected extensive refining, storage and distribution capacity in the South African centre for oil they have shipped from their wells elsewhere. This has helped South Africa to build its industrial base. It has also augmented the dependence of neighbouring nations which must buy oil products through them from South Africa.

REFERENCES

CHAPTER EIGHT

1. Cited in Corporate Information Centre, *Church Investments and Southern Africa*, (New York, 1973).
2. Ibid.
3. *Financial Mail*, 5 March 1971.
4. Mobil Oil Co., *Mobil in South Africa*, 1972.
5. No. A16868.
6. Texaco reply to Corporate Information Centre, letter to R.L. Phillips, Research Director, CIC, from K. King, 8 September 1972, in Corporate Information Centre, *op. cit.*
7. Determined by the Institute of Social Research, University of Natal, as around $140 in 1973. It is the minimum income necessary for subsistence, and excludes expenditures for education and recreation.

Chapter IX

U.S. Financiers in South Africa

The growth of U.S. investment in South African mines, manufacturing, and refining and distribution of oil has been accompanied and facilitated by the simultaneous intrusion of U.S. financial interests. U.S. banking and financial concerns appear to provide the key link in the complex network which binds together the firms engaged in the other sectors. Most of the largest U.S. firms with investments in South Africa are represented on the boards of the two largest U.S. banks most directly involved. This provides them, on the one hand, with the necessary contacts with the South African private and state capitalist sector. It assures them, on the other hand, of additional direct conduits to high U.S. Government circles, facilitating their task of influencing U.S. Government agencies to adopt policies favourable to their interests there.

Until 1974, U.S. financial and insurance investment in South African was incorporated, in U.S. Dept. of Commerce data, in the category dubbed 'other'.* In 1974, the U.S. Dept. of Commerce provided a breakdown which indicated that about 22 per cent of the 'other' category of investment in South Africa was in finance and insurance. The rate of profit in this business was about 30 per cent, the

*This category then also included trade and additional 'other' investments. It had doubled from 1968 to 1973. In 1973, its reported rate of profit in South Africa was about 41 per cent, the highest in all sectors, and almost four times the rate of profit in this category in the rest of Africa. As a result, although less than half of all U.S. investment in this category in Africa was reported to be in South Africa, over threefourths of the profit obtained in Africa in this category came from South Africa.

highest of all sectors reported for that country in that year. It was almost three times the profit rate reported for financial and insurance business in the rest of Africa.

Despite this high rate of profit, the reported dollar amount of U.S. investment in finance and insurance in South Africa appeared to be almost insignificant, only about 2.3 per cent of all U.S. investment there. Examination of the techniques adopted by U.S. banking interests for penetrating the South African political economy suggest, however, that the officially reported data on US investments in this category are particularly misleading. For the most part, the biggest U.S. banking firms concentrated on strengthening their ties and controls through British banks, especially Standard and Barclays, which have long played a crucial role in financing South African economic growth.

TABLE 9.1
FOREIGN BANKS IN SOUTH AFRICA, 1972

Bank	Foreign Ownership of South African Bank as percentage of its Total Equity	Total Assets ($mn)
Sanbic (Standard's Holding Company	86	3326
Barclay's National	85	2989
Trust Bank	3	1192
Western Bank	8	416
French Bank	54	180
Citibank	100	124*
Hill Samuel	77	109
UDC Bank	40	86
Bank of Lisbon	90	77
Bank of Athens	97	25

PERCENTAGE TOTAL ASSETS HELD BY FOREIGN BANKS, MID- 1970

Type of Deposit	Total Assets	Percentage Held by Foreign Bank
Commercial Bank Deposits	4928.6	73%
Merchant Banks	4322.3	10.5%
Other	1673.0	23%
TOTAL	7035.0	56%

SOURCE: Counter-Intelligence Services, *Business as Usual: International Banking in South Africa.* (UK: 1972)

*Figure for September 1972, returns to the Registrar of Financial Institutions.

Two Rockefeller Banks

The contribution of U.S. financial firms to the South African economy cannot be adequately measured in dollar terms. Rather, it is to be judged from their assistance to U.S.-based multnational corporations through counselling and arrangement of contacts needed to expand their profitable South African business. The two leading U.S. banks, Chase Manhattan and the First National City Bank of New York*, have become increasingly significant in this business in the last decade.

Both of these banks are enmeshed in the Rockefeller Group in the United States. Together, they own about 15 per cent of the assets and deposits of all commercial banks in the United States itself. Most of the largest U.S. mining, manufacturing and oil firms with investments in South Africa are represented on their boards of directors.

Both banks have taken advantage of the Edge Act, which permits U.S. commercial banks to create overseas corporations to engage in a wide range of activities abroad which anti-trust legislation prohibits in the United States. An Edge Act authority has explained that an important role of Edge Act corporations lies in their facilitation of U.S. firms' entry into overseas markets and investments:[1]

> ... the financing corporations devote a considerable amount of total staff time (30 percent according to one source) to being helpful to customers of their parent banks and other interested parties ... [in arranging] licensing agreements, joint venture partners, distributors, acquisitions.

These two U.S. banks have been able to work both directly and through their Edge Act affiliates to facilitate the expansion of the U.S. manufacturing, mining and oil firms in the context of the oligopolistic structure of the South African political economy.

Chase Manhattan

David Rockefeller, Chairman of Chase Manhattan, boasted at a 1974 press conference in Pretoria, South Africa, that his organization had substantial investments in South Africa. He asserted blandly, 'People I have talked to are of the opinion that foreign investment here is advantageous to all concerned.'[2] The expansion of Chase's own involvement in South Africa suggests that, at least from Chase's own point of view, it is indeed advantageous.

*After this went to press, its name was changed to Citibank.

Chase Manhattan initially set up its own branch bank in South Africa in 1959. By 1965, it had three branches there.* In that year, it purchased what appeared to be a controlling 15 percent stake in the Standard Bank, which, along with Barclays, controls two thirds of South Africa's commercial banking assets.[3] Standard in 1969 had 822 branches in South Africa. The number had more than doubled since before the Sharpeville Massacre. Standard's subsidiaries are engaged in a wide range of business in South Africa, including investment, credit facilities, insurance and computer leasing services. Its total assets in South Africa exceed $4 billion. Standard handles South Africa's gold sales through a British broker.[4]

In 1974, Chase executives sat on the Standard Board of Directors, and a Chase officer in London served with Standard's central management group. As the 1974 Chase Annual Report put it,[5] Chase officers at various levels of management in Standard bring the facilities of that bank to bear on the needs of Chase customers, especially U.S. corporations active in Africa'.

Several directors of the largest U.S.-based multinational corporations with investments in South Africa sit on Chase Manhattan's board,[6] including J.T. Connor, of General Motors; R. Lazerus, of General Electric; E.R. Black, of International Telephone and Telegraph; W.R. Hewell, of Chrysler; W.C. Butcher of Firestone. Chase directors also provide direct contact with official U.S. Government circles. J.T. Connor, for example, was formerly U.S. Secretary of Commerce (1965-67). He is also a director of Engelhard Minerals and Chemicals Company. E.R. Black was president of the International Bank for Reconstruction and Development (World Bank) from 1949 to 1962.

Through Standard, Chase became a major influence in the South African economy, and a conduit for U.S. firms interested in expanding their profitable investments there. In 1975, however, the U.S. Federal Trade Commission required Chase Manhattan to divest itself of its Standard holdings.[7] The reasons had nothing to do with Chase's involvement in South Africa. Since Standard itself had entered the U.S. banking field the FTC held the liaison permitted collusion

---

*In 1965, Chase Manhattan Bank's vice president for Far Eastern Affairs explicitly indicated that U.S. support was an important consideration in its efforts to facilitate expanding investment. Although he referred to Vietnam, he might as well have been talking of Southern Africa. 'In the past, foreign investors have been somewhat wary of the overall political prospect for the Southeast Asia region. I must say, though, that the U.S. actions in Vietnam this year--which have demonstrated that the U.S. will continue to give effective protection to the free nations of the region—have considerably reassured both Asian and Western investors.'

between two firms engaged in U.S. banking, in violation of U.S. anti-trust law. Chase, therefore, made new arrangements to continue its profitable business.

Chase exchanged its shares of ownership in Standard for a seven per cent share of Midlands, another of the largest commercial banks in England. Midlands also participates in South Africa as a member of the European banking consortium, EBIC, which owns an office in Johannesburg. Chase reports it sold its Midland shares and re-established its own representative office in South Africa, headed by the officer who used to handle its business through Standard Bank [8], although there is no other outside evidence of this.

First National City

The other big Rockefeller bank, the First National City Bank of New York, had preceded Chase Manhattan in setting up a South African branch by a year. By 1973, it had increased its branches there to eight located in the major industrial centers. It also acquired a 40 per cent share of the British National Grindley's Bank. The Chairman of the National Grindley Board sits on the board of Citicorp, the Edge Act subsidiary through which the First National expands its investment activites overseas. [10] These ties give First National a direct entree into a number of Southern, Central and East African countries where National Grindley's has branches.

Like Chase, the First National City Bank has direct links through its board of directors with other U.S. firms investing in South Africa. W.B. Wriston, Chairman of the Bank's Board, is a director of General Electric, one of the U.S. firms with the biggest South African interests. Other directors sit on the boards of the Coca-Cola Company, the Scott Paper Company, the American Express Company, Texaco, Penny, Abbott Laboratories and the Chrysler Corporation. First National City Bank also shares directors with Morgan Group companies in the U.S. itself.

Financing Apartheid

Throughout the post-Sharpeville Massacre period, Chase Manhattan and First National were part of a consortium of ten American banks

---

*EBIC was initially organized by several large European banks, including Midlands, to deal with the growing penetration of European financial business by U.S. banks.

which supplied the South African Government with a $40 million revolving loan.[11] The consortium was formed and administered by Dillon, Reed and Company, one of whose senior partners, Douglas Dillon, was President Kennedy's Secretary of the Treasury. The consortium was finally dissolved, after extensive public protest in the United States, when the South African Government indicated it no longer needed the credit.

A third U.S. bank involved in the consortium, the First National Boston Corporation, has two affiliates in South Africa: the City Credit (Transvaal) Ltd, Johannesburg, and International Factors (South Africa) Ltd, Johannesburg.

Bank of America

The largest bank in the United States — for that matter, the largest bank in the world—the Bank of America, has not opened branches directly in South Africa, although its latest detailed report on overseas investments indicated that it had invested in a 'financial institution in Salisbury', Rhodesia.   It did, however, participate in the consortium of U.S. banks contributing to the $40 million revolving loan for the South African Government after Sharpeville.

In 1967, the Bank of America joined the British bank, Barclays, together with four other leading European banks, to form the Societe Financiere Europeanne 'to help... companies established in Europe solve the problems arising from their international operations'.[12] As Barclays Chairman explains,[13] the Société Financière Européanne 'is able to supplement the resources of the founding banks and give banking and financial help of all kinds, especially by way of medium and long-term credits and participations, and has built up a management team of international character made up of members seconded by each of the partners'.

In 1972, almost thirty per cent (28.52 per cent) of Barclays international accounts were located in Southern Africa. Barclays South African branches in 1969 totalled 963, almost triple the pre-Sharpeville Massacre number, making it by far the largest bank in South Africa. Barclays is also involved in insurance, merchant bank finance, and other financial activities in South Africa. The Bank of America's relations with Barclay's would appear to provide its customers with extensive contacts in South Africa.

The Others

The linkages of the biggest U.S. banks with the South African financial system have undoubtedly facilitated rapid expansion of U.S.

investment in other sectors of the economy. A network of other U.S. - based financial, insurance and management consultant firms has radiated out from this hub to service the needs of expanding U.S. business in South Africa. Kidder, Peabody and Company, associated with the Morgan Group in the U.S., provides a financial consultancy firm.

As this book went to press, in the mid-1970s, owing to an internal economic recession, worsening balance of payments deficits and increased military expenditures, the South African Government, state corporations and parastatals began to borrow heavily on the international market. The South African Government devalued its currency twice in little over a year. A sharp increase in foreign loans, which reached $5.5 billion in mid-1976, saved it from more serious difficulties. Many loans were made directly to the South African Government and parastatals. The unique feature of these loans was the support of U.S. banks, which mobilized over a third of them. The U.S. Government's Export-Import Bank facilitated the provision of credit by providing various kinds of guarantees for amounts equal to about 10 per cent of the total loaned through U.S. banks.[14] Private U.S. banks most deeply involved were Citibank, * Chase Manhattan, Manufacturers Hanover, and Morgan Guaranty, often in co-operation with major foreign banks.

Summary

The expansion of U.S.-based multinational companies in South Africa's racist political economy has been facilitated by the simulataneous growth of U.S. banking and financial penetration of British banks with extensive interests there. Prominent among these are two of the largest banks in the United States, Chase Manhattan and the First National City Bank of New York, both of them in the orbit of the Rockefeller Group. A third giant, The Bank of America, has cemented ties with the British bank, Barclays, which is the leading commercial bank in South Africa. Through these boards of directors and financial and government relationship, these banks provide the final links in the network tying together the interests of the U.S. multinationals operating in South Africa. In the economic crisis confronted by South Africa in the mid-1970s, U.S. banks played a major role in providing financial assistance on a scale far greater than ever before.

* Formerly First National City Bank-of New York.

REFERENCES

CHAPTER NINE

1. T.M. Farley, *The 'Edge Act' and United States International Banking and Finance* (New York: Brown Brothers and Harriman and Co., 1962 typescript in Baker Library, Harvard Business School), p. 47.
2. *South Africa Scope*, 24 January 1975, p. 9.
3. *Moody's Bank and Finance Manual*, 1974, p. 673.
4. World Council of Churches, *Business as Usual: International Banking in South Africa*, especially pp. 4 and 22.
5. Chase Manhattan Bank, *Annual Report*, 1965, p. 6.
6. All information relating to memberships of boards of directors is from Dunn and Bradstreet, *Reference Book of Corporate Management*, 1974/5 (New York: Dunn and Bradstreet, Inc., 1974); Standard and Poore, *Register of Corporations, Directors and Executives*, 1975 (New York: Standard and Poore Corp., 1974): Vol. II; and *Who is Who in Finance and Industry* (Chicago: Marquis Who's Who, Inc., 1973).
7. *New York Times*, February 1975.
8. Tim Smith: Interfaith Center on Corporate Responsibility, based on interview with Chase Manhattan Bank Official.
9. *Moody's Bank and Finance Manual*, 1974, p. 894.
10. Citicorp, *Annual Report*, 1973. See also, First National City Bank, *Annual Report*, 1968.
11. *The South African Connection, Western Investment in Apartheid*, op. cit.,
12. Barclay's Bank, Ltd., *Report of Board of Directors and Accounts*, 31 December 1973, p. 54.
13. J. Thomson, 'Address', in Barclay's Bank, Ltd., *Report of Directors and Accounts*, 31 December 1967.
14. *Financial Mail* (Johannesburg) July 2, 1976; *South African Digest*, 15 October 1976; and Senator Dick Clark, *Opening Statement*, U.S. Senate Subcommittee on Foreign Affairs, 23 September, 1976.

Chapter X

United States Labour Unions in Southern Africa

The expansion of United States corporate investment in Southern Africa in the last decade has been paralleled by the establishment there of an affiliate of the United States trade union movement, the African-American Labour Center (AALC). Available evidence suggests, that AALC's role has not been to mobilize African workers for a militant struggle to end the system of *apartheid* which ensures payment of wages below the breadline and record profits for the firms investing there. Rather the AALC appears to seek to shape African resistance in channels conducive at most to marginal reforms in the context of the *status quo*.

The AALC in Africa

The AALC was founded by the AFL-CIO in 1964 at the time when nation after nation across the African continent was attaining political independence. Its stated objectives are: [1]

1. To strengthen African trade unions so they can better serve their members and participate in the development of their countries.
2. To provide direct assistance to African trade unions in union development and leadership training, workers' education, professional training, cooperatives and credit unions, labour economics, communication, and other areas related to the welfare of the workers; and
3. To promote solidarity between African and American workers...

The AALC undertook nearly 200 projects between 1965 and 1974, in 'workers' education and leadership training, vocational training, cooperatives and credit unions, social services, information and communications, and study tours and visitors programmes...' They were implemented in 34 countries. Major programmes were mounted in Botswana, Dahomey, Ethiopia, Ghana, Kenya, Liberia, Mauritania, Niger, Nigeria, Senegal, Sierra Leone, Swaziland, Upper Volta and Zaire.

Official and Covert U.S. Government Backing

The AALC is officially a creature of the AFL-CIO Executive Board. It is, however, financed primarily by the U.S. Government through AID. It spent over $8 million in Africa from the date of its establishment to the end of 1972. The rate of expenditure has been increasing in recent years. AALC itself reports that the funds 'come from the U.S. labour movement and from the[U.S. Government's] Agency for International Development'.[2] The only publicly reported figures as to sources of AALC funds[3] show that four out of five dollars are provided by the U.S. Government. The U.S. labour movement contributed less than 20 per cent.

The CIA has also, apparently, played a role in the expansion of AALC in Africa in the post-independence decade. It was estimated as early as 1967 that the CIA had paid more than $100 million to organized labour for activities in foreign countries. An indeterminant part of that money went to AALC which 'spends CIA money in Africa'.[4] Top leaders of the AFL-CIO are reported to have received CIA payments. Jay Lovestone, who has been called AFL-CIO President George Meany's 'minister of foreign affairs', and Irving Brown, a founder of the AALC and until recently its director, have been reported as major recipients. Brown prepared the AALC's policy statement on Southern Africa at its 'Exchange of Views' meeting in Geneva in 1975.[5]

Irving Brown's ties with the CIA date back to 1947, when the French CGT led a massive strike in Paris. One of his CIA colleagues says: [6]

Into this crisis stepped Lovestone and his assistant, Irving Brown... they organized Force Ouvriere, a non-Communist union. When they ran out of money, they appealed to the CIA.

More recently, Brown became involved in Portugal and Italy[7]

...after the Caetano dictatorship fell, Brown arrived in Lisbon to see what he could do to develop anti-Communist unions in

Portugal. In July he travelled to Rome, where his goal was to try to encourage splits in the Italian trade union government and stop the trend towards a unified Communist-dominated union movement.

Under Brown's leadership, the AALC vigorously attacked the All-African Trade Union Federation (AATUF) because it 'entered into signed agreements with the WFTU (World Federation of Trade Unions) and... passed resolutions which indicate increased reliance on "revolutionary" ideology'. This AALC position, as the *AALC Reporter* explains, was founded on Brown's objection to government affiliated union structures and policies. [8]

And who are the predominant members of AATUF? So-called trade union organizations in Algeria, Guinea, Tanzania, and the UAR—countries where workers are totally indifferent to trade unions, recognizing that unions in those countries serve primarily as instruments of a party or the state.

These are, in reality, the African nations which a number of Africanist scholars have held to be working most effectively to achieve self-reliant development designed to raise the levels of life of the working people.

The fact that the AALC claims to receive its financial support from AID is not inconsistent with CIA involvement. Numerous studies have exposed the role of AID in providing cover and funds for CIA operations. [9] That the CIA is working through AALC, a U.S.-supported labour centre, is not a new tactic, either. The CIA has long worked with what the AALC has proclaimed as a 'sister institution' [10] in Latin America, the American Institute for Free Labour Development (AIFLD). Like AALC, AIFLD is affiliated to the AFL-CIO. It receives 90 per cent of its funds from AID. AIFLD's role in fostering the unrest that preceded the Chilean coup has been recognized as extensive. [11] The CIA's role in Chile's unions lends interest to Brown's comments in 1974. [12]

Now is the time to assist trade union organization in these areas, in Mozambique, Angola, Guinea-Bisseau and southern Africa... even if there is independence tomorrow, the problem will still be whether there will be trade union movements, trade union organizations functioning as trade unions.

Brown cannot really suppose that liberation movements, built on the support of workers and peasant, will not organize unions. What he appears to fear is that they will adopt policies like those he rejects in Tanzania, Algeria and elsewhere.

AFL-CIO Support

The role of the AFL-CIO   and AALC in Africa is perhaps best explained by the characteristics of its top leaders. These may be illustrated in the case of George Meany, president of the   AFL-CIO, as well as of the AALC itself. From his post as secretary-treasurer of the AFL, the craft union federation, he became president of the combined   AFL-CIO in 1955. *Time* magazine pictures him vividly: [13]

> ...Meany is used to having people pay him respect and listen to what he says. After all his years of power he would be hard put to imagine life any other way... (In his comfortable summer home) Meany held court while a number of men came by to pay obeisance or ask a favour...

He has invested in (among other things) 'a Dominican Republic resort, along with... other labour and management figures'. [14]

Meany supported the U.S. Government's aggression in Vietnam, even when countless surveys showed the majority of U.S. workers were opposed to it. He is virulently opposed to detente with the Soviet Union. He insists detente 'has got to lead us to eventual disaster'. [15]

The notion of utilizing trade unions to maintain the *status quo* in Africa is not new. In 1959, some years before the founding of the AALC, as Britain prepared to grant independence to its African colonies, a British Cabinet paper suggested that trade unions could play a valuable role in avoiding radical change which might threaten foreign investments in Africa. [16]

> Since it is difficult to accuse unions of serving colonialism, with their aid it should be possible to establish harmonious relations with the new social and political institutions of Africa... Trade union help will be needed to check irresponsible nationalization and to maintain   control of the key sectors of the economy in the newly created African states.

The Cabinet paper made a revealing observation at that early date as to what at the time was merely an incipient interest of U.S. trade union officialdom in Africa: [17]

> The Americans are not interested in the creation in Africa of genuine trade unions... America has no labour party. Her trade

union movement has been built from above by highly paid trade union bosses... [who] are isolated from the rank and file... As a result, the American trade union leaders such as Meany... can afford directly and openly to execute government and particularly CIA policy.

AALC Structure

The AALC maintains that it is democratically run. 'Policy guidance', its 1963-73 Report asserts, 'is provided by the African-American Consultative Committee... which meets at least once a year, although informal consultation takes place on a continuing basis.' The AALC staff also receives additional direction during 'Exchange of Views' meetings held during the International Labour Conference at Geneva every year. These are attended by 'top African labour and government representatives'.

It seems doubtful that a committee can exercise effective control when it meets only once a year. Furthermore, the AALC could only charitably be considered so naive as to believe that four 'top' African union leaders, chosen by the AALC executives themselves to participate in the Consultative Committee, can meaningfully 'represent' the views and concerns of African workers in more than forty nations throughout a continent three times the size of the United States.

The assertion that there is 'informal consultation' can, at best, add to the illusion that the AALC is managed with African participation. No structures have been built to make this illusion a reality. The AALC Report, itself, declares that, 'Full administrative and programme control rests with the Board of Directors and the Executive Director.' The Board is chaired by George Meany. The other members are 'presidents or top officers' of U.S. unions. Not all espouse positions parallel to those of Meany, but they are too preoccupied with their own unions to devote much attention to African labour problems. In effect, the Executive Director and other staff members exercise the real control. There are no Africans on staff.

The man who replaced Irving Brown as Executive Director of AALC in 1973 was one of the few U.S. trade union leaders who has apparently never worked in a factory.[18] He served as sergeant in the U.S. Marine Corps for three years between high school and college. Upon graduation he joined the U.S. Department of Labour, Bureau of Labour Statistics... three years later, in 1962, he left to become research associate with the United Steelworkers. The new Executive

Director went to Ghana to help establish the AALC in 1967, after the coup which ousted President Nkrumah there. He became Deputy director of the AALC two years later.

The Deputy Executive Secretary, Jerry Funk, never worked in a factory, either. He began his career in the Steelworkers when they 'sent him to the Caribbean, where he worked with the Caribbean Bauxite Mineworkers Federation for three years'. He was then employed in Denver by the International Federation of Petroleum and Chemical Workers before going to Ethiopia to work with the AALC in 1968. He moved back to New York when he became Deputy Director of AALC in 1973.[19]

In Francophone Africa the AALC has been working with the Force Ouvriere. This is the union that split off from the French CGT with the encouragement of Meany, Lovestone and Brown, who still maintain that the CGT, which represents the majority of French workers, is 'communist dominated'. As Meany boasted in 1964, 'We financed this split—we paid for it.' [20]

The Force Ouvriere remains the smallest labour group in France. Nevertheless, the AALC decided in 1967 to collaborate with its Institute Syndical de Cooperation in Francophone Africa

The AALC in Southern Africa

In independent Africa, AALC has maintained that trade unions should support 'a stable industrial relations system [which]... is indispensable'[21] for development. It does not seek fundamental changes in the political-economic structures inherited from colonialism. It argues that foreign investment is the key to development. Hence it emphasizes skills training for African workers. '[I]nvestments from abroad will be made if... skilled African workers are available.'[22]

Over the years, AALC has made its views on South Africa clear. The political stance of AALC in the region is essentially that advanced in Option 2 of the U.S. National Security Council's Memorandum of 1969. It argues against guerilla warfare to end white supremacist rule in Southern Africa: 'Eventual war in Southern Africa in which Soviet-trained (sic) African cadres can overwhelm the existing regimes [will] reverse the whole peaceful, constructive and stable development in most of Black Africa.'[23] It does not seem to trouble the AALC that, if the peoples of Mozambique, Guinea-Bisseau, and Angola had not used arms to free themselves, they would still be ruled by Portuguese colonialists.*

In opposition to the stance taken by the South African liberation movement, the AALC supports the United States veto of United Nations action to oust South Africa from that body: [24]

> ... [the] expulsion of South Africa from the United Nations will not... weaken or modify the policies and government of Verwoerd; nor has the usual general consumer boycott there been of much effect.

The AALC financed the trip of Lucy Mvubelo of the South African National Union of Clothing Workers to the International Labour Conference in Geneva.[25] There she sought to convince the conference to reject the idea of an economic boycott of South Africa. She also attended the AFL-CIO's annual conference in Miami, along with Arthur Grobelaar of the white-led Trade Union Congress of South Africa, Harriet Bolton and Norman Daniels. There she played a critical role in persuading the delegates to adopt a watered-down resolution voicing vague support for trade unions 'inside and outside of South Africa', instead of a strong stand in favour of the South African Congress of Trade Unions, the trade union affiliate of the African National Congress. She thus successfully hindered attempts of progressive American unionists to put teeth into their support for liberation in South Africa.

In 1974, the AALC invited a group of handpicked South African unionists to Gaborone in Botswana to discuss union policies in South Africa. Lucy Mvubelo and Arthur Grobelaar were included. It should comes as no surprise that this group, in the face of world-wide efforts to impose an economic boycott on South Africa, endorsed continued investment there by U.S. and other foreign firms. [26]

> Rather than pull out of South Africa, U.S. and other foreign firms should institute far-reaching changes... for their black employees. Pullout would hurt only blacks, and joblessness would literally amount to starvation and lead to the forced removal of blacks from the urban areas...
> The discussions we had in Gaborone have helped define other

---

*Most of these arms, it is true, were provided by socialist countries. Western nations, including the U.S., supplied arms to the Portuguese colonial rulers through NATO.

possible areas of cooperation, notably in South Africa, with TUCSA...

The AALC has initiated contact with the leadership of the Bantustans in South Africa. They have 'been in touch with Chief Gatsha Buthelezi... about the possibility of making use of the AALC's training resources'. [27] It might be noted that Buthelezi came to the United States in 1975, as he himself explained, [28] to try to convince Americans, particularly in the World Council of Churches, to end their efforts to persuade U.S. firms to withdraw their investments from South Africa. The AALC apparently would like to cooperate with leaders like Buthelezi, but AALC Reporter expresses some question as to whether Kwa Zulu actually can exercise meaningful 'independence under the homeland policy'. This initial contact may be something of a trial balloon to assess the reaction of other African countries before the AALC becomes too directly involved with the leaders of South Africa's main instrument for bolstering up *apartheid.*

Finally, AALC's negative response to the great strike wave that spread throughout South African industry in the early 1970s illuminates AALC's view of its own role in Southern Africa. [29]

Unless responsible black leadership is encouraged... the next series of strikes could be disastrous. If the government does not permit blacks to form and run responsible trade unions, industrial chaos and the resulting explosion may in the end destroy the very fabric of South African society.

In other words, AALC seeks ways to control and shape black resistance to *apartheid,* rather than to mobilize a head-on challenge which might destroy the system altogether.

The AALC has expanded its network of bases in Botswana, Lesotho, Swaziland and other Southern African states as U.S. involvement has grown in the region. In Angola, AALC has, since 1969, materially supported the CGTA and LGTAG, exiled trade union movements based in Zaire, which merged in 1973 to form the Centrale Syndicale Angolaise. This is affiliated to GRAE, [30] and through it to the FNLA which, by 1975, the U.S. and South African Governments were openly supporting. The AALC also reported sending medical aid to GRAE. [31]

Summary

The expansion of United States Corporate investments in Southern Africa has been accompanied by increased U.S. Government involvement including CIA - financed activities of the African American Labour Centre. Analysis of the structure of the AALC shows that it is dominated by the most conservative elements among the AFL-CIO leadership. Any pretense of African participation is little more than window-dressing. The policies adopted by the AALC do not challenge the system of apartheid which has condemned the masses of African workers in South Africa to poverty. Rather they seem designed to control and shape African labour's resistance into an acceptance of the very foundations of the system.

REFERENCES

CHAPTER TEN

1. *AALC Reporter*, August-September 1974.
2. *AALC, 1965-73*
3. *AALC Geneva—June 1967.*
4. Drew Pearson and Jack Anderson, 'CIA Figure in Reuther-Meany Riff', *Washington Post*, 24 February, 1975.
5. *AALC Reporter*, August-September, 1974.
6. Thomas Braden, 'I'm Glad the CIA is Immoral', *Saturday Evening Post*, 20 May, 1967.
7. *London Sunday Times*, 27 October 1974.
8. *AALC Reporter*, December 1971.
9. Bruce Oudes, 'The CIA and Africa', *Africa Report*, July-August, 1974.
10. *AALC Reporter*, May 1972.
11. Cf. Fred Hirsch, 'An Analysis of Our AFL-CIO Role in Latin America, or Under the Covers with the CIA', (San Jose, Calif: mimeo, 1974). ILO, The Trade Union Situation in Chile (Geneva: International Labour Office, 1974).
12. *AALC Reporter*, August-September 1974.
13. *Time*, 3 March 1975.
14. *Business Week*, 12 October 1974.
15. *Time*, 3 March 1975.
16. Annex to British Cabinet Paper on Policy in Africa, 1959, quoted in George Morris, *CIA and American Labour* (New York: International Publishers, 1967).
17. Ibid..
18. *AALC Reporter*, June 1973.
19. *AALC Reporter*, December 1973.
20. Quoted in G. Morris, 'Meany, Brown, the CIA and Africa', *World Magazine*, May 26, 1973.
21. *African-American Labour Centre, 1965-1970.*
22. *AALC Reporter*, December 1971.
23. *AALC Reporter*, May 1973.
24. Ibid.
25. *Garment Worker*, 9 September 1973.
26. *AALC Reporter*, June 1973.
27. *AALC Reporter*, May 1973.
28. Talk at Harvard University, 18 Novermber 1975.
29. *AALC Reporter*, June 1973.
30. *AALC Reporter*, December 1973.
31. *AALC Reporter*, April 1973.

APPENDIX TO PART III

Prepared by Davidson Anyiwo

1. DIRECTORSHIP IN OTHER FIRMS INVESTING
   IN SOUTH AFRICA AND FORMER HIGH U.S.
   GOVERNMENT POSTS HELD BY SELECTED
   DIRECTORS OF LEADING U.S. FIRMS
   WITH INTERESTS IN SOUTH AFRICA—1975

Leading U.S. Firms Investing in South Africa	Present (or former) Director or Officer of Leading U.S. Firms Investing in South Africa	Names of other companies with direct involvement in South Africa in which Directorships are held	Dates on which held high U.S. Government Posts (partial list)
Banking			
Chase Manhattan Corporation	Rockefeller, David	Chase International Investment	Chairman, President's Commission on White House Fellows, 1966 - Director, Overseas Development Council
	Butcher, Willard C.	Firestone Tire & Rubber Co., Chase International	
	Connor, J. T.	Allied Chemical Corp; General Motors Corp.; Chase Manhattan Bank	U.S. Secretary of Commerce, 1965-1967 Director, General Motors Company
	Dilworth, J. Richardson	Chrysler Corp. Chase Manhattan Bank, Diamond Shamrock Corp.	
	Furlaud, Richard M.	Squibb Corp, Olin Corp; American Express Co.	
	Jamieson, J. K. Lazarna, Ralph Lilley, Robert D. Loudon, John H.	Exxon Corp. General Elec. Co. A.T. & T. Royal Dutch Petroleum Co.	
	Myers, Charles F.	U.S. Steel Corp. Burlington Industries, Inc.	

Chase Manhattan Bank

	Pratt, Edmund T.	Pfizer, Inc.
	Smith, J. Henry	Colgate-Palgate-Palmolive
	Stone, Whitney	American Express Co.

First National City Bank of N.Y.	Palmer, Edward L.	Borg Warner Corp. Del Monte Corp. Corning Glass Works	
	Costanzo, G.A.	Owens-III Co. Nat'l Cash Register	Econ. & Financial Advisor, Depts. of Internat'l. Commerce. State & Treasury 1941—51
	Spencer, William	Phillips Petroleum Corp.	
	Batteu, William deButts, John D. Eilers, Louis K. Garvin, Jr., C.C.	J.C. Penny Co. U.S. Steel Corp. Eastman Kodak Co. Exxon Corp.	
	Grace, J. Peter	Ingersoll-Rand Co; Kennecott Copper Corp; Deering Milliken, Inc.; Braden Copper Co. (subs. of Kenne cott Copper); W.B. Grace & Co.	
	Gray, Harry Jack Hatfield, Robert S. Haynes H. J. Houghtoh, Amory McCoy, Charles B. Milliken, Roger	Aetna Insur. Co. Kennecott Copper Corp. Standard Oil of Calif. Corning Glass Works E.I. duPont de Nemours Westing house Elec. Corp.	
	Pigott, Charles M. Rees, William Sheldon, Eleanor	Standard Oil of Calif. Chubb Corp.	Pres., Social Science Research Council
	Smith, Darwin	Kimberly-Clark Corp.	

MINING FIRMS

AMAX	Burden, W.A.M.	Asst. Sec. of Commerce for Air, 1943-47, Spec. Aviation Asst. to Sec. of

Commerce, 1942-43
Dir., Nat'l Aviation
Corp. 1939-41
Mem., Nat'l Adv.
Comm. for Aeronautics
1942-47
Spec. Asst. for Res.
& Dev. to the Sec.
of Air Force. 1950-52
Ambassador to Belgium
1959-61
Chairman, Internat'l
for Defense Analysis
Dir., Council on
Foreign Relations
(Aerospace Corp., A
private Corp. which
carries on high level
military related
research for U.S.
government)

	Donahue, D. J. Hauge,Gabriel	Tsumeb Corp.	Spec. Asst. to the Pres. for Econ. Affairs, 1956-58

Engelhard	Harlan, John G.		Dep. Commissioner Defense Materials Service (1958-66) Commissioner, Defense Material Serv. 1966 Commissioner, Prop. Mgmt. and Proposal Service, 1966-69 Rep. President's Comm. on Econ. Impact & Def. & Disarmament
	Reilly, G. W. A.	Anglo-Amer. Corp. Charter Consol, Ltd.	
	Hale, Gerald A.	Chemstone Easton Magnesora Talc Co.	
	Rosenthal, Milton	European-American Bembry Corp. Euro-American Bank & Trust Co. Ferro Corp.	
	Blake, Alfred A.	Chemstone Corp. Eastern Magnesora Talc Co.	Dir. (Ops.) Training in Industry War Man- power Comm. 1942-45

Newmont Mining	Pearce, A.O.	O'Kiep Copper Co. Tsumeb Corp. Magna Copper Co. AMAF Prospect, S.A.	
	Malozemoff, Plato	O'kiep Copper Co. Palabora Mining Co., Ltd. Tsumeb Corp.	U.S. Gov't. Engineer (1943-45)
	Coolbaugh, Frank	AMAX, Inc.	

Union Carbide	Brown, R. M. Jackon, J. B. McNeill, R.E. Ferguson, J. L. Ward, J.H.	Morgan Guaranty Trust; J.P. Morgan J.C. Penney Chrysler Continental Ins. Pres., Chief Execu- tive of General Foods International Harvester Company Continental Corp.	
	Nicholson, W. B. Lambert, A. T.	Union Carbide Southern Africa, Inc. Westinghouse (Canada) IBM Canada	
	Rush, Kenneth		US Ambassador to Germany, 1969-72 Deputy Secretary of Defense, 1972-3 Deputy Secretary of State, 1973- Economic Advisor to President Ford, 1976

Manufacturing

Caterpillar Tractor Company	Martin, W.M. Jr. With firm since 1941 and now Chairman of CEO		(Director, New York Stock Exchange) Chairman, Ex-Im Bank, 1946-48 Asst. Secretary of Treasury, 1949 Exec. Dir., IBRD, 1949-52 Chairman, Federal Reserve Board, 1951-
	Franklin, W. H.	Exxon Corp.	Chairman, Federal Res. Bank of Chicago
	Freeman, Gaylord	Borg-Warner Corp. A.R.C.O.	

	Blackie, William	Shell oil Co.	
		Ampex Corp.	
	Morgan, Lee	3M Company	
	Packard, David	Hewlett-Packard	Chairman and Chief Exec. Officer, Hewlett-Packard Co., 1964–69; Deputy Secretary of Defense, 1969-

Chrysler Corporation	Hewlett, W.R.	Chase Manhattan Bank; FMC Corp.	
	Hauge, Gabriel	AMAX; Mfrs.-Hanover Corp.	
	Coleman, John H.	Colgate-Palmolive Ltd.	
	Clark, H. L.	American Express Co.; Pan Am-Grace Airways	
	Townsend, Lynn	Mfrs.-Hanover Trust Company	
		Burroughs Corp.	First VP, Vice Chairman and Director Ex-Im Bank, 1960-62 US Exec. Director, Inter-American Development Bank & Special Ass't' to Secretary of Treasury, 1962-66

Firestone Tire & Rubber Company	Floberg, J.F.		Ass't. Secy. of Navy 1949-53; Commissioner Atomic-Energy Commission, 1957-60
	Karch, George F.	Rockwell Internt'l Standard Brands, Inc; Warner-Swasey Co.	

Ford Motors Corp.	Bennett, George F.	Hewlett-Packard Corp. N.E. Elec. System	
	Burgess, Carter L.	Morgan Guaranty Trust Co., J.P. Morgan Co.; Smith Kline & French Labs	
	Cullmann, Jos. F. III	I:B.M. World Trade Corp.	
	Gadsten H.W.	Merck & Company	

	(Robert S. McNamara President, 1960-1)		U.S. Secretary of Defense, 1961-68 President, International Bank for Reconstruction & Development, 1968-
	Oelman, Robert S.	Nat'l. Cash Register Co.; Citicorp; First Nat'l City Bank; Procter & Gamble Co.	
	Taylor, A. Thomas	DelMonte Int'l (Deltee)	
General Electric Company	Austin, J.P.	Coca-Cola Co. Morgan Guaranty Trust Co.	
	(Day, Virgil B. VP. Personnel & Industrial Relations Services)		Management Representative, National Labour Management Panel, Federal Mediation & Conciliation Service
	(Dent F.B. Director to 1973)		Secretary of Commerce, 1973-
	Dickey, Jr., C.A.	Scott Paper Co.; J.P. Morgan & Co.; Morgan Guaranty Trust Co.	Special Agent F.B.I. (1941-43)
	Henley, Jr., H.H.	American Express Co; Bristol-Myers Co; Mfrs-Hanover Trust Co;	
	Littlefield, E.W.	Chrysler Corp. Hewlett-Packard Corp.	
	Humphrey, G.W.	Texaco	
	Scribner, H.H.	Abbott Labs.	
	Wriston, W.B.	First Nat'l. City Corp.; J.C. Penney Co.	Officer, Spec. Div., State Dept., 1941-42
General Motors Corporation	Connor, J.T.	Chase Manhattan (President, Chief Executive Officer, Merck & Co., 1955-67)	U.S. Secretary of Commerce, 1965-67
	(Hafstad, L.R. VP Research Labs)		Chairman, General Advisory Committee, US Atomic Energy Commission, 1966-.
	(Malone, R.L.)	(Partner, Atwood & Malone, 1937-67)	US Deputy Attorney General, 1952-55

Goodyear Tire & Rubber Company	Anderson, R. B.	Pan Am World Air-Ways, Inc.	Sec. of Navy; Dept. Sec. of Defense; Sec. of Treasury
	Dodd, E. D.	Owens-Illinois, Inc.	
	Geier, P.O. Jr.,	Armco Steel Corp. Procter & Gamble	
	Harper, J.D.	Procter & Gamble COMSAT: Alcoa	Director, U.S.-Korea Economic Council
	Charles, R. Milone		Energy Commission, 1952-60
	Wright, J.D. DeYoung, Russell	TRW, Inc. Kennecott Copper Corp.; Lykes-Youngstown Corp.	
	Smith, L.B.	A.O. Smith Corp; Deere Company	

I.B.M.	(Brown, Harold) (Consultant, Aeroyet-General Corp., (1956-61)		Secretary of Air Force, 1961-
	Davies, Paul L	FMC Corp; Lehman Bros., Inc.	Trustee, Committee on Internat'l Development; Director, Ex-Im Bank
	Fox, John Michael (Chairman and Chief Executive Officer, United Brands, 1967-71)		US Secretary of Commerce, 1965-67; Dir., Federal Res. Bank of Boston (current)
	Cary, Frank T.	Morgan Guaranty Trust Co.	
	(Katzenbach, N.)		US Attorney General, 1965-66; Under-Secretary of State, 1966-69
	MacNaughton, D.S. (Moore, W. H.) Watson, T. J.	Exxon Corp. RCA Corp.	Director, Economic Development Council Member, Council on Foreign Relations
	Williams, A. L.	Mobil Oil Corp; First Nat'l City Bank; Eli Lilly & Co.	Chairman, President's Comm. on Internat'l Trade & Investment Policy (1970-71)
	Learson, T. V.	Exxon Corp; Caterpillar Tire & Rubber	

International Tel. & Tel. Corporation (I.T.& T.)	Black, E.R.	Chase Manhattan Bank; American International Investment Corp.	Exec. Dir. for the I.S.I.B.R.D. 1947-49 Pres. & Chairman Internat'l Finance Corp. 1961-62; Member, Nat'l Comm. for Internat'l Dev. Member, Perm. Adv. Comm. Evaluate U.S. Foreign Aid Programs
	Brittenham, Raymond		Dir., Nat'l Foreign Trade Council-1961-
	Lannan, J.P.		Special Asst. to Sub-Comm. on Education & Labour (U.S. Congress) 1947
	Eestfall, Ted. B.	Grace Line, Inc.	Dir. (auditing) U.S. General Account. Off. 1944-52
Minnesota Mining & Manufacturing Co.	Barr, J. W.	Burlington Indus. Inc. American Security & Trust Co.	(36th Congress, 11th draft) Asst. to Sec. of Treasury 1961-64 Chairman F.D.I.C., 1964-65; Undersec. of Treasury, 1965-68
	Binger, J.H.	Honeywell, Inc.; Chase Manhattan Corp.	
	Hansen, I.R.	First Nat'l Bank of St. Paul; Minnesco Corp.	
	Heltzer, Harry	General Motors Corp.	
	Cross, Bet S.	Exxon Corp; Morgan Guaranty Trust	
Oil Companies			
Gulf Oil Corporation	Dorsey, B.R. Chairman and Chief Executive Officer	Director, American Petroleum Institute	
	Pearson, Nathan Matthew, Beverly	Ampex Corp. Westinghouse (Canada) 3M (Canada) Ltd.; Rheem (Canada) Ltd.	
	Higgins, James H.	Mellon Bank; Joy Manufacturing Co,; First Boston (Europe) Ltd. Mellon Nat'l. Corp., etc.	
	Brockett, E.A.	Mellon Nat'l. Bank & Trust Co.; Alcoa	

Mobil Oil Corporation	Williams, A. L.	First Nat'l City Bank of N.Y. Eli Lilly & Co.	Chairman, Pres. Committee on Internat'l Trade & Investment Policy 1970 – 71
	Warner, Rawleigh Riordan, J. Q.	Caterpillar	Attorney, Treas. Div Dept. of Justice 1952 – 55
	Borch, F.J.	American Home Products	
	McGhee, George F.		Ambassador to Turkey and West Germany
Standard Oil of California	Haynes, Harold J.	First Nat'l City Corp.; First Nat'l City Bank	
	Wasson, E. H.	Bank of America N.T. & S.A.; Prudential Insurance Company	(Member, Bd. of Trustees Aerospace Corp.)
	Peterson, Rudolph	Bank of America N.T. & S.A.; Bank of America International; Kaiser Steel Corp.; Kaiser Aluminum & Chem. Corp.	Director, COMSAT Administrator, United Nations Development Programme
Texaco	Graham, Donald M.	Abbott Labs. Marcor, Inc.	
	Humphrey, G. W. McCall, Howard W.	G.E. Co., Liggett & Myers, Inc. Lyles Youngstown Corp.	
	McGill, Wm. J. Roosa, Robt. V.	McGraw-Hill, Inc. American Express Co, Owens-Corning Fibergla ss Internat'l; Banks Ltd. (London); Anaconda Co.	

Bibliography

Dunn & Bradstreet *Reference Book of Corporate Management*, 1974-75, (New York: Dunn & Bradstreet, Inc., 1974).
Standard & Poore, Register of Corporations, Directors & Executives, 1975 (New York: Standard & Poore Corp., 1975).
Who is Who in Finance and Industry (Chicago: Marquis Who's Whos, 1973).

PART IV

Exploitation of the Periphery

Chapter XI

South Africa's 'Outward Reach'

South Africa's rapidly growing industrial complex, spurred on by the inflow of foreign capital, confronts sharp internal limitations on its continued growth. The impoverishment of the masses of the African population on the one hand, an important factor contributing to that profitable growth, on the other hand, restricts the possibility of expanding the internal market. The military build-up, required to maintain the white minority regime in power, has provided only a temporary, unstable solution to this intractable market constraint. By the 1970s, it had become increasingly apparent to South African officials and their allied multinational economic interests that new markets and new sources of profitable investment were essential to continued prosperity. At the same time, South Africa's burgeoning industrial sector required new sources of raw materials. These interrelated factors were and continue to create an underlying pressure behind South Africa's augmented efforts to foster 'detente' and extend its 'outreach' to its neighbours to the north. U.S. - based multinational corporations with investments in South Africa have been inextricably bound up in this process.

South African Interdependence

This is not to imply that South Africa's involvement in the political economies of her neighbours has just begun. On the contrary, South Africa's industrial growth has, from the outset, been dependent in part on the exploitation of the neighbouring territories in several critical ways. In this sense, South African development has taken

137

place at the expense of the continuing underdevelopment of its neighbours.

In the first place, South Africa's mining and agricultural concerns have long depended upon neighbouring countries as a critical reserve of the low cost wage labour essential to reaping the accumulation of profits which have been a major source of finance of South Africa's industrial growth. The total number of workers migrating to South Africa annually in recent years has been estimated at almost 600,000.[1] By 1973, they constituted about 8 out of 10 workers on the gold mines. Over a fourth of the gold miners came from Malawi (28.3 per cent). Almost as many came from Mozambique (23.1 per cent); a fifth came from Lesotho (20.2 per cent); a little over five per cent came from Botswana (4.7 per cent) and, Swaziland (1.2 per cent).

TABLE II.A
MIGRANT LABOUR IN SOUTHERN AFRICA, 1973

Country of Origin	
Malawi	280,000
Mozambique	220,000
Lesotho	210,000
Botswana	60,000
Zambia	40,000
Swaziland	30,000
Destination	
South Africa	580,000
Rhodesia	220,000

TABLE II.B

ORIGINS OF MINERS IN SOUTH AFRICA

Country of Origin	1969		1973	
	No.Employed	%	No.Employed	%
Malawi	69,748	18.8	106,860	28.27
Mozambique	99,799	26.9	87,129	23.05
Lesotho	64,925	17.5	76,280	20.18
Botswana	14,840	4.0	17.803	4.71
Swaziland	5,194	1.4	4,573	1.21
South Africa	116,494	31.4	85,050	22.50
Total	371,000	100.0	377,695	100.00

SOURCE: Rhodesian Farmer Publications *Development Magazine*, March 1973, B. *African Research Bulletin*, Vol. 11, No. 5.

MINE
RECRUITING DEPOTS

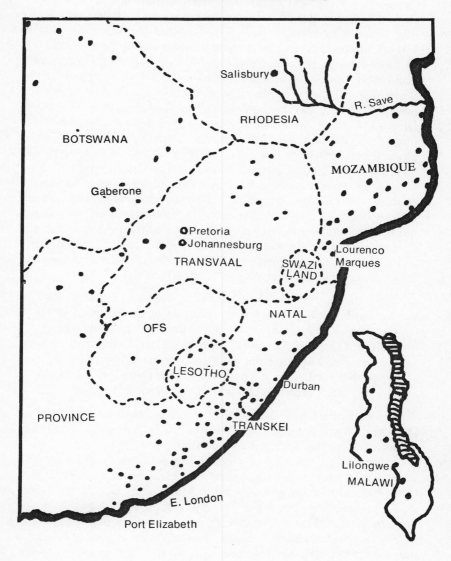

Financial Mail, January 17, 1975

The migrant labour system, drawing on a much larger labour reservoir than was available in South Africa, ensured that mine wages could be held even below the depressed national average. Furthermore, employment of contract labour from outside the country made it harder to unionize the workers, who could be deported at any time at the mine owners' wish. The fact that the miners are kept in 'tribal coumpounds' is used to foster disunity among the workers.

The African mine workers, nevertheless, have a militant history. Continuous unrest has persisted on the mines in recent years. In September 1973, eleven miners, participating in a mass demostration over wages, were shot by the police at Anglo-American's Carltonville Deep Level Mine. Riots, mostly over wages, led to more than sixty miners' deaths in the eighteen months ending in December, 1974. Since then there have been many miners' strikes. For example, in January 1975, 12,000 miners struck on the Vaal Reefs mine.

South Africa has been having trouble maintaing her traditional sources of migrant labour as independence has swept south. Independence in Mozambique means a government which will not allow exploitation of its nationals. In addition, Malawi ordered an end to recruiting, after a plane carrying Malawi migrants crashed in April 1974. According to the *Financial Times* 2 these countries have been less dependent on migrant labour than South Africa.

> The low-geared economies of Malawi, Lesotho and Mozambique which together supply in normal times over 60 per cent of mines labour, would be damaged by a recruitment ban, but they would survive, as Malawi has done for the past six months. The argument goes that they have less to lose than does the highly-geared South Africa economy, where maintaining a high growth rate is an important political priority.

The mine owners have been forced to raise wages to attract South Africans. In the same period, however, the gold price has more than quadrupled, so that their profits have risen still further.

The mining companies have begun to turn to more capital-intensive technology to reduce their dependence on migratory labour. They have announced plans to invest $150 million in new machinery and equipment on the mines. This is undoubtedly one of the factors attracting increased U.S. investment and technology.[3] The importance of maintaining a regular flow of cheap migratory labour in the meantime, however, appears to have been an important factor fostering South Africa's attempt to achieve detente with its neighbours.

A second feature of South African penetration into neighbouring territories has been the investment by South African firms, alone or, more frequently, in joint ventures with foreign partners, in their rich mineral deposits. These investments have contributed to South African economic growth in two ways. First, they have, through sale of increased crude mineral exports abroad, contributed to the growing foreign exchange earnings and profits of South African mining companies. These have helped to finance the import of machinery and equipment for South Africa's new manufacturing industries. Second, South African investment in the mines and agricultural wealth of neighbouring countries has provided a regional source of raw materials for South Africa's factories. The growing pressure of independent African nations for a world-wide boycott of South Africa makes attainment of direct control by South African firms of sources of raw materials within the region increasingly necessary.

Official South Africa data (see Table 11.2) reveals the sharply increased involvement of South African capital in other countries. This reflects the growth of South African investment in neighbouring countries, as well as the increased interlinkages of South African capital with overseas multinational corporations. (See Chapter 3 above) About four out of five dollars of direct private South African investment 'abroad' are in the 'sterling area', which includes most of South Africa's African neighbours. It also includes Australia and Britain, where Anglo, in particular, has been making extensive investments as part of its entry into the world of multinational corporate enterprise.

Two thirds of South Africa's non-direct investment, half of its short term private capital, is also in tthe sterling area. Most of the rest is in Western European banking business. This may reflect a flight of some South African capital as the long-run domestic perspective appears more and more uncertain. Or it may constitute speculation by South Africans seeking to cash in on the profitable financial manipulations taking place in Europe. South African capital in the dollar area makes up only about 10 per cent of all South African investment overseas. Four fifths of this is in non-direct investments, over half of it in the banking business.

South Africa's current outreach policy, in short, must be viewed in terms of its traditional dependence on its neighbours for cheap labour reserves, profitable areas of investment and raw materials for its growing manufacturing sector. The growth of the South African manufacturing sector, spurred by further foreign investment, has

TABLE 11.2

SOUTH AFRICAN INVESTMENTS IN OTHER COUNTRIES, 1972

(in millions of $US and as a per cent of all South African investment by area)

	1966 $m	1966 %	Total $m	Total %	Sterling Area $m	Sterling Area %	Dollar Area Internat. Organ. $	Dollar Area %	Other $	Other %	Western Europe $	Western Europe %	Other Areas $	Other Areas %	Gold Reserve & SDR $	Gold Reserve & SDR %
DIRECT INVESTMENT[1]																
Central govt. & banking sector																
Long-term	3	0.1	4	0.1	—	—	—	—	—	—	3	0.3	—	—	—	—
Short-term	—	—	—	—	—	—	—	—	—	—	—	—	—	—	—	—
Total	3	0.1	4	0.1	—	—	—	—	—	—	3	0.3	—	—	—	—
PRIVATE SECTOR																
Long-term																
Shares, nominal value	88	7.1	352	7.7	276	14.4	—	—	28	7.0	43	4.6	4	8.8	—	—
Reserves	81	6.6	794	17.3	589	30.7	—	—	54	13.5	147	16.0	4	8.8	—	—
Branch & partnership	68	9.5	88	1.9	73	3.8	—	—	0	—	15	1.6	0	0	—	—
Mortgages, long-term loans, debentures, etc.	33	2.7	130	2.4	119	6.2	—	—	2	0.5	6	0.6	3	6.6	—	—
Real estate	36	2.9	39	0.8	44	1.7	—	—	2	0.5	4	0.4	—	0	—	—
Total long-term	307	24.9	1,402	30.6	1,089	56.8	—	—	85	21.2	216	23.5	12	26.6	—	—
Short-term	63	5.0	158	3.5	147	7.7	—	—	—	—	4	0.4	4	8.8	—	—
Total	369	30.0	1,560	34.1	1,234	64.4	—	—	86	22.0	220	23.9	16	35.5	—	—
TOTAL DIRECT INVESTMENT[2]	372	30.3	1,564	34.2	1,238	64.6	—	—	86	22.0	223	24.3	16	35.5	—	—
NON-DIRECT INVESTMENT[2]																
Central govt. & banking sector																
Long-term	143	11.6	591	12.9	57	2.9	452	100.0	—	—	79	8.6	3	6.6	—	—
Short-term	205	16.7	791	17.8	121	6.3	=	—	222	55.5	447	48.7	1	4.4	—	—
Gold reserves	238	19.4	794	17.3	—	—	=	—	—	—	—	—	—	—	794	94
Special Drawing Rights	—	—	49	1.0	—	—	—	—	—	—	—	—	—	—	49	5
Total	587	47.7	2,226	48.3	177	9.2	452	100.0	222	55.5	526	57.3	4	8.8	843	100
PRIVATE SECTOR[3]																
Long-term																
Shares	69	7.2	165	3.6	138	7.1	—	—	7	1.7	19	2.1	0	0	—	—
Mortgages, long-term loans, debentures, etc.	73	5.9	160	3.5	113	5.8	—	—	3	0.7	43	4.6	2	4.4	—	—
Total long-term	142	11.5	326	7.1	252	13.2	—	—	10	2.5	63	6.9	2	4.4	—	—
Short-term	129	10.5	460	10.1	248	12.9	—	—	82	20.5	106	11.6	23	51.4	—	—
Total	271	21.8	726	15.9	501	26.1	—	—	92	23.0	168	18.3	25	55.5	—	—
TOTAL NON-DIRECT INVESTMENT	958	69.7	3,012	65.8	678	35.3	452	100.0	314	78.5	694	75.7	30	60.6	843	100
TOTAL FOREIGN ASSETS	1,230	100.0	4,577	100.0	1,916	100.0	452	100.0	400	100.0	917	100.0	45	100.0	843	100

NOTES: South Africa's foreign assets in the form of direct investment refer to all liabilities towards South Africa of foreign undertakings 'controlled' from South Africa, that, is organisations in which South Africans have an effective say in the policy of the organisation, whether by virtue of share ownership, agreement or otherwise.

[2] In general, the non-direct investment sector has been obtained by deducting direct investment items from the total of the appropriate items of foreign assets reported by South African residents.

[3] Listed securities were valued at the average market values as at the end of 1956 in the case of non-direct investment. All other securities were included at nominal values or book values.

SOURCE: Calculated from South African Reserve Bank, *Quarterly Review,* September 1975.

provided an added impetus for formulation of new 'outreach' policies.

The remainder of this chapter aims to indicate the limits imposed on the continued expansion of South Africa's manufacturing sector, unless new markets can be found; and why the military 'solution' to this problem is inadequate and unstable. The following chapters in Part IV outline the impact of South African penetration in distorting the political economies of its immediate neighbours. The historical drain of hundreds of thousands of migratory labourers and South African-foreign exploitation of their agricultural and mineral wealth have aggravated the external dependence of their national production structures. The sale of South African manufactured goods and the direct and indirect drain of investible surpluses have stunted their industrial growth. The final chapter of Part IV will focus on the special situation in Zambia to show the contradictory factors which have shaped that pivotal nation's reponse to South African initiatives.

South Africa's Narrow Internal Market

South Africa's Bantustanization policies, the suppression of trade unions, and the banning and detention of African leaders has pushed the levels of life of the masses of Africans below the breadline. The resulting widespread misery, even starvation, have been documented and analyzed in Chapter 2, above. The impact of these measures on national economic growth has been a serious problem which even South African officials recognize. The Government's Commission on Exports found: [4]

> the continued process of import substitution necessitating the development of heavy industry impeded by the limited size of the local market in relation to optimal production scales.

The domestic market which results from apartheid policies is far smaller than required for the continuing expansion of the manufacturing sector. The limits imposed by the low incomes of Africans is graphically illustrated by a breakdown of South African income distribution for 1973: [5]

	African	White
Per cent of total population	71.2	16.7
Per cent of all incomes received	17.2	73.9

Real per capita incomes of Africans have been falling in recent years.[6] The total income of all African wage earners and peasants in

1970 had risen about 61 per cent in money terms from 1958 to 1970. In real terms, due to rising prices, the increase was only about 20 per cent. In the same period, the African population grew by 40 per cent. The resulting decline in real per capita income has further reduced potential African purchasing power for the technically sophisticated items produced by South Africa's new manufacturing industries.

The narrowness of the South African market especially hampers the expansion of basic industries which require large investments and large outputs to benefit from the economies of scale available to modern industry. In the highly capital-intensive chemicals industry, for example, a large plant may produce ten times the output of a smaller plant, but cost only four times as much to build.[7] One of the two biggest chemicals firms in South Africa, AE&CI, is building a $300 million coal-based chemicals plant to produce 80,000 metric tons of polyester vinyl chlorine (PVC), the basic input for a wide range of plastic products annually. By 1977 AE&CI, alone, expects to produce 1,220,000 tons yearly. Another firm is building a similar plant, also to come onstream by 1966, with capacity for another 80,000 tons output a year. But South Africa's total demand for this basic product by 1977 was estimated at only 120,000 tons a year, far less than that needed to absorb the two firms' total output.

The smallness of South Africa's market hindered plans to undertake commercial production of a new material, despite subsidization of exploratory costs. The Government developed production of silicon monolithic integrated circuits (small electronic control devices used in computers, military equipment, measuring instruments, etc.) at considerable expense. It has been admitted, however, that 'local manufacture does not look encouraging' because the market is too small.[8]

These examples only illustrate a much larger problem. The fact is that South Africa today is faced by the necessity of finding new markets if its industrial economy is to continue to grow. As one South African authority put it:[9]

> The small domestic market is in part due to the size of South Africa's population... and little can be done about this except to attempt to expand the area of free trade in southern Africa. The limited domestic market is, however, also due to the fact that a majority of the South African population also has only a very low level of consumption. The... whites have on the average a relatively high standard of living, but the... non-whites live for the most part very little above a bare minimum standard.

The Instability of the Military 'Solution'

A partial and temporary 'solution' to the problems of the smallness of the domestic market has been provided by the growth of the Government's defense budget over the last decade. The white minority regime can only stay in power in South Africa through the use of massive force. The attainment of independence of over forty African nations in the decade of the 1960s, the successes of the guerilla movements in the neighbouring Portuguese territories and Zimbabwe, and the declared intentions of the African liberation movement to free South Africa itself, have stirred deep fears among the white ruling group which have spurred their efforts to build a powerful military force. These growing military expenditures have created an increasingly important market for industry, especially for basic manufacturing industry.

In the 1960s, alone, South African military expenditure multiplied over six times from $65 million to $405 million a year.[10] By 1974/75, it had more than doubled again, to $1,045 million.[11] Direct military spending had risen from 12 to 16 per cent of the government budget in the two years from 1972 to 1974. In 1975/76, military spending jumped another 36 per cent to $1,000,000, or 19 per cent of the budget.[12]

TABLE 11.3
DEFENCE EXPENDITURES

	1974/5		1975/6		
	$ million	% total	$ million	% total	Increase
Total Government Budget	6,374.5	100.0	7,553.0	100.0	18.5
Defence	1,038.1	16.3	1,412.7	18.7	37.1
African Education	89.4	1.4	102.7	1.3	14.8

SOURCE: Republic of South Africa, *Estimate of Expenditure to be Defrayed from Revenue Account During the Year Ended 31st March, 1976.* (Government Printers, 1975)

Since 1970, the South African Army has been introducing the most modern equipment available. The share of the defence budget allocated for armament procurement and special equipment to replace obsolete gear rose steadily from 32 per cent in 1971 to 53 per cent in 1973.[13] About $280 million was spent on aircraft, $125 million on ammunition, and $110 million on radio, radar and other electro-technical equipment between 1970 and 1973.

TABLE 11.4
SOUTH AFRICAN ARMED FORCES

South Africa

Military service: 12 months
Total armed forces: 50,500 (35,400 conscripts)
Estimated GNP 1974: $32.5 bn.
Defence expenditure: 1975—76: 948.1 m rand ($1,332 m.)
$1 0.712 rand (1975), 0.667 rand (1974)

Army 38,000 (31,000 conscripts)
1 armoured brigade *
1 mechanized brigade *
4 motorized infantry brigades.*
2 parachute battalions.*
6 field and 1 medium artillery regiments*
2 light AA artillery regiments *
6 field engineer regiments *
5 signals regiments *
5 signals regiments *
141 Centurion, 20 Comet med tks; 1,000 AML-245/60, AML-245/90
Fland, 50 M-3 armed cars and 80 Ferret scout cars; 250 Saracen,
about 100 Commando APC; 25-pdr gun/how, 155mm how; 17 pdr.,
90 mm ATK guns; ENTAC ATGW; 204GK 20 mm, K-63 twin 35mm,
1,-90 40mm and 3.7-in. AA guns; 18 Cactus (Crotale), 54 Tigercat
Sam.

Reserves 138,00 Active Reserve (Citizen Force)
Reservists serve 19 days per year for 5 years

Navy: 4,000 (1,400 conscripts)
3 Daphne-class submarines
2 destroyers with 2 Wasp ASW helicopters
6 ASW frigates (3 with 1 Wasp ASW hel each)
1 escort minesweeper (training ship)
10 coastal minesweepers

* Cadre units that would be brought up to full strength on mobilization of the Citizen Force and form II divisions.

South Africa

4 patrol craft (ex-British Ford-class)
(6 Corvettes, with Exocet SSM, being built)
Reserves 10,400 trained Citizen Force with 2 frigates and 7 minesweepers.

Air Force: 8,500 (3,000 conscripts); 108 combat aircraft
1 light bomber sqn with 10 Buccaneer S-50 with AS-30 ASM.
2 fighter sqns with 32 Mirage IIIEZ and 8 III IIIDZ
1 fighter recce sqn with 16 Mirage IIICZ, 4 IIIBZ and 4 IIIRZ with
AS-20 ASM. Matra R-530 AAM
2 MR sqns with 7 Shackleton MR3, 18 Piaggio P-166S Albatross (2
more P-166S

4 hel sqns, 2 with 20 Alouette III each, 1 with 20 SA-330 Puma, 1 with
15 SA-321L. Super Frelon. 1 flight of 7 Wasp (Naval-assigned) 1
comms and liaison sn (army-assigned) with 16 Cessna 185/A/D/E
(being replaced by AM-3C) Trainers incl Harvard; 160 MB-326M
Impala (some armed in a COIN role); 30 Vampire FM Mk 6, Mk 9, T
Mk 55: T-6; TF-86; C-47 and Alouette II/III. (32 Mirage F-142
and 16 F-1C and 15 MB-326K on order.)

Reserves 3,000 Citizen Force 8 sqns with 20 Impala, 40 AM-3C,
Boshok, 100 Harvard IIA. III, T-6G Texan; Cessna 185 A/d A185-E

Para-Military Forces: 75,000 Commandos-armed civilian military
organized in infantry battalion-type units grouped in formations of 5
or more units with local industrial and rural protection duties.
Members undergo 10 months' initial and periodic refresher training.
There are 12 Air Commando squadrons with private aircraft.

SOURCE: The Military Balance, 1975-1976. International
Institute for Strategic Studies (London: 1975).

TABLE 11.5

EXPENDITURE ON CAPITAL EQUIPMENT BY SOUTH AFRICAN
ARMED FORCES,
1969/70 - 1972/73

	R000
Total	534,150
Radio, radar, & other electronics	75,141
Guided 'weapons	23,166
Ammunition	85,422
Vehicles mobility equipment	29,477
Combat vehicles	43,070
Weapons	34,592
Vessels	53,214
Aircraft	190,072

SOURCE: UN Unit on Apartheid, 'Call for an End to All Military Cooperation
with South Africa', Notes and Documents No. 18/73, Annexe

The South African Government has taken steps to stimulate local
manufacture of the necessary parts and equipment for its growing
military establishment. The United Nations, effort to impose an arms
boycott in the 1960s was undoubtedly a significant factor in this
decision. Although the boycott was broken, mostly by France and
Italy, it did push up the price of South Africa's military imports. In
1974, arms imports alone added over $500 million to its import bill.
Oil and arms together totalled $1,500 million in import costs, [14] the
major cause of South Africa's persistent balance of payments deficit.

Domestic military purchases contributed significantly to the
expansion of demand required to stimulate domestic manufacturing
industries. The American military journal, *Armed Forces Journal
International,* observed that South Africa's increasing expenditure on
capital goods for the military, 'has resulted in development of skils
locally, and has provided economic growth to the country' [15]

International Defence reported that as early as 1971, South
Africa could manufacture:

Explosives and propellants—South Africa is so self-sufficient
that she can consider exports.
Ammunition—the position is extremely satisfactory. About
100 various types are being made. Regarding heavy calibre
ammunition, South Africa is self-sufficient. With infantry
ammunition, she is either self-sufficient or has reached the
production stage. The country will be self-sufficient in naval

ammunition within the foreseeable future, and is already producing all the pyrotechnical supplies she needs.

An automatic service rifle... and a submachine gun (unconfirmed reports indicate the Israeli USS) as well as mortars, are already being locally made. A start has been made on a 90 mm cannon.

There are facilities to manufacture almost any armoured vehicle.

Aircraft, radios, mine detectors and other classified electronic equipment can already be locally designed and made.

More recently it was disclosed that South Africa is building its own 25 pounder guns, manufacturing napalm bombs, the full range of aerial bombs up to 1,000 lb and is continuing to develop its own guided missiles (including a Mach 2 air-air missile, thought to be IR homing, which was successfully test fired from a *Mirage* at a supersonic target in September). The missiles, I was informed, might be available for export.

This is not to suggest that South Africa had achieved complete self-sufficiency in arms production. The Institute for Strategic Studies' magazine, *Survival*, reported in 1972: [16]

Although South Africa has made considerable progress towards her goal of becoming more self-sufficient in weaponsment, she remains vulnerable to external sanctions, especially in the area of supersonic jet aircraft, heavy armour and warships. So a total, as distinct from partial, embargo of South Africa by the external industrial powers would certainly pose major problems for these programmes which rely primarily on sophisticated weapons... it can be argued that South Africa's current indigenous production plans provide adequate quantities of small arms and ammunition to overcome a total embargo. All other programmes, even for relatively simple weapon systems such as the locally produced Italian *Impala* counter-insurgency aircraft and the French *Panhard* armoured cars, would probably suffer from a total embargo.

From the official South African perspective, given the imminent danger of internal uprisings, it was perhaps more important that, as the Institute study pointed out, [17]

...in a relatively short time South Africa would probably be able to produce all her own counter-insurgency equipment, apart from helicopters and large transport aircraft.

By 1974, the *Evening News* was able to announce[18] that South Africa planned to build its own El Mirage fighterplanes under licence from the French firm Desault. As a first step, it had bought fifty kits for local assembly. It was already producing 'in whole or nearly so... advanced versions of Impala aircraft (the Italian Aermacchi MB-326), Eland armoured cars, and many small arms including the Belgian FN rifle'.[19] According to its Defence Minister,[20] South Africa was ex pected to start building its own tanks soon.

In cooperation with the French, South Africa was reported to have developed the Cactus surface-air missile, providing 80 per cent of the funds to finance its development and production.[21]

The South African Government has become directly involved in military production, in much the same way that it has invested directly in the overall manufacturing sector, by creating a parastatal holding company. It set up a firm, ARMSCOR, in 1969, providing it with an initial capital of about $150 million. The President of the Government Armaments Board, Professor H. J. Samuels, asserted that, in 1972, seventy per cent of the Government's defense expenditures for armaments went to ARMSCOR's seven wholly-owned subsidiaries and to private industry. Private contractors were awarded $52 million worth of contracts for military production in 1971/72, and double that amount in 1972/3. Most of these funds were spent for engineering and electronics equipment and machinery.[22] In 1973, the Defense Department reported that half of the total armaments expenditures were paid to about 200 contractors and sub-contractors in South Africa itself. These expenditures provided a considerable demand for expanded manufacturing production.

The military 'solution' to South Africa's market problem is, however, inherently unstable. The expansion of military expenditures by the Government has, on the one hand, inevitably added to the inflationary pressures which plague the economy. The Government has been forced to pile up an increasing internal debt to pay for its' weapons build-up. The 1974 military budget, alone, accounted for about 70 per cent of the total Government debt. The increased debt represents the creation of new money supplies, which are not matched by the expanding production of consumer goods. At the same time, the oligopolistic manufacturing firms, especially those in basic in-dustries, take advantage of the existence of the guaranteed military market for their products to maintain rigid high prices throughout the rest of the economy, despite the low incomes of the masses of the consumers. The main consequence in the context of South Africa's already distorted income distribution, is to siphon off the profits and high salaries to the already-rich, further reducing the real incomes of the masses of the population.

On the other hand, the production of military goods and equipment is a once-and-for-all business, even with the renewal of obsolete equipment, unless it is used up in actual warfare. South Africa was able to sell 'certain heavy armaments... abroad', according to Minister of Defence, Botha.[23] Most of these transactions were not publicized, but it is probable that most of them were sales to bolster the illegal white minority regime of Rhodesia [24] and to aid the Portuguese fascists to maintain their rule in Angola and Mozambique. The coup which ended Portuguese rule also seemed likely to spell a sharp reduction in South Africa's military sales abroad.

The need to continue expanding military output to maintain economic growth was a significant factor pushing the fascist states of Germany, Japan and Italy towards outright warfare to occupy and exploit neighbouring territories during the Great Depression of the 1930s. For the South African regime, however, any kind of expanded sales of manufactured goods, military included, is preferable to war itself. The only obvious area for military expansion of South Africa is towards the independent black African countries to the north. Any effort to achieve military expansion in that direction might well provide the spark in the tinder to explode the foundations of the entire oppressive racist South African apparatus.* Hence, in the long run, the expansion of military production appears likely to at most provide only a temporary and inadequate 'solution' to the need for an expanding market for the mushrooming manufacturing sector.

The Limits on South African Exports to Developed Nations

The only alternative available to South Africa is to expand its markets abroad. An International Monetary Fund economist, writing in the *South African Journal of Economics*, [25] argues that expansion of exports is essential to enable South African industry to achieve economies of scale 'which are denied to small countries establishing industries solely to supply the limited home market'.** The Govern-

---

*This seems to be the most likely reason that South African military forces in Angola were pulled back to the border in 1976 when it became apparent that they faced either a prolonged battle or outright defeat when the U.S. Congress refused to send military support.

**With a population of 24 million plus, South Africa is not such a small country; rather, its market is limited because the wages of Africans are systematically held below the poverty line. But the white South African regime is not voluntarily about to alter the foundations of its profitable rule.

ment has adopted this policy specifically, declaring that further growth must depend on increasing exports of manufactured goods. [26]

Sean Gervasi has summed up South Africa's dependency on world trade in a UNO document:[27]

> South Africa is in fact rather more dependent on world trade than [the] figures would indicate. There are many countries with a volume of trade which is important. Most of them, however, could produce substitutes for the goods which they import. In some cases, they could redirect their exports to the domestic market. South Africa is not in such a favourable position. Its exports cannot be marketed at home and most, or many, of its imports are irreplaceable. Qualitiatvely speaking, it is highly dependent on world trade.

South Africa has little choice of new outlets for the sale of manufactured goods. Its traditional markets in the developed countries of Western Europe, North America and, today, Japan, are open primarily only for raw and semi-processed materials in the typical neo-colonial pattern. In exchange, South African purchases from these nations the capital and intermediate goods and equipment required to build up its own manufacturing sector. (See Table 11.6).

As South African manufactures cannot compete in developed country markets due to high tariffs and the cost of transport, the Government still promotes the sale of crude and semi-finished raw materials to them to earn the foreign exchange to purchase the manufactured goods and equipment South Africa must still import. [28]

In 1974, South Africa's exports to her most important trading partner, the United Kingdom, were 47.8 per cent of its total precious stones and metals sales (Section 14 of the BTN), and 22.5 per cent vegetable products, prepared footstuffs, beverages and tobacco (Sections 1, 2 and 4).

South Africa's two most important exports to West Germany (her second largest trading partner since 1973) were gold and copper in 1973: these totalled almost a third of South Africa's total exports to that country. The only manufactures in the fifteen most important of South Africa's exports to that country were tinned fruit and fruit juice, 2.7 per cent of total exports. The share of raw materials has apparently increased slightly since 1969.

On the other hand, South Africa's imports from the United Kingdom in 1974 were 24.2 per cent machinery and equipment (Section 16 of the BTN) and 26.6 per cent transport equipment (Section 17). Her imports from West Germany in 1974 were 26 per

TABLE 11.6

SOUTH AFRICA'S EXPORTS TO AND IMPORTS FROM
SELECTED COUNTRIES AS PER CENT OF TOTAL TRADE, 1974.

A. *Trade in Agricultural Products:*

*African countries and USA are major sources of South African imports

*South Africa exports these kinds of products to England

BTN SECTIONS	Africa I %	Africa E %	Britain I %	Britain E %	W. Germany I %	W. Germany E %	U.S.A. I %	U.S.A. E %	Total SA R thousands I	Total SA R thousands E
1. Live vegetables, animal products	33.2	14.1	5.6	8.1	2.7	1.6	9.1	25.5	R60,794	54,067
2. Vegetable products	24.0	13.0	4.4	19.8	1.5	8.2		0.6	R100,900	381,914
3. Animal & vegetable products	12.5	14.1	2.0	13.9	1.2	5.8		0.3	R40,575	21,577
4. Foodstuffs, beverages	31.4	0.7	19.5	21.9	1.9	5.6		5.9	85,399	446,491
Sub-Total	26.8	10.5	18.8	22.5	7.9	7.3		5.3	287,668	804,049

B. *Light Manufactured Goods Trade:*

*African countries now produce their own, neither sell nor buy much from South Africa

*South Africa sells a major share of its exports of these products to England and West Germany

*England, West Germany and the USA are major sources of imports for South Africa

	Africa		Britain		W. Germany		U.S.A.		Total SA R thousands	
	I	E	I	E	I	E	I	E	I	E
11. Textile & textile products	8.8	8.6	12.2	20.1	10.5	15.9	11.5	2.8	465,402	152,413
8. Leather & leather products	6.6	1.3	19.2	33.0	9.3	10.9	11.5	2.2	23,550	55,838
Sub-Total	8.7	6.3	12.5	23.6	10.5	14.1	11.5	2.6	488,952	207,751

C. *Crude Metals and Minerals Trade [including gold]*:

*These constitute South Africa's main exports to England, West Germany and the U.S.A.. England is South Africa's main market for its gold (almost half of South Africa's gold exports).
*South Africa imports some in crude form from Africa, exports some processed metals to Africa.

	Africa		Britain		W. Germany		U.S.A.		Total SA	
	I	E	I	E	I	E	I	E	I	E
5. Mineral products	25.9	4.0	3.8	12.7	3.8	15.1	12.8	9.0	97,585	288,941
14. Precious & semiprecious stones & metals (incl. gold)	26.0	4.1	3.8	12.7	3.8	22.1	12.8	9.1	99,585	288,921
1 Base metals & allied products	5.9	17.8	11.1	7.7	27.4	12.0	10.5	19.8	506,317	487,435
Sub-Total	19.6	6.6	12.4	28.3	22.4	14.4	10.6	10.3	646,573	1,525,898

D. *Complex Manufactured Goods Trade:*
*Africa is South Africa's main export market for these industries.
*South Africa itself must still import some of these items from England, Germany and the U.S.A.

	Africa		Britain		W. Germany		U.S.A.		Total SA	
	I	E	I	E	I	E	I	E	I	E
6. Chemicals & allied products	1.6	54.9	18.9	4.0	17.0	3.4	20.7	4.1	448,792	116.278
7. Plastics & rubber products	0.2	88.9	19.6	1.8	18.2	0.3	15.1	0.3	278.533	21.620
10. Paper & paper products	0.8	26.6	17.5	36.9	6.7	3.3	28.2	14.0	203.533	77,733
13. Stone, cement, glass & allied products	0.8	77.5	23.8	2.3	13.3	0.3	12.1	4.2	70.983	14.233
16. Machinery & mechanical appliances, incl. elec. equipment	0.8	72.7	19.6	6.8	24.2	2.6	19.7	5.0	1,322.538	12.947
17. Vehicles, aircrafts, vessels & parts	0.3	67.2	19.8	4.2	26.6	0.7	14.9	6.4	789,891	4.537
18. Optical, photographic & recording instruments	0.5	37.2	15.1	19.3	17.7	0.8	20.7	14.0	179.546	1,117
20. Miscellaneous manufactured articles	12.5	59.0	17.5	13.0	10.1	0.5	15.0	11.7	40.076	260
Sub-Total	0.9	58.2	19.3	11.3	21.7	2.1	18.7	6.6	3,323.567	41,848

E.   Total Trade:

*England is still South Africa's leading export market, but West Germany has become its leading source of imports, and the U.S. has almost caught up.

*Africa is South Africa's second most important export market, especially when gold is excluded from total exports. Africa is the only area with which South Africa has a trade surplus.

	Africa		Britain		W. Germany		U.S.A.		Total SA	
	I	E	I	E	I	E	I	E	I	E
Totals										
1974	4.9	13.6	16.7	28.7	18.8	9.5	16.5	7.1	4,915,954	334,507
1975	5.8	13.0	19.3	26.6	18.5	7.2	16 1	6.2	3,283,066	262,697
Total less precious stones & metals (Section 14)* including gold-1974		24.0		32.1		10.7		7.6	4,873,283	187,743

19. Relates to military imports and is therefore excluded by South Africa Government.

* = 22.4% of total exports

NOTES: (1) BTN = Brussels Trade *Nomenclature* (2) Subtotals refer to country's trade in category as percentage of S.A.'s total trade in that category.

SOURCE: Republic of South Africa, *Monthly Abstract of Trade Statistics*, June December, 1975 (Pretoria: Gov't Printer, 1975).

cent transport equipment, 25 per cent machinery, and 18 per cent chemicals.

South Africa is building a new productive capacity to expand the sales of crude and semi-processed materials for export to the developed countries. For example, Lonrho recently opened a $3 million platinum refinery at Brakpan, with exports expected to be worth 'at least $372 million by the late 1980s'. [29]

Triomf fertilisers (see p. 52 above) has signed contracts for exports worth $ 2,980 million over twenty years. To fulfill these, it is building a giant phosphoric acid plant in Richards Bay, to produce 400,000 tons a year. This will increase South Africa's production of fertilisers by a factor of ten. [30]

Consolidated African Mines contracted to supply the Japanese steel industry with 8.6 million tons of mangaferrous ore over eleven years. It has opened a mine in Sishen to fill these orders. [31]

Coronation Collieries, an Anglo subsidiary, has contracted to supply 850,000 tons of low-ash coal to Japan for five years from 1976, and then 500,000 tons a year for five years thereafter. [32]

A new fluorspar mine is to be opened by Marico Fluorspar (which represents North American interests) to produce 170,000 tons a year of both acid and metallurgical grade concentrates 'almost entirely for export to world markets'. [33]

Johnnies and a Japanese company, Showa Denko, are establishing a high-carbon ferrochrome plant with a capacity of 120,000 tons of charge chrome. Showa Denko will buy 30,000 tons at ruling prices. Capital expenditure is to be $37 million. Annual earnings at full capacity should be over $45 million. [34]

Palabora Mining Company contracted to export almost nine million tons of magnetite concentrates to Japan in the ten years to 1976. This was one of the main reasons for establishing the company.

The motor industry is in a special position, because of the import restrictions imposed by the South African Government to encourage local production. These restrictions have apparently led the multinational vehicle firms operating in South Africa to develop exports of auto components and cars to the U.S. and Europe, as well as Africa. In 1972, Ford South Africa was reportedly trying to find an export market for its Cortina light pick-up truck 'which was designed and developed in this country [South Africa]'. General Motors exports components to Europe, and VW exports assembled cars to the rest of Africa. [35] The recent serious drop in local demand for cars, due partly to the oil boycott and high prices, seemed likely to accelerate this trend.

The Government has played a major role in encouraging exports. [36] As with the process of industrialisation itself, the Government intervenes both indirectly, through encouragement and financing for private exports, and directly, through exports by parastatals.

One of the main tasks of the Industrial Development Corporation as noted in Chapter 4 above, has been to assist South African firms to export their produce. In 1974 alone it loaned $425 million to South African firms in the export business. [37] In conjunction with the South African Reserve Bank and the Department of Commerce, it made a credit of $270 million available to finance the export of capital goods. The basic principle of IDC export policy was to provide financing on 'a virtually breakeven basis to ensure competitiveness in the international market'. [38] With the cooperation of British banks, [39] the IDC also arranged $22 million in credit for South African industrialists selling goods in England.

ISCOR takes the lead in direct exports by Government parastatals. It completed a ten year contract to supply five million tons of pig iron to Japan by 1974 which earned $211 million. [40] Its Saldanha-Sishen Scheme is expected to produce primarily for export, bringing in about $150 million in foreign exchange earnings annually. [41] An ISCOR subsidiary, Veldmaster, manufactures agricultural discs and other earth-engaging parts, mainly for export, benefitting considerably from export promotions schemesfi. [42]

ISCOR has formed a steel trading corporation, ISKOOR, with the largest Israeli steel processor, the Koor Group. The corporation is 49 per cent Iscor and 51 per cent Koor. It will buy steel on the world market for Israel, presumably purchasing as much of it as possible from ISCOR. [43]

The Government's oil-from-coal company, SASOl., is also producing for the export trade. A new plant came on stream in the early 1970s, to produce 'hard wax powder... used, among other things, in printers ink'. Most of the output is to be exported to the U.S., Europe and the Far East (probably Japan). [44] The Government's fertilizer parastatal, FOSKOR, expects to export a significant portion of the phosphate concentrates to be produced by the new capacity it is adding. The bulk of its output will be sold to Triomf which is expected to sell phosphoric acid for 'substantial' foreign exchange earnings. [45]

The Pattern of South African Trade with Africa

In contrast to her trade with developed Western countries and Japan, South Africa's exports to the 'rest of Africa' consist predominantly of manufactured goods: machinery and equipment (in 1974, 73 per cent of total exports of these items); chemicals (55 per cent); plastics and rubber products (89 per cent); stone, cement, and glass products (77 per cent); and transport machinery and equipment (73 per cent). (See Table 11-6. above.) Most South African imports from 'the rest of Africa' consist of light consumer goods and raw materials: vegetable products, prepared foodstuffs, beverages and tobacco (27 per cent of these items); textiles (8.6 per cent); mineral products (26 per cent).

It should be noted that South Africa does not publish statistics for individual African countries, probably to avoid embarrassing them as well as to conceal the extent of her trade with the racist Rhodesian regime. The data given for 'the rest of Africa' excludes Botswana, Swaziland and Lesotho, because they are incorporated within the Southern African Customs Union.

Africa is the only area of the world with which South Africa has a trade surplus. If Botswana, Lesotho and Swaziland were included in this data, Africa's importance as a market for South Africa's manufacturing industry would be shown to be even greater.

The vital necessity of maintaining and expanding this market for her growing manufacturing sector constitutes the economic foundation of South African Prime Minister Vorster's renewed efforts toward an 'outward reach', his declared goal of achieving an African detente.[46]

The alternative is military conflict. He argued, early in 1975,

Either we come to an understanding with Africa or there will be an escalation of confrontation. Either the Rhodesian situation is settled or... Either South Africa's stated policy with regard to South West Africa is accepted... or...

He did not then spell out the alternative, but he had previously asserted that it was 'too ghastly to contemplate'.

Summary

The impoverishment of the masses of the African population, while making possible the high rates of profit reaped by investors in South Africa, also inevitably limits the possible expansion of the domestic market. The national military build-up has provided a temporary but inherently unstable 'solution' to this market problem. It fosters inflation, and, in the long run, cannot continue unless there is war; and war might well spark a revolutionary confrontation which would destroy the white minority regime. Exports to western developed countries and Japan are limited to crude and semi-processed materials in a typical neo-colonial pattern. The only apparent market for exports of South African manufactured goods is in the neighbouring countries to the north. This is a fundamental reason underlying the search for detente. Prime Minister Vorster has declared the alternative 'too ghastly to contemplate'.

REFERENCES

CHAPTER ELEVEN

1. *Africa Research Bulletin*, Vol. 11, No. 5.
2. Quoted in *African Research Bulletin*, Vol. 11, No. 9.
3. Johannesburg *Star*, 6 July 1974.
4. H.J.J. Reynder, 'Export Status and Strategy', *South African Journal of Economics*, Vol. 43, No. 1, March 1975. Reynder headed the Government Commission of Inquiry into the Export Trade of the Republic of South Africa , 1972.
5. *Financial Mail*, 21 February 1975.
6. R. First, C. Gurney, J. Steele, *South African Connection* (London: Maurice, Temple, Smith Ltd., 1972).
7. Ibid.
8. *Financial Mail*, 21 December 1973.
9. D. Hobart Houghton, *The South African Economy* (Cape Town: Oxford University Press, 1973), third edition.
10. Institute for Strategic Studies, *Survival*, June – July 1972.
11. Ibid.
12. Republic of South Africa, *Estimate of Expenditure to be Defrayed from Revenue Account During the Year Ended 31st March, 1976* (Pretoria: Government Printers, 1975).
13. *Survival*, op. cit.
14. *Financial Mail*, 13 September 1974.
15. *Armed Forces Journal International*, June 1973 (Washington, D.C.).
16. June-July.
17. Ibid.
18. 19 February 1974.
19. *AFJI*, op. cit.
20. Ibid.
21. *Evening News*, 19 February 1974.
22. *Guardian*, 5 December 1973.
23. *Evening News* (London) 19 February, 1974.
24. See eg. *Manchester Guardian*, 5 December, 1973; also *Financial Mail*, 23 October, 1970.
25. D. Lachman, 'Import Restrictions and Exchange Rates', in *South African Journal of Economics* Vol. 42, No. 1, March 1974.
26. Cf. Republic of South Africa, 'Commission of Inquiry into the Export Trade of the Republic of South Africa', (Pretoria: Government Printers, 1972).
27. Sean Gervasi, *Industrialisation, Foreign Capital and Forced Labour in South Africa* (New York: UN Unit on Apartheid, 1970).
28. Trade statistics are from Republic of South Africa, *Monthly Abstract of Trade Statistics,* January-December 1975 and January-December 1970 (Pretoria: Government Printers), data for West Germany is from *Financial Mail*.
29. Rhodesian Farmers Association, *Development Magazine*, August 1974.
30. *African Research Bulletin*, Vo. 11, No. 4; Economist Intelligence Unit Ltd., *Quarterly Economic Review*, 3rd Quarter, 1974.

31. Economist Intelligence Unit, *Quarterly Economic Review*, 2nd Quarter, 1974.
32. *South African Digest*, 25 October 1974; *African Research Bulletin*, 11, No. 5.
33. *African Research Bulletin*, Vol. 11, No.3.
34. *African Research Bulletin*, Vol. 11, No.1.
35. *South African Digest*, 28 January 1972; see also, Da Gama Publishers, *An Industrial Profile of South Africa* (Johannesburg: H. & G. Dagbreek, 1966).
36. Da Gama Publishers, *State of South Africa, Economic, Financial and Statistical. Year Book for the Republic of South Africa* (Johannesburg: 1973).
37. *Development Magazine*, op. cit., August 1974.
38. *South African Digest*, 25 October 1974.
39. *Financial Mail*, 11 October 1974.
40. *South African Digest*, 25 October 1974.
41. Counter Intelligence Services, *Business as Usual: International Banking in South Africa* (London: 1974).
42. Union Steel Corporation. *Annual Report*, 1974.
43. Iscor, *Annual Report*, 1973.
44. *Development Magazine*, op. cit., August 1974.
45. Ibid.
46. *New York Times*, 1 April, 1975.

Chapter XII

Namibia: An Outright Colony

Namibia, which the South African Government persists in calling South West Africa, is South Africa's only political, as well as economic, colony. It was mandated to South Africa after World War I by the League of Nations. After World War II, the International Court of Justice declared continued South African occupation of the territory to be illegal. But South Africa has refused to accept this ruling. It has, instead, proceeded to impose an *apartheid* system there as the foundation for prolonged indirect, if not direct, rule.

The population of Namibia is a little less than a million. Its per capita output is barely $8 a head,* one of the lowest in Africa. Primary resources—minerals, fish, cattle and a persian wool called karukul—provide its most important commercial produce. In 1969, diamonds and base minerals provided about a third of its gross product. Agriculture and fishing provided about 15 per cent.

Export Orientation

Under South African tutelage, the Namibian economy has been increasingly distorted towards the export of crude materials. Mining, the most externally dependent sector, has been the fastest growing in recent years. The value of mineral exports doubled in the five years from 1962 to 1967 to over $200 million, equalling over a third of the national output in the latter year. Fishing earned almost $100 million,

*South Africa does not publish statistics for Namibia, so most figures are estimates.

162

agriculture $60 million, and tourism about $75 million in 1967. [1]
Agricultural output grew about 6.5 per cent between 1965 and 1965,
while the fishing sector's production remained about the same.

TABLE 12.1
NAMIBIAN EXPORTS, 1966-1973

	1966	%	1973*	%
	R000		R000	
Karakul pelts	15,375	7.3	32,000	10.3
Livestock	14,115	6.7	40,000	12.9
Livestock products	2,525			
Other agricultural		1.2	...	
products	120			
Fish meal	22,400	10.7		
Canned fish	14,000	6.6	65,000	20.96
Other fish				
products	12,500	5.9		
Diamonds	85,014	40.6	127,000	41.0
Blister Copper	19,242	9.2		
Refined lead	12,287	5.8		
Lead/Copper/Zinc				
concentrates	8,876	4.2	40,000	12.9
Other minerals	3,339	1.5		
Total exports	209,293	100.0	310,000	

NOTE: In 1966 imports were estimated to total 154 million rand and 90 per cent
were obtained from South Africa. The breakdown of imports is not available since
Namibian statistics are combined with those of South Africa. Almost all the
requirements of the modern sector of the economy must be imported.
*Estimated.
SOURCE: Economic Commission for Africa, Summaries of Economic Data,
Namibia, 6th Year, 1974.

Namibia is the second largest producer of lead in Africa, and the
third largest producer of zinc. In 1973, its zinc output constituted 14
per cent of all African production. [2] Namibia also produces about half
the world's karakul fur, all of which is exported. [3] In 1974, about ten
million cartons of pilchards, a small type of fish related to herrings,
were exported. [4] The only manufacturing of any significance is fish-
canning, which is essential before export because of the perishability
of fish.   In 1963-4, Namibia had only 212 industrial establishments,
employing 8,400 people. Of the total manufacturing output of $25
million, processed fish constituted almost two thirds. Other food and
drink industries produced about a fifth of the manufactured goods
output. Although mining produces by far the greatest share of exports, local metals processing added barely a tenth of the total
manufacturing value. [5]

Chart 6: Mine Company Links in Namibia

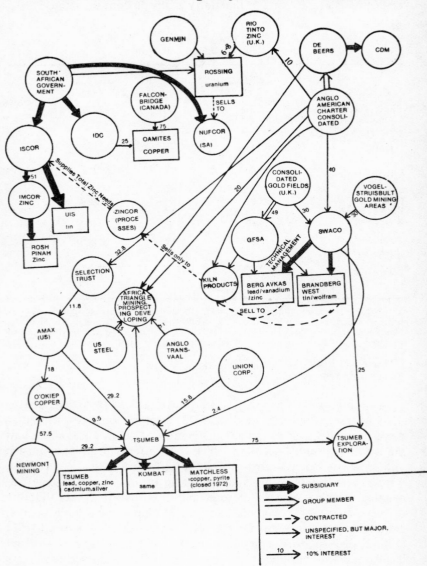

Note: CDM and Tsumeb account for over 90% of all Namibian mineral production.

Source: Report of the UN Council for Namibia; company reports.

South Africa has encouraged the expansion of the profitable primary sectors which are predominantly controlled by South Africans, while preserving the country as a market for South African manufactures.[6] It was estimated in 1966 that Namibia exported over $300 million worth of produce and imported $230 million worth. These figures have undoubtedly risen since 1966, but no more recent estimates are available. The UN Economic Commission for Africa reports, 'Almost all the requirements of the modern sector of the economy must be imported.'[7] At least 90 per cent of Namibia's imports come from South Africa. Most of her exports, being raw materials, were sold on the world market to provide the necessary foreign exchange to pay for her South African imports.

South African and United States Investments

South Africa's rule in Namibia has permitted the extension into that country of the oligopolistic and state capitalist structure of the South African economy. The mining finance houses are deeply involved, in cooperation with the state, in controlling and directing Namibian mining development. If a company, not composed of South Africans or Namibians, seeks to obtain mining rights in Namibia, they must offer a share of at least 50 per cent to the territorial administration. The actual amount is determined by the South African Government.[8] This ensures that foreign investment in Namibia takes place on South African terms. It is in this context that U.S. mining interests have become deeply involved in Namibian mines, both directly and indirectly through their intertwined relationships with South Africa's mining finance houses.

South African and United States mining companies dominate the two biggest mining companies that produce over 90 per cent of all mineral production in Namibia. One of these is Consolidated Diamond Mines of South West Africa, Ltd (CDM), a subsidiary of De Beers and a member of the Anglo American Group. The other is the U.S.-owned Tsumeb Corporation Ltd, whose major shareholders are AMAX, Newmont, Union Corporation, and the O'okiep Copper Company.

Consolidated Diamond Mines produces over 90 per cent of Namibian diamonds. The world's largest producer of gem diamonds,[9] it is a subsidiary of De Beers, which owns 98.43 per cent of its shares.[10] Its profits in the first half of 1973 (to June 30) were $56 million after tax, about 40 per cent higher than in the previous year. It paid taxes of $46 million, most of which was used to help bolster up South African rule in Namibia.[11]

The other of the two biggest mines, Tsumeb, produces copper, lead, zinc, silver and cadmium. It is owned by AMAX (29.2 per cent), Newmont (29.2 per cent), Union Corporation (15.6 per cent) O'okiep Corporation (9.5 per cent), and the South West Africa Company (2.4 per cent). Newmont and AMAX own, respectively, 57.5 and 18 per cent of O'okiep. [12]

Tsumeb controls the Tsumeb, Kombat, and Matchless mines (the last was closed in 1972). It refines and smelts the ores at Kombat and Tsumeb. Production is 80 per cent of Namibia's total base mineral production, and 20 per cent of Namibian exports. [13] Tsumeb also announced plans to begin development of a US $960m. copper mine in 1974. [14] In 1972, sales proceeds were $55 million, and profits after tax were $7.5 million. [15]

Tsumeb is the larger employer in the country, with four to five thousand African employees. [16]

Tsumeb has increased the capacity of its concentrator in Namibia to reduce the cost of shipping the ores extracted out of the country, but it has not built facilities to refine the metals there. In fact, Tsumeb and O'okiep announced plans to build a refinery in South Africa itself, near Cape Town, to produce 120,000 tons of cathode copper from Namibian concentrates. The plant was to begin production in late 1976. [17] Apparently they planned to follow the pattern of neo-colonial powers all over the world by refining crude ores shipped from the periphery to their factories in the centre. In 1974, however, these plans were reported to have been shelved as UN pressure mounted to force South Africa to give up its rule over Namibia.

South African interests own most of the remainder of the smaller Namibian mines. U.S. interests, while more difficult to detect, appear to be both directly and indirectly involved in these, as well. An exploration firm, the African Triangle Mining, Prospecting and Developing Company (Pty) Ltd , is owned 36 per cent by Anglovaal; 20 per cent by Anglo; and 15 per cent by US Steel. De Beers and Tsumeb also have shares. The company is exploring concessions of 1,500 square kilometers for copper and silver [18]

Johnnies is opening a $34 million copper mine at Otjihas. Johnnies owns 52.5 per cent; the rest is owned by Minerts. [19]

Strathmore Services and Finance Corporation, Ltd , a subsidiary of General Mining/Federale Mynbou, has a diamond mine in Terrace Bay and a tin mine in Cape Crest. It also has offshore prospecting rights for oil. [20]

The South West Africa Company (SWACO) is owned 90 per cent by a consortium of Anglo, Charter Consolidated and Gold Fields

TABLE 12.2

NAMIBIA: OWNERSHIP OF MINES

Mines	Product	Year End	Volume [tons]	Total Sales [in rands]	Company	Shareholders	Percentage of holding
Oranjemund and the Spergebiet	Diamonds (million carats)	1971	1.7	56.9	CDM[a]	De Beers	98.3
						Public	1.7
Tsumeb	Copper (thousands)	1972	19.0	...	Tsumeb Corporation[b]	Newmont Mining	29.2
Kombat	Lead (thousands)	1972	51.0	...	"	American Metal Climax	29.2
Matchless	Zinc (thousands)	1972	6.0	...	"	Selection Trust	11.2
	Cadmium (thousands)	1972	116.0	29.0	"	O'okiep Copper	9.5
						SWACO	2.4
Berg Aukas	Lead vanadates (thousands)	1971	8,197.0	...	SWACO	Union Corporation	9.0
						Anglo American	44.0
Brandberg West	Zinc/lead sulphides	1971	7,319.0	...	SWACO	Consolidated Gold Fields	11.0
Rosh Pinah	Sinc silicates	1971	23,674.0	...	SWAPO	...	...
	Tin/Wolfram	1971	595.0	4.6	SWACO		—
	Zinc concentrates	1972	23,201.0	...	ISCOR	ISCOR	—
	Lead concentrates	1972	9,556.0	c	ISCOR	ISCOR	—
Uis	Tin concentrates	1972	1,228.0	...	ISCOR	ISCOR	—
Klein Aub	Copper concentrates	1972	8,600.0d	2.7	Gen. Min. Federale Mynbou	—	
Oamites	Copper	1971	416.0	e	Oamites Mining	Falconbridge Nickel*	75.0
						SA Industrial Devel. Corporation	25.0

Notes and Source: See footnote p. 168

*Falconbridge is a subsidiary of the Superior Oil Company, U.S.A.

South Africa. GFSA owns 40 per cent and administers the company. [21] SWACO operates a mine at Berg Aukas (lead, vanadate and zinc ores), and another at Brandberg West (tin/wolfram). The latter was placed on a care-and-maintenance basis in 1973 because of low wolfram prices. After tax profits were £118,819 in 1973 (up from £23,976 in 1972). [22]

Namibian mineral wealth has contributed significantly to the development of the jointly owned state-private-parastatal sector in basic industry in South Africa itself. Iscor, the giant South African iron and steel parastatal, obtains essential supplies of minerals like zinc and tin, required to produce important iron and steel products from Namibia. A consortium dominated by Gold Fields South Africa (61 per cent) and Anglo, buys the residues and concentrates from the Berg Aukas mine for processing and sale to Zincor, the Zinc Corporation of South Africa. Zincor supplies Iscor's entire requirement of zinc, which is essential for making galvanized iron and to rustproof sheets of metal.widely used throughout Africa for roofing. Iscor itself owns 51 per cent of the Namibian firm, the Industrial Mining Corporation (Imcor). This company controls the Rosh Pinah mine in Namibia, which in 1973 produced 29,700 tons of zinc concentrates and 8,100 tons of lead concentrates. Its zinc output was processed by Zincor. A second, richer zinc mine, was opened near Rosh Pinah in 1973. [23]

ISCOR also owns Namibia's Uis tin mine through its wholly-owned subsidiary, Industrial Minerals Mining Corporation (Pty) Ltd. In 1973, it produced 1,100 tons of tin concentrates, over half of ISCOR's requirements. [24] The opening of Iscor's tinplate factory in 1969 saved South Africa an estimated $22 million in foreign exchange every year. [25]

The South African Industrial Development Corporation (IDC) is also involved in Namibia. In cooperation with Falconbridge, it invested $8.3 million in the Oamites copper mines, [26] which started production in 1972 at 55,000 tons a month. IDC owns 25.1 per cent, and Falconbridge controlled by Superior Oil of U.S.A. owns the rest. [27]

SOURCE: 'Desert Deadlock. South West Africa: *Financial Mail* Special Survey', *Financial Mail* (Johannesburg, 2 March 1973, p. 60.)

[a] Diamond account (R38.8 m) plus cost of production (11.3m tons treated at R1.6 a ton). Not including diamonds on hand at cost of production (R10.6). [b] Together CDM and Tsumeb produce more than 90 per cent by value of minerals in Namibia. [c] Undisclosed by South African authorities. [d] Tonnage was low owing to the migrant labourers' strike. The value of sales is calculated on an average of R320 per ton.
[e] Pre-Production; 1972 figures not available.

Charter Consolidated, Anglo's associate, owns over $600,000 of Falconbridge's equity capital.[28]

Namibia is to become an important source of uranium for South Africa's expanding nuclear power industry. In partnership with Rio Tinto Zinc, the South African Government is developing an open pit uranium mine at Rossing. GM&FC owns 6.8 per cent. The mine is to cost US$140 million and be opened in 1976.[29] Reserves are about 100,000 tons (a third of total South African reserves). The ore will be treated by the South African parastatal, NUFCOR, at Pelindaba in South Africa.[30]

Commercial agriculture and fishing are also controlled from South Africa. Over 60 per cent of the commercial farmers are white South Africans. The rest are mostly German. Commercial agriculture is entirely in karakul and cattle, which are white controlled. Most slaughtering is by two South African companies, Suide-Afrikaanse Vleisprodusente (Sentraal Kooperatif) Bpk. ('Vleissentraal'), and Afrikaanse Sake-Ontwikkelinas Korporasie (ASOKOR). Vleissentraal operates two abattoirs and meat packing factories at Otavi and Windhoek. A third company, the Karroo Meat Exchange, owns an abattoir and a factory. These are the only abattoirs and meat-packing factories in the country.[31]

Fishing contributes about 20 per cent of export earnings. Capital investment is about $30 million for a fleet of about 240 purse-seine trawlers. Nine commercial fishing companies or groups were registered in 1972, all of which are closely interconnected. They are all, of course, white controlled.[32]

Namibian investments have been very profitable for the foreign firms involved. Between 1946 and 1962, it has been estimated that about a third of the national income was shipped out of the country in the form of profits, interest and dividends. Profits alone totalled $125 million in 1971,[33] about a fifth of the national income. South African Governmental control of Namibia's mineral resources is reinforced by a complex set of financial and licensing arrangements. The two thirds of Namibia's revenues provided by mineral taxes[34] is not enough to maintain its repressive regime. As a result, it must borrow from South Africa. In 1974, for example, the South West African Administration had a deficit of $24 million. It borrowed $9 million from the South African treasury, and the balance on an overdraft from the South African Reserve Bank. The expansion of this kind of debt entangles Namibia further in a web of financial controls from South Africa. It also ensures a continued outflow of interest as well as principal to

South African government and banking concerns in a typical colonial/neo-colonial pattern.

Impoverishment of the Namibian People

The high profits the foreign private and parastatal firms reap in Namibia are, of course, the result of low wages they pay there, as well as the relatively free hand they have been given to extract Namibia's mineral wealth. In 1968, there were 65,998 non-white male workers in the Police Zone (the white areas which take up most of the land). 21,230 Africans were in semi-skilled work, mostly domestic service. [35] Forty per cent were migrant workers from Angola. [36] Almost all African employment on the mines was contract labour. The three biggest mining companies employed almost 10,000 African workers. [37]

Wages and conditions are as bad or worse in Namibia than in South Africa. An observer has described a typical mine compound for Ovambo migrant workers. [38]

The men are housed in barracks–type buildings with only concrete locker-type beds for each man. The kitchen is quite unsanitary, with flies all over the place and cats chasing each other throughout the place. The food is served through openings in a wire fence separating the cooking area from the dining area. Porridge is slapped in a bowl with a shovel, a conglomeration of liquified vegetables is poured over the porridge and a piece of bread is also given each man. For meat, a hunk of bone is given on which there is some slight bit of beef.

Wages paid in Namibia are less than a fourth of the South African poverty level. Prices are about twenty per cent higher than in South Africa. [39]

According to an unofficial survey, African wages in Namibia in 1972/3 were: [40]

	Lowest	Highest	Average
Farming	$6.70	$44.00	$9-15 (per month)
Domestic Service	—	—	$32.33 (per month)
Railway	—	—	$9.60 (per week)
Construction	—	—	$10-17 (per week)

Most mines recruited workers for twelve months at 25 to 33 pence a shift (between $15 and $19 a month). Monthly wages on the U.S.-owned mine, Tsumeb, were somewhat higher:[41]

(US Dollars)	African		White
Minimum	$24		$300
Maximum	$146		—
Average	$39	in cash	$490
	$32	in kind	

Although the African wages in Tsumeb were reportedly the highest in the mining sector, the average was still only about half the Poverty Datum Line, even with the non-cash wage component included. The average was less than a twentieth of what the same firms would have had to pay workers back in the United States.

When wages have been increased to reduce worker complaints, the way they have been raised has tended to augment the inequality of the wage structure. When the partially U.S.-owned O'okiep copper mines provided increases of 15 per cent for its white staff and 30 per cent for its white hourly paid staff, it gave only a 20 per cent raise to Coloureds and a 25 per cent increase to Africans. Since white employees were much better paid in the first place, this means their increase, in absolute terms, far exceeded that of the blacks.

At these wages, it is not surprising that African workers have had to be forced to work in the mines. The Namibian reserves have all the horrific characteristics of South African Bantustans. They were designed for the same purposes: to force labour.[42] In addition to mass impoverishment, arbitrary police violence has been an added cause of migration to the mines. As one worker told an interviewer:[43]

Some people really want to come back [to the reserves], but others see soldiers and police and feel safer outside Ovambo. Many huts have been burned down and people shot.

Much of this violence has been directed against SWAPO, the Namibian liberation movement, but its side-effects have also been useful in intimidating any Namibians who might seek to avoid labour on the mines. The violence has mounted, especially since the big mine strike of 1971.

U.S. Vetoes Proposed United Nations' Action

The United Nations, seeking to end the continued illegal rule of Namibia by South Africa, voted that member governments should discourage their nationals from investing in Namibia as long as South

Africa remained in power. Where vast profits are to be made, however, a mere vote by the sovereign nations of the world does not appear to have been a serious deterrent. The U.S. Government, although initially accepting the UN decision, took no significant measures to enforce it against its own U.S.-based multinational firms.

In 1975, the overwhelming majority of the United Nations membership sought, therefore, to put teeth into their efforts to end continued foreign firm exploitation of Namibia under the illegal rule of South Africa. They voted that UN member governments should seize all minerals exported from Namibia by firms investing there until South Africa withdrew from Namibia altogether. The United States, together with Britain and France, vetoed this measure.

Summary

To sum up, South Africa has shaped Namibia into a typical colonial-type economy during the decades of its illegal reign there. Namibia's key productive sectors, controlled by foreign firms, dominated by the South African mining finance houses, are geared to the export of crude materials. Namibian minerals provide essential ingredients for South Africa's basic industrial sector as well as earning essential foreign exchange through sales overseas. The masses of Namibians are forced to provide cheap labour at wages and living standards even lower than those of Africans in South Africa.

Namibia must import machinery and equipment for the expanding operations of foreign firms, as well as most of the consumer goods demanded by South African and German farm owners and the highly paid managerial and salaried personnel engaged in export activities. It provides, thus, a significant market for South African manufactured goods.

The bulk of the resulting profits of Namibia's export-import trade—almost a third of the gross domestic product, year in and year out—are shipped to South Africa and beyond to associated foreign firms. U.S.-based multinationals have been very much involved in this profitable business.

REFERENCES

CHAPTER TWELVE

1. Economic Commission for Africa, *Summaries of Economic Data,* Namibia 5th Year, No. 2.
2. United Nations General Assembly, 'Report of the UN Council for Namibia', *Official Records, 28th Session,* Supplement No. 24 (A/9024). Hereafter referred to as 'Report of the Council for Namibia.'
3. Ibid.
4. Economist Intelligence Unit, *Quarterly Economic Review for Southern Africa,* 3rd Quarter, 1974.
5. ECA, op. cit.
6. Report of the Council for Namibia, op. cit.
7. ECA, op. cit.
8. Report of the Council for Namibia, op. cit.
9. Ibid.
10. Consolidated Diamond Mines of South West Africa, Ltd., *Annual Report,* 1973.
11. *Quarterly Economic Review,* op. cit., 4th Quarter, 1973.
12. Ibid.
13. Report of the Council for Nambia, op. cit.; Anglo American Corporation, *Annual Report.* 1974.
14. *African Business Review,* March/April 1974.
15. AAC, *Annual Report,* 1975.
16. Report of the Council for Namibia, op. cit.
17. *African Research Bulletin,* Vol. 11, op. cit.
18. Report of the Council for Namibia, op. cit.; Anglo Transvaal *Annual Report,* 1974.
19. *African Research Bulletin,* Vol. 11, No. 9.
20. Report of the Council for Namibia, op. cit.
21. Consolidated Gold Fields, *Annual Report,* 1974.
22. Anglo American Corporation, op. cit.
23. ISCOR, *Annual Report,* 1973.
24. Ibid.
25. Da Gama Publishers (Pty) Ltd , *State of South Africa, Economic, Financial and Statistical Year Book for the Republic of South Africa* (Johannesburg, 1973).
26. *African Research Bulletin,* Vol. 11, No. 9.
27. *African Business Review,* op. cit.
28. Charter Consolidated Ltd., *Annual Report* 1973.
29. General Mining and Finance Corporation, *Annual Report,* 1974.
30. Report of the Council for Namibia, op. cit.
31. Ibid.
32. Ibid.
33. Ibid.
34. *Quarterly Economic Review,* op. cit., 2nd Quarter 1974.
35. United Nations, Special Committee on the Situation with Regard to the Implementation of the Declaration of the Granting of Independence to Colonial Countries and Peoples. *Activities of Foreign economic and other interests which are impeding the implementation of the Declaration on the granting of independence to colonial countries and peoples in Southern Rhodesia, Namibia and territories under Portuguese domination and in all other territories under colonial domination and efforts to eliminate colonialism, apartheid and racial discrimination in Southern Africa,* General Assembly, Official Records, Supp. No. 23A (A/7623/Rev. 1/Add.1)
36. Report of the Council for Namibia, op. cit.
37. Ibid.
38. Counter Intelligence Services, *Consolidated Gold Fields, Anti-Report,* (UK: 1972), quoting Judge William Booth of the International Commission of Jurists.
39. African Bureau, Grafton Way, London, 'Rhodesia: Effects of the Sanctions War', *Fact Sheet No. 34,* February 1974.
40. Report of the Council for Namibia, op. cit.
41. Ibid.
42. Cf. R. First, J. Steele and C. Gurney, *The South African Connection* (London: Maurice Temple Smith, 1972)
43. *CGF Anti-Report,* op. cit.

Chapter XIII

South African Captives

Swaziland, Botswana and Lesotho obtained political independence from England in the mid-1960s. In a very real sense, however, they have remained economic captives of South Africa. The entire set of institutional arrangements established during the colonial period continued to shape their economies into a typically neo-colonial relationship with South Africa. Their basic industries are predominantly owned by South African or interlinked, especially U.S.-owned, firms, and are geared to export. The major commercial banks which handle their financial transactions are Barclays and Standard. The handful of wholesale trading houses which import manufactured goods are almost wholly owned by South Africans. Their experience illustrates the impossibility of attaining meaningful development in the Bantustans if they should be granted 'political independence' in the framework of the political economy prevailing in southern Africa.

More than a decade after Botswana, Swaziland and Lesotho attained political independence, they remained incorporated in a Customs Union which bound them to South Africa. The basic outlines of this union were established more than half a century ago, back in 1910. On the surface it is only a customs-sharing arrangement: South Africa collected the duties on all goods shipped through its territory to the smaller countries. They, in turn, received a tiny fraction, 1.31097 per cent, of all South African customs duties.

An expert noted, however, that.
The trade aspects of this relationship benefit South Africa more than the three smaller partners. The prices they receive

for their exports are governed by world commodity prices, but the existence of the Customs Union raises their import bill by giving preferential access to relatively expensive South African manufactures.

Both Swaziland and Botswana have begun to make efforts to reduce their dependence on South Africa. While still in the Customs Union, they have issued their own currencies. Bordering on Mozambique and Zambia, respectively, they may, over time, have the option of opening new trade routes outside the South African orbit. Their success will in the long run, however, depend on two fundamental interrelated factors.

In the first place, the balkanization fostered by colonialism left both economically too small to establish fully viable economies at high levels of productivity. They will need to unite with their neighbours into larger self-reliant, increasingly integrated units, capable of restructing the regional economy. Even for Botswana and Swaziland, whether this option is open depends in large part on their neighbours' success in withstanding the political and economic pressures exerted by South Africa and its western allies. In the case of Lesotho, geographically an island in a sea of South African apartheid, this option is in no way even conceivable until the masses of South Africans are liberated.

In the second place, whether Swaziland and Botswana are in fact able to join together with their neighbours in a larger, self-reliant regional unit will depend on their own ability to build the sets of new institutions required to end South African dominance. The remainder of this chapter will examine how that domination has, in the past, rendered their political economies lopsidedly dependent on South Africa in a typical neo-colonial relationship.

Swaziland

In terms of population, Swaziland is the smallest of the three BLS countries. Living in lovely rolling vales among mountains sandwiched between South Africa and Mozambique, its population is estimated at about half a million. But only half of Swaziland's 'national territory' is actually owned by Swazis. The remainder was essentially given away through a series of colonial-type agreements, to foreigners in the nineteenth century. The rapid growth of the Swazi population in the twentieth century has aggravated the problems of overcrowding on the remaining land. This has been a major factor forcing some thirty thousand Swazi males to migrate annually to work on South African mines and farms.[2]

A land purchase commission was set up in 1970 with British assistance to try to buy back some of the land which had been given away a century earlier.[3] The cost of the valuable alienated lands is high and progress in recovering it in this manner is slow and expensive.

Swaziland's national product is officially estimated at about $160 per capita, but the incomes of the majority of the Swazis are far below that average. About 20 per cent of its national income is shipped out in the form of profits, interests, dividends, etc., to the foreign firms and individuals who dominate the export sectors of the economy. In the early 1970s, over 20,000 workers were employed in the agricultural sector, forestry and fishing; about 3,000 in mining; almost 6,000 in manufacturing; and about 5,000 in commerce. [4]

The South African *Financial Mail* asserted[5] the obvious fact that, 'without doubt... South Africa's private sector stake in Swaziland is proportionately massive enough to dominate the economy.'

Sugar is Swaziland's largest crop in terms of sales, exports, employment and land area utilized.[6] In 1972, sugar exports were worth $28 million, about a fourth of total exports. Most of the sugar exports go to England.

Citrus fruit is the second largest crop produced in Swaziland. It is grown only by non-Swazi commercial farmers employing Swazi labourers. In 1971, exports totalled $6. 5 million. About two thirds of all citrus fruit production is exported fresh to Europe by the South African Citrus Exchange. Most of the profit is in the canning process, but little of that is done in Swaziland. The only fruit-canning factory there in 1971 was operated by the U.S.-owned Del Monte Company. Most of the juice is produced from Swazi fruit in South Africa. Only 10 per cent is exported directly from Swaziland. The third largest crop, rice, is grown entirely for sale in South Africa. The 1971 crop was worth $1.2 million.

The value of the fourth commercial crop, cotton, was slightly less than that of rice.

The biggest direct South African stake in Swaziland, as in Namibia, is in mining. Iron ore is the second largest export, next to sugar. Most of the iron is currently being sold to Japan on a thirteen-year contract due to terminate in 1978.[7] As is common with Japanese mining agreements in Africa, none of the ore is locally smelted. The mine is owned and operated by an Anglo subsidiary, the Swaziland Ore Development Company.

Anglo also works a 'small drift colliery', the Mpaka Colliery, to produce coal. Its output satisfies the requirements of 'the Swaziland railways, local industrial, agricultural and domestic

TABLE 13.1

EMPLOYER IN THE PRIVATE SECTOR BY INDUSTRY AND SEX, IN SWAZILAND SEPTEMBER, 1970, AND 1972

Industry	Males		Females		Total				% Increase
	1970	1972	1970	1972	1970	%	1972	%	1970–1972
110 Agriculture, etc.*	11,781	14,999¹	2,574	5,202	14,355	43.3	20,201	46.1	40.7
120 Forestry	2,645	3,513	438	445	3,083	9.3	3,958	9.0	28.4
200 Mining	2,827	2,877	80	73	2,907	8.8	2,950	6.7	1.5
300 Manufacturing	5,017	5,788	366	724	5,383	16.2	6,512	14.9	21.0
500 Construction	969	2,093	33	14	1,002	3.0	2,107	4.8	52.4
600 Distribution etc.	2,499	2,701	924	1,141	3,423	10.3	3,842	8.8	12.2
710 Transport, Storage	453	732	26	43	479	1.4	775	1.8	61.8
800 Finance, etc.	220	403	124	177	344	1.0	580	1.3	68.6
900 Social Services	1,435	1,735	765	1,107	2,200	6.6	2,842	6.5	29.2
Total	27,846	34,841¹	5,330	8,926	33,176	100.0	43,767	100.0	31.9

SOURCE: Swaziland, *Annual Statistical Bulletin [Mbabane; Central Statistical Office, 1973].*

¹ The large increase in agricultural employment in 1972 — mainly due to better coverage in the Agricultural Census—falls exclusively in the male employment.

*Does not include subsistence sector.

demands, and a small export market'.[8] Rand Mines operates the Swaziland Collieries, Ltd It produced about 120 thousand tons of coal in 1970 and employed 337 workers.[9] Swaziland's total cash exports earned about $402,000 in 1971.

South African business interests have built up tourism in Swaziland as they have in the other two BLS countries. In this area, one perceives the impact of one of the most degrading aspects of the development of underdevelopment.

There are four hotels near Mbabane (one of them is the U.S. - owned Holiday Inn). The Southern Suns Group, a South African hotels group, is to build 'a vast holiday complex... with golf courses, a new casino, and a 300-room hotel'.[10] The estimated cost will be $6.7 million. There may be a limited Swazi participation, but the project is to be predominantly foreign-owned and financed.

The UN Economic Commission for Africa reports:[11]

> Tourism: this is a rapidly developing industry in Swaziland and very large numbers of South African visitors come by car for a short stay (a week-end's gambling).

What it does not say is that the other big attraction is black prostitutes, forced by the synthetic impoverishment of their families to earn a little cash in the only way they can.

It is unlikely that the tourist industry brings much income to Swaziland's impoverished economy. The consumer luxuries consumed must all be imported from South Africa. Most of the profits are shipped back to the Republic and associated foreign firms by the firms which own the hotels.

Swaziland's manufacturing sector appears deceptively large in terms of its contribution to the national product, primarily because of the extensive agro-industrial sector linked to the predominantly foreign-owned farming sector. In 1971, net manufacturing output was worth about $21 million. There were only 33 manufacturing firms, however, which employed about 6,000 workers. Most of these are huge, capital-intensive enterprises owned by foreign agro-businesses: two sugar mills, a cannery, a slaughterhouse, a cotton ginnery, four sawmills and a pulpmill [12] The cotton ginnery cannot compete with South African ginneries, so it operates at about 50 per cent of capacity.

One factory recently built manufactures concentrates for the food industry. It has been developed by a consortium of Canadian, Israel and South African businessmen, called Food Industries (Swaziland). It will utilize some local sugar and import large quantities of honey from South Africa. Total investment will be about $600 thousand. All production will be for export to Europe and the Far East. An International Monetary Fund Report suggested1[13] the reasons for this new type of foreign investment in Swaziland:

...relatively cheap labour, natural resources for processing industries, well-developed infrastructure, relatively low corporate tax (33 1/3 per cent) and a liberal investment allowance (30 per cent).

An added inducement, as the Report points out, is Swaziland's potential for expanding exports to other nations which have refused to 'buy South African':[14]

Also of importance is Swaziland's access to both a Customs Union area of 22 million people and African nations not receptive to exports from South Africa.

Almost all other manufactured goods are still imported, over 90 per cent of them from South Africa. This gives South Africa a trade surplus vis-a-vis Swaziland that exceeds Swaziland's total agricultural exports. Machinery and equipment for the foreign-owned commercial agricultural and mining sectors constitute about a fourth of the imports. The remaining three fourths consist of consumer items, many of them luxuries for the limited high income group, many of them foreigners engaged in the export business and tourists.

The wages paid in Swaziland are somewhat above those of Namibia, but below those of South Africa, as Table 13.3 shows.

TABLE 13.
AVERAGE MONTHLY EARNINGS OF MALES BY
SKILL CLASSIFICATION IN SWAZILAND
SEPTEMBER 1972 (IN U.S. DOLLAR EQUIVALENT)

| Industry Group | Non Manual | | Manual | | |
	Admin. & Technical	Clerical	Semi-Skilled	Semi-Skilled	Un-Skilled
110 Agriculture	229	*	113	34	22
120 Forestry	426	116	177	70	33
200 Mining, Quarrying	687	158	629	118	58
300 Manufacturing	551	155	359	115	51
500 Construction	526	92	338	106	37
600 Distribution, etc.	404	158	256	88	48
700 Transport, Storage	495	386	317	67	65
800 Finance, etc.	560	186	*	82	54
900 Social Services	502	143	334	83	43
Average All Industries	435	162	310	83	34

*Data not available

SOURCE: Swaziland, *Annual Statistical Bulletin*. (Mbabane: Central Statistical Office, 1973).

In short, economic growth in Swaziland, the most 'developed' of the three BLS countries, has left that country as externally dependent on the South African and associated multinational corporations as ever, while the majority of the population live at subsistence levels. Swaziland must spend most, if not all, the foreign exchange earned from its overseas sales to buy imports and pay for the chronic outflow of capital in the form of profits, interest, dividends, and high salaries paid to the foreign firms, as well as their personnel who shape its externally-dependent economy.

Like Namibia, Swaziland remains financially dependent on South Africa. Sixty per cent of its revenues derive from its tiny share of South African Customs Union duties. In 1972/3, this equalled less than $20 million, barely enough to cover basic administrative expenditures. At the same time, the Swaziland Government has been forced to borrow from South Africa to build the infrastructure needed, much of which was to enable South African and associated interests to expand their exploitative activities. In 1969, for example, the Swazi Government borrowed $3 million from Anglo to build the railroad to ship out Anglo's iron ore to Japan. It also owed Barclays Bank $2 million, and Standard Bank another $55,000.[14]

Botswana

Botswana's population is somewhat larger than Swaziland's, inhabiting a far larger land area, much of which is near-desert. Its 1972 population was estimated at about 625,000 persons actually living in Botswana. Botswana, like Swaziland, has been systematically underdeveloped by its political-economic ties to South Africa. Almost 50,000 more Botswana males are forced by poverty, as well as enticed by South African labour recruiters, to add to South Africa's low-cost labour supply. Almost half the migrants work in South African mines, most of the rest on farms. In 1971, the 21,592 Batswana working on the mines remitted only $1.5 million, or about $70 apiece, for their year's labour.

Botswana's national product in 1971 was about $133 million, over $200 per capita, and more than twice the 1964 figure.

Until the 1960s, agriculture had remained Botswana's most productive sector. This began to change rapidly, as a result of the rapid development of two new mining complexes, one producing diamonds, the other, copper and nickel. These did little to alter the low income or the lives of most Botswana, but they did establish a new export-oriented sector and change national income statistics.

TABLE 13.3
A. BOTSWANA EMPLOYMENT BY SECTOR, 1967/8 AND 1972[1]

Sector	1967/8 Number	%	1972 Number	%	% Increase 1967/8-1972
Agriculture & forestry	7,570	26.9	5,058	10.5	-33
Mining & Quarrying	814	2.9	1,680	3.5	106
Manufacturing	1,566	4.8	2,639	5.5	94
Construction	1,566	5.6	6,468	13.4	313
Commerce	5,508	19.6	6,342	13.2	15
Transport & Communication	1,135	4.0	1,121	2.3	-1
Services	10,148	36.2	24,892	51.6	144
Total	28,148	100.0	48,200	100.0	71

B. BATSWANA WORKING ON THE SOUTH AFRICAN MINES,
1967-1972

	1967	1970	1972
Recruits (No.)	22,735	35,921	23,678
Deferred Payments & Remittances	$ 1,636,000	$1,615,000	$139,000

Southern African statistics typically refer only to employment in the commercial sector.

SOURCE: Economic Commission for Africa, *Summeries of Economic Data* Botswana, 1974, Sixth Year (Addis Ababa: mimeo)

TABLE 13.4
BOTSWANA GDP AT CURRENT FACTOR COST

1964	1967/8	1971/2	% Increase 1964/1974
$48,750,000	$59,110,000	$133,210,000	173%

SOURCE: Economic Commission for Africa, *Summaries of Economic Data, Botswana*, 1974, Sixth Year (Addis Ababa: Mimeo)

The new mining complexes were financed largely by South African and U.S. -based multinational corporate funds. One of them, the Orapa diamond mine, started production in 1970. It quickly became the most profitable mine of the South African firm, De Beers. Some 2.4 million carats were recovered from it in 1972, over a fifth of De Beer's total output. The cost per ton was roughly 11 per cent lower than the De Beer's average, while the average ton of Orapa ore contained about three times the carat value of the average De Beer's output. Diamond exports, worth about $30 million in 1972, had jumped by a fourth to over three million carats in 1973. [15]

De Beers had invested $31 million in the Orapa Mine and is planning to open a second, smaller, mine nearby. [16] It gave the Botswana Government 15 per cent of shares, 'free of consideration'. The Government, however, borrowed $3 million from Anglo to pay for the necessary infrastructure for the mine. It will, of course, have to repay this loan with interest out of its future earnings from its shares.*

With two of its largest and most profitable diamond mining operations in Botswana and Namibia, Anglo American's associate, De Beers, would seem to have reason for a special concern with the maintenance of South Africa's neo-colonial relations with these two neighbours.

Botswana's other large newly-developed mining project is at Selebi-Pikwe. These large open pit copper/nickel mines have proven reserves of 33 million metric tons. The grades of ore run from 0.70 per cent nickel to 1.56 per cent copper, but it was expected that their relatively low metal content would be offset by the low cost of operating the mines. [17] This was still probably true, although technical problems encountered after the mine opened in 1974 required refinancing, raising the cost by $65 million to a $365 million total. [18]

Selebi-Pikwe is operated by Bamangwato Concessions, which is 85 per cent held by Botswana Roan Selection Trust (RST) and 15 per cent by the Government. Botswana RST is held 30 per cent by the American firm, AMAX/RST, 30 per cent Anglo-Charterd Consolidated, six per cent Fusco Mineral Separations and 34 per cent public. Botswana RST itself invested $178 million which was raised partly from a consortium of West German banks and partly from the South African Industrial Development Corporation. The Botswana Government borrowed from the World Bank, Canada and USAID to finance the $90 million required for essential infrastructure. In other words, for its nominal 15 per cent of the shares, the Botswana Government in this case contributed 30 per cent of the investment. [19]

---

*Prospects for Business in Developing Africa, published by Business International in Geneva, a publication for investors in Africa, says: 'A large number of Western investors in Africa consider joint ventures attractive or at least the surest way to gain acceptance by the host country... Local participation will ensure that managerial control lies with the foreign investor, and at the same time satisfies many of the requirements of "national interest". Anglo and associates have apparently taken this to heart.

The agreements reached between the companies and the Botswana Government actually served to increase, rather than reduce, Botswana's dependence on its South African neighbour and U.S.-based multinational corporations. AMAX and Anglo insisted that all machinery and equipment be bought from South Africa, rather than its copper-producing neighbour, Zambia. They also insisted that the ores be shipped crude to an AMAX refinery in New Orleans, and from there to Metalgesellschaft in Germany, though Zambia has long been refining copper on the other side of the border. To ship the ores to Zambia would, it is true, have necessitated improvement of rail facilities to the north, but in the long run this would have significantly reduced Botswana's dependence on South Africa. [20]

On paper, the Botswana Government could expect a considerable amount of revenue from the new mining operations at Selebi-Pikwe. The Government of Botswana is to get a 7.5 per cent royalty on the mines' profits. The stated company tax is a minimum of 40 per cent and a maximum of 65 per cent at Selebi-Pikwe, and 40 per cent for Orapa. Total ordinary Government revenue in 1972/3 was $34 million. The two mines were expected to contribute almost a third of that amount in 1973, and two thirds of it in 1975/6[21] In 1975, however, unexpected technical difficulties interfered with production. Furthermore, the fall in the world copper price reduced potential foreign exchange earnings and government revenues from the mines.

The Botswana Government also proposed to take over half the shares of Orapa. It was hoped that this might raise its share of profits to 75 per cent.[22]*

Anglo American has opened a coal mine, the Moropule coal mine near Palapye, to supply Selebi-Pikwe and a power station. Production was to be 200,000 tons per annum, starting in 1974. This could increase to 640,000 tons a year, 'if new markets can be secured'. Anglo owns 80 per cent of the operating company, Moropule Collieries (Pty) Ltd , through its subsidiary, Anglo American Corporation Botswana, Ltd (AMBOT).[23]

AMBOT holds the interests of Anglo and 'certain other associated companies' in Botswana. These include an indirect interest of 18 per cent in Botswana RST, as well as the share in Moropule. In additions, AMBOT owns wholly West End Property Company (Pty)

---

*The Zambian government, with a similar goal, bought 51% of the shares of ownership of the Anglo-Amax owned mines some years earlier; however, (see pp. 236 below) a number of factors caused it to experience a sharp drop in actual government revenue.

Ltd (WEPCO). WEPCO is building Botsalano House in Gaborone, a multi-storey office building.

Another industry may be built to utilize Botswana's crude materials to satisfy South Africa's requirements for soda ash. According to the *Quarterly Economist Review,* the Makgadikgadi Soda Project probably would be feasible after transport costs from Britain to South Africa rose: 'a R30 million [$45 million] plant would take two years to build and satisfy South Africa's needs'.

Although the mines have contributed to an increase in Botswana's national product and government revenues, they have contributed little to improve the levels of living of the majority of the nation's people. Relatively capital intensive, they provide little in the way of new jobs. Even today, services provide the greatest number of paid jobs for Botswana citizens remaining in the country, followed by commerce and agriculture. [24]

The entire manufacturing sector is smaller than Swaziland's, absolutely as well as in comparison to the national product. The major manufacturing projects, as in Swaziland, are primarily linked to processing agricultural produce.

In 1971, the largest manufacturing industry in the country was the Botswana Meat Commission. Depending on the level of production, it employs 700 to a thousand workers, and provided, in 1972, over a third of Government direct tax revenue. There were 22 licenced manufacturing firms in the country: two breweries, one distillery, six clothing manufacturers, two firms processing wild animal skins, two furniture and two engineering firms, three firms producing construction materials, and so on. (The Meat Commission, mills, bakeries, mines, quarries, construction firms and service industries do not need licences.)

Sir Seretse Khama, Botswana's Prime Minister, claimed that, in 1973, $3 million was invested in industry, employing 700 people. By 1974, investment had reportedly risen to $10 million, employing 2,000. [25]

Most of the new industries are relatively small-scale light consumer goods industries, located in Lobatse, Gaborone, or Francistown, and owned by non-Batswana. [26] The second largest manufacturing firm [27] is a $3 million brewery and soft drink bottling plant owned by a West German firm, Brau Finanz Ltd. A Swiss finance corporation is building a textiles (weaving, finishing and dying) mill in Gaborone, said to be 'the largest and most sophisticated of its kind in Southern Africa'. [28] It will employ between 2,000 and 2,500 Batswana. Machinery worth $2.2 million had already been ordered by 1975. By 1985, investment in manufacturing was expected to reach $30 million. It seems highly possible that the investors, who may include South Africans operating incognito through the Swiss company, are eager to benefit from the cheap labour available in Botswana while at the same time expanding output for sale throughout Africa and the European Common Market without the stigma of the made-in-South Africa label.

As late as 1972, rough UN Economic Commission for Africa estimates indicated that Botswana's main exports were cattle carcasses, hides and skins, abattoir by-products and other animal products worth an estimated $40 million. The United Kingdom remained the largest market for the cattle carcasses. [29]

As in Swaziland, the rapid growth of Botswana's tourist trade has been dependent on South Africa, with parallel consequences for the people of Botswana: 'The opening of the (U.S.-owned) Holiday Inn in Gaborone in 1972 has led to a large increase of tourists on short stays from South Africa to enjoy a weekend's gambling at the casino'. [30]

Botswana, like Swaziland, continues to provide an important market, not only for South Africa's expanding manufactured goods output, but also for Rhodesia's. The latest concrete figures are available only for 1968, when about 70 per cent ($23 million) of Botswana's imports came from South Africa. About a third was in the form of food and live animal imports, despite the fact that agriculture was still the primary economic activity in the country. Manufactured goods for the limited consumer market constituted a little more than a third of the imports. Machinery and transport equipment, mostly for the new mines, constituted most of the remainder. [31]

Two years earlier, imports from Rhodesia had officially been reported as worth about $10 million, bringing over 90 per cent of the total. It is hard to know to what extent this remains true, but there is little reason to believe that it has changed significantly. Until recently, all of Botswana's imports had to come from Rhodesia or through South Africa. There were no all-weather roads to the North. Botswana's border touches Zambia only at a narrow point; most is cut off by the Caprivi Strip controlled by South Africa.

Yet the Botswana Government has been trying to reduce its dependence on South Africa. An all-weather dirt road to Zambia has been constructed under contract with USAID by a U.S. firm. The road should facilitate direct export of Botswana's cattle products which Zambia had begun to import by air after the closure of the Rhodesian border. Zambia's new manufacturing sector could provide

TABLE 13.5

BOTSWANA'S TRADE

Major Exports	1968 R000	%	1969 R000	%	1973 R000	%
Live cattle	793	7.5	5.4	—		
Cattle carcasses	6,911	65.2	8,561.6	79.6		
Sheep & goat meat	68	0.6	168.3	1.6	29,000	52.0
Canned meat	670	6.4	9.6	—		
Meat extract	125	1.2	—			
Abattoir by-products	362	3.4	294.8*	2.7		
Other animal products	541	5.1	299.6	2.8	4,300	7.7
Hides & skins	893	8.4	811.3	7.5		
Beans & cow peas	192	1.8	121.2	1.1	...	
Groundnuts	23	0.2	...	1.0		
Sorghum	6	—	123.7	1.1	...	
Manganese ore	10	0.1	365.2	3.3	—	
Diamonds	—		—		22,000	39.8
Copper. nickel. sulphur					10,000	
TOTAL	10,594	100%	10,755.4	100%	55,318	100%

Imports by SITC Section	1967	%	1968	%
Food & live animals	5,549	24.8	5,800	24.7
Beverages & tobacco	1,615	7.2	1,701	7.3
Crude materials	...		349	1.5
Mineral fuels, etc.	2,430	10.9	2,451	10.6
Chemicals	812	3.6		
Manufactured goods[a]	3,808	17.2	4,817	20.7
Machinery & transport equipment	4,642	20.7	4,025	17.3
Miscellaneous manufactures	2,300	10.3	2,375	10.2
Other	1,205	5.4	906	3.9
TOTAL	22,370	100%	23,231	100%

[a]Classified chiefly by materials.

NOTE: Most imports are from South Africa and Rhodesia, and for the cattle carcasses exported, the United Kingdom is the biggest market.

SOURCE: Economic Commission for Africa, Summaries of Economic Data, Botswana. 6th Year, 1974.

some of the consumer goods and mine imports still imported from South Africa and Rhodesia. The road definitely will not, however, be able to carry Botswana's heavy ores to Zambia's smelting-refining facilities on the Copper Belt. As yet there are few signs that Botswana has been able to significantly reduce the controls exercised by South

African and U.S. based multinational concerns over its externally dependent political economy.

Lesotho

Lesotho's population is over a million, making it the largest of the three BLS countries in terms of inhabitants. The mountainous country is, however, completely surrounded by South Africa. Its crowded valleys and agricultural areas are badly eroded. Of a total land area of 3,036 square miles, only 353 are arable. Permanent meadows and pastures add up to 2,495 square miles. As a result, a very high percentage of Lesotho males are forced to migrate annually to South Africa, mostly to work on the mines. In 1970, it was estimated that about four out of every ten adult men were working there. By 1973, about 80,000 Basotho were employed on the mines, an 11 per cent increase over the preceding year. Remittances from the miners totalled only $130 thousand,[31] barely $11 per worker.

Even with the vast annual migration to South Africa, unemployment remains a primary feature of Lesotho's economy. In 1969, it was estimated that only seven per cent of all Lesotho males had paid employment in their home country.

Lesotho's national product is $68 million, the lowest in absolute terms of all three countries. The national per capital income is only about $50, one of the very lowest in the world. The largest productive sector in the country is agriculture, which contributes about two thirds of the total national product. Government administration and welfare services provide most of the paid jobs.[32]

Aside from the annual exodus of almost half of its adult males, Lesotho's main exports are like those of Botswana and Swaziland, crude raw materials, but their value is far smaller. In 1972, the total value of wool, Lesotho's main export, was only $3 million. Its mohair and live animal exports each earned about half that amount. Lesotho has never had its own modern textiles or apparel factory. Its pre-existing handicrafts weaving industries were put out of business by cheap imported South African products, some of them actually made out of Lesotho's own wool.

Diamonds may become a more important export. In the first six months of 1974, Lesotho exported diamonds worth $683 thousand. The Government revenue from taxes levied on these exports was about a sixth of that amount.[33] De Beers planned to start diamond mining at Letseng by 1976 at a rate of 4000 tons of ore a day. The total investment was to be $30 million, with $4.5 million to be spent on infrastructure and $25 million on capital equipment. The Lesotho Government will receive 25 per cent of the equity and representation on the board of directors.

Lesotho's manufacturing sector is the smallest of all three countries, both in absolute and relative terms. In 1969, there were only 16 industrial establishments in all of Lesotho. They had a net output of $561 thousand and employed only 714 persons.

TABLE 13.6
LESOTHO'S EXPORTS AND IMPORTS, 1966 AND 1972

Major Exports	1966 R000	%	1972 R000	%
Live animals	542	11.2	944	15.5
Wheat	57	1.1	140	2.3
Peas and beans	124	2.5	503	8.2
Wool	1,861	38.5	2,040	33.5
Mohair	943	19.5	1,122	18.4
Hides and skins	94	1.9	48	0.8
Diamond	697	14.1	196	3.2
Total	4,837	100.1	6,093	100.0
Imports by SITC Section				
Foodstuffs, drinks and tobacco	7,057	30.4	11,687	27.2
Crude materials	353	1.5	529	1.2
Mineral fuels, lubricants	1,036	6.7	2,440	5.7
Animal & vegetable oils	174	0.7	381	0.9
Chemicals	1,280		2,172	5.1
Manufactures*	5,740	25.0	9,095	21.2
Machinery & transport equipment	2,038	8.3	5,042	11.7
Misc. manufactures	4,019	17.5	11,626	27.0
Other	1,220	5.3	--	--
Total	22,917	100.0	42,972	100.0

*Classified chiefly by material
NOTE: Most trade is conducted with South Africa but details are not available.
SOURCE: Economic Commission for Africa, *Summaries of Economic Data*, Lesotho, 5th Year, 1973.

The Government claims to be attempting to improve this situation by creating a public development corporation, the Lesotho National Development Corporation (LNDC), in the image of those established in almost every former British colony. [34] 'It is financed by the United Nations Development Programme and British Funds. The UNDP provides an average of $2.3 million annually. The UK gave $16 million in 1973/4 and in 1975/6. The World Bank's 'soft money' affiliate, the' International Development Association, and   USAID

together provided $2.6 million for a rural development scheme at
Thabu Bosiu. [35] The corporation also obtained $21 million in direct
investment from South Africa. The chief industrial advisor of the
Development Corporation since Lesotho became politically independent in 1966, has been a South African millionaire, Dr Anton
Rupert. [36] By 1972, the corporation claimed it was attracting 20 times
as much foreign capital as it invested directly. [37] In 1972, it had paper
plans for investments totalling $90 million, targeted to create 9,400
jobs directly and 5,600 indirectly. The direct employment was, in
other words, expected to be extremely costly, about $9,500 each. This
implies the imposition of a highly capital intensive economic structure, hardly appropriate given Lesotho's capital scarcity and
widespread unemployment.

The new Poverty Datum Line survey, prepared at the University
of Botswana, Lesotho and Swaziland, was estimated to be $92.23 a
month in 1975 in the capital, Maseru. Sixty per cent of Maseru
households were, at this figure, 'unable to satisfy their basic needs'.
The rural figure was estimated to be higher, $111.75, because of the
added costs of transporting basic necessities over almost impassable
mountain roads. The average mineworker in South Africa was then
earning a minimum of only $85.22. The University staff who prepared
the report maintained, furthermore, that it would be necessary for a
family to obtain 195 per cent of the PDL estimate to full basic needs
'adequately'.

The *Financial Mail,* summarizing the results of this report,
asserted that the inadequacies of the Lesotho Government policies and
other factors as causes of these conditions are 'negligible in comparison with the true historical origin of Lesotho's poverty: The
country's sheer economic thralldom to South Africa'. [38]

The biggest single project of the Lesotho National Development
Corporation in 1971 was the establishment of the U.S.-managed
Holiday Inn in which the Development Corporation invested about
$10 million. The remainder of the cost was financed by foreign,
mostly U.S., investment. [39] The Development Corporation has now
invested another $10 million in a second hotel and night club complex
at Maseru. The result of such investments is that the tourist traffic
from South Africa has risen to 100,000, from 6,000 four years ago. [40]

The Development Corporation has also built a "modern block of
27 apartments" at a cost of $380,000, most of it from the Com-
monwealth Development Corporation.

An LNDC subsidiary, the National Motor Company of Lesotho,
opened a $216 thousand workshop in Maseru in 1974. This has a

franchise for Mercedes and VWs, as well as Bosch equipment and spares. [41] The LNDC plans also established a basic assembly project at Beribe Technical School, which was expected to have an annual turnover of $120 to 135 thousand and provide 60 jobs. [47] Anglo and De Beers have jointly financed a $90 thousand fly-spray factory at Matsieng, 40 kilometres from Maseru. This will be managed by Main Tin Manufacturers, a subsidiary of the Metal Box Company of South Africa. [43]

None of these so-called 'manufacturing' industries are capable of significantly altering Lesotho's external dependence. They are mainly last-stage assembly and processing plants using imported parts, mainly from South Africa. They are typically too capital-intensive to help significantly in relieving Lesotho's unemployment problem.

Lesotho's economy has become more closely knit to that of South Africa in another way in recent years. In 1968, the Lesotho Electricity Supply Department was linked into the South African electrical utility by the South African electrical utility, ESCOM. This apparently represented a deliberate South African policy to render Lesotho increasingly dependent on South Africa's electricity output, rather than developing its own potentially extensive capacity. A proposed hydro-electrical power project which was to have been built within Lesotho itself to supply power to South Africa was shelved. The International Monetary Fund reported in 1971: [44]

> The Electricity Corporation has continued this arrangement and accelerated the replacement of locally generated electricity with power purchased from the South African Electricity Supply Commission (ESCOM)... [although] Lesotho is comparatively rich in water resources.

Lesotho does not publish its own trade statistics. Most of its trade is clearly, however, with South Africa. Even more than in the case of Swaziland and Botswana, Lesotho provides a captive market for South Africa's manufactured goods. In 1972, its imports totalled about $42 million worth of goods. Of this total, about a fourth constituted food, drink and tobacco, reflecting the underdevelopment of Lesotho's own agro-industrial sector. Only 12 per cent of imports constituted machinery and equipment for its limited so-called 'modern' sector. Most of the rest constituted luxury items for the narrow high-income market and the tourist trade, and some imported parts and materials for the limited last-stage assembly and processing manufacturing sector.

Lesotho's total dependence on South Africa was sharply illustrated when its Prime Minister Chief Jonathan started making some tentative moves at the Organization of African Unity and United Nations meeting against South Africa in 1974. Immediately some 10,000 Lesotho miners were arbitrarily sent home. The result was a major increase in unemployment and riots in Lesotho. [45]

Summary

The economies of Swaziland, Botswana, and Lesotho, despite their attainment of nominal political independence in the mid-1960s, continues to be shaped to provide raw materials, areas of profitable investments and markets for the manufactured goods of South Africa's oligopolisitc corporate system. Their commercial banking and trading systems are intertwined with South Africa's at every point. Although Swaziland and Botswana have broken out of the South African Customs Union and issued their own currencies, South African-based settler and corporate interests, together with associated foreign multinational corporations, run their mines and agricultural export sectors. The masses of the peoples in all three countries live at levels among the lowest in Africa. In this sense, they do in fact remain captives of South Africa's political economic rulers in all but name.

REFERENCES

CHAPTER THIRTEEN

1. Europa Publications Ltd , *Africa South of the Sahara, 1974* (London: 1974).
2. Economic Commission for Africa, *Summaries of Economic Data, Swaziland,* 1972,Fifth Year, no. 2.
3. International Monetary Fund, *Surveys of African Economies* (Washington, D.C., 1971) Vol. 5.
4. *Standard Bank Review,* September 1974.
5. *Financial Mail,* 17 November 1974.
6. For data re Swaziland agriculture, see IMF, *Surveys of African Economies,* op. cit.
7. Anglo American, *Annual Reports.*
8. *Standard Bank Reviews,* July 1974.
9. Rand Mines, *Annual Reports.*
10. *Financial Mail,* 11 October 1974.
11. *ECA, Swaziland,* op. cit.
12. IMF, *Surveys of African Economies,* op. cit.
13. Ibid.
14. Ibid.
15. Economic Commission for Africa, *Summaries of Economic Data Botswana 1972.* Fifth Year, No. 17.
16. State of South Africa, *Economic, Financial and Statistical Yearbook for the Republic of South Africa* (Johannesburg: 1973); African Research Bureau, Vol. 11, No. 10.
17. The Economist, *Quarterly Economic Review,* Annual supplement.
18. *Financial Mail,* 11 October 1974, 'ZCI, Review by Dr. Z.J. De Beer'; *Quarterly Economic Review Annual Supplement,* op. cit.
19. Europa Publications, Ltd., *African South of the Sahara,* 1974, op. cit.
20. M. Selitshena, 'Mining and Development Strategy in Botswana', in A. Seidman, ed., *Natural Resources and National Welfare: The Case of Copper,* (New York: Praeger, 1975).
21. Europa Publications, *Africa South of the Sahara,* 1974, op. cit.
22. *African Research Bulletin Vol. 11, No. 10.*
23. *Anglo American Corporation, Annual Report,* 1975.
24. ECA, *Botswana, 1972,* op. cit.
25. *Standard Bank Review,* August 1974.
26. IMF, *Surveys of African Economies,* op. cit.
27. *African Research Bulletin,* Vol. 11, No. 5.
28. *African Research Bulletin,* Vol. 11, No. 5.
29. ECA, Botswana, op. cit.
30. Ibid.
31. *Quarterly Economic Review,* Second Quarter, 1974.
32. Europa Publications, *Africa South of the Sahara,* 1974, op. cit.
33. *Standard Bank Review,* September 1974.
34. Cf. A. Seidman, *Planning for Development in Sub-Saharan Africa* (New York and Tanzania: Praeger and Tanzania Publishing House,1974), pp. 140—146.
35. *Standard Bank Review,* June 1974.
36. *Financial Gazette,* 7 January 1972.
37. Ibid.
38. *Financial Mail,* 1 August 1975.
39. IMF, *Surveys of African Economies,* op. cit.
40. *Standard Bank Reveiw,* August 1974.
41. *Standard Bank Review,* September 1974.
42. *Standard Bank Review,* August 1974.
43. *African Research Bureau,* Vol. 11, No. 9.
44. *Surveys of African Economies,* op. cit.
45. *Quarterly Economic Review,* First Quarter, 1974.

Chapter XIV

Mozambique and Angola

The Portuguese clung to their rule over Mozambique and Angola, the largest colonial empire left in the vast African continent, for almost a decade after most of the rest of Africa had attained political independence. South Africa had come to view Portugal as a valuable ally bolstering white rule in Southern Africa. Then, weakened by a decade of guerilla warfare, the Portuguese dictatorship in Europe was overthrown by a coup led by young military officers who had learned through years of war that continued enslavement of the Africans was impossible. One of the first steps taken by the new Portuguese Government in Lisbon was to pledge independence for the colonies. This was an important factor causing the South Africa regime to proclaim its 'new' strategy of 'detente' with its neighbours to the north.

It is impossible, in the limited space here available, to discuss the political and economic transformations which the independent nations of Mozambique and Angola will bring about in southern Africa. The aim here is only to outline the extent of South African multinational corporate interests which laid the foundation for the evident concern of the South African Government and its allies in the United States with the future of those new nations.

Mozambique

The new nation of Mozambique is one of the biggest of the more than 40 independent nations of Africa. Its population, estimated in 1970 at over eight million, is almost as large as Kenya's or Ghana's. Until

193

1975, its lop-sided political economy had been shackled to one of Europe's most underdeveloped countries, Portugal. Its main exports were cotton, cashew nuts, sugar, and sisal, mostly grown on Portuguese settler estates employing African labour. In recent years, as the national liberation front, FRELIMO, mobilized the guerilla movement throughout the rural areas, the Portuguese dictatorship had, in desperation, welcomed increased South African economic penetration in order to bolster its fast-weakening position.[1]

Mozambique had long provided one of the most important sources of cheap immigrant labour for the South African mines. About 86,000 Mozambicans, driven by poverty and systematic Portugese recruitment worked annually in South Africa. A quarter of their annual earnings of $60 million were paid directly to the Portuguese Government in gold at the official rate.[2] The incomes of migrant labourers, small as they were in absolute terms, equalled almost a fourth of the value of the manufacturing output of Mozambique's stunted industrial sector. Over three fourths of Mozambique's handful of factories produced foodstuffs, clothing, drink and tobacco. Most of the manufactured goods used in the colony were imported, providing an important market for Portuguese factories at home.

The most important project in which South African business became engaged in Mozambique was the Cabora Bassa dam, one of the biggest hydro-electric projects on the African continent. The South Station alone is to produce 2000 MW. Most of the electric power was originally planned to be sold to South Africa to earn the foreign exchange desperately needed by the Portuguese colonial rulers to finance their war effort.

The Portuguese Government had also hoped that Cabora Bassa would involve international interests in its efforts to defeat FRELIMO, and stimulate an increase in white immigration to strengthen its fight against the liberation forces. As the reality of the situation unfolded, especially as European protest movements frightened away West German and other foreign firms, however, an estimated three fourths of the investments were provided by South African-based companies.[3] Anglo American became especially deeply involved, both directly and through its subsidiary, LTA Construction. Anglo itself is a member of the ZAMCO consortium which built the Cabora Bassa project. LTA obtained civil engineering projects worth 445 million to build three substations, 220kv transmission lines, and preliminary work for the eventual establishment of the North Bank station.[4]

Anglo American had been the most important South African investor in Mozambique even prior to the inception of the Cabora Bassa project. By 1969, it had about $30 million invested in various projects there. In association with a French company, Société Nationale des Pétroles d'Aquitaine, and a German firm, Gelsenkirchner Bergwerk, it had been prospecting for the oil South Africa required to reduce its dependence on traditional oil producing countries.[4]

Anglo also had a controlling interest in Industrias de Caju Mocita, the leading Mozambique exporter of unroasted cashew nuts, with a capital of about $800,000. A subsidiary operated a processing factory producing an almost equivalent amount of cashews.[5] Another South African company, Tiger Oats and National Milling, which holds an interest in Industrias de Caju Mocita, also owns one of the largest fishing companies in Namibia, the Lamberts Bay Fishing Co. [6]

Anglo had a large interest in Banco Standard-Totta Mozambique which was jointly controlled by the Portugese Bank, Banco Totta Alianca and Standard. It will be recalled that the U.S. bank, Chase Manhattan, owned 15 per cent of the parent bank of Standard in England, and hence was also involved in Mozambique. (See above, p 114).

Messina (Transvaal) Development Company, in which Anglo has a major interest, owned another $6.5 million worth of assets in Mozambique in the mid-1960s.

Anglo shipped the ore from its Swaziland mines to Japan down a railroad through the port of Lourenco-Marques. South African traffic through that port was another source of needed foreign exchange earnings for the Portuguese colonial administration.

The South African Government-owned Industrial Development Corporation itself had, by 1969, invested about $26 million in Mozambique. In cooperation with the Banco de Fomento Nacional, it had loaned about $9 million to a Portuguese sugar company, Marracuene Agricola Acucareira.[8]

South Africa's expanding trade with Mozambique reflected her increasing presence there in the latter years of Portuguese rule. South Africa sold five times as much to Mozambique in 1973 as in 1969. Its share of Mozambican imports multiplied from 3.2 per cent to about 16.3 per cent, or $62 million dollars in the later year. Thus Mozambique constituted an important and growing market for South African manufactured goods exports. Machinery and equipment, largely for the dam project constituted the bulk of Mozambican imports from South Africa.

Although South Africa began to increase its purchases from Mozambique in the same period, it never bought as much as it sold there. Mozambique's trade deficit with South Africa had, by 1972, mounted to $37 million. This was offset by the Mozambican miners' earnings. The overall Mozambique trade deficit with all countries, however, reached $165 million in 1972, a significant feature of the worsening financial situation confronting the colonial administration.

TABLE 14.1

MOZAMBIQUE'S FOREIGN TRADE BY REGION,
JAN-JUNE 1974 IMPORTS AND EXPORTS
IN ESCUDOS AND AS PERCENTAGES OF TOTALS

	Imports		*Exports*		*Balance*
	$000	*%*	*$000*	*%*	*$000*
Total	116,175	100.0	54,290	100.0	—61,885
Metropolitan					
Portugal	19,655	6.9	8,835	16.3	—10,820
South Africa	22,828	19.7	6,647	12.3	—16,181
West Germany	17,684	15.3	1,455	2.8	—16,228
U.K.	7,535	6.6	3,169	5.9	—4,366
U.S.	6,997	6.0	8,021	14.8	—1,024
Japan	9,216	8.0	1,345	2.5	—7,870

SOURCE: Instituto Nacional da Estatística, Delegado do Estado Portugues de Mocambique, Directo Provincial dos Servicos da Estatística, *Boletim Mensal da Estatística,* Nov., 1974.

Exchange rate: 54.43 escudos — U.S. $1.00

By the 1970s, to sum up, the Portuguese-ruled Mozambican political economy had become increasingly integrated with that of South Africa in several respects. It provided cheap contract labour for the South African mines, an expanding market for South African industry, and profitable business for the leading South African mining finance house, Anglo American.

All of this began to change after the Mozambique liberation movement won independence. ⁹ The banks were nationalized by the post-coup Portuguese Government in Lisbon and handed over to the new Mozambique administration. The newly installed Frelimo Government made it quite clear that existing links with multinational corporations and agri-business conglomerates were to be severely scrutinized, with every expectation of further nationalizations. In the short run, Mozambique workers were to continue to migrate to South Africa to work on the mines, though Mozambique officials declared they would press for better conditions and wages. In the longer run, the new government planned to restructure the economy along self-reliant lines so these workers could be absorbed at home. The same approach was adopted to creating alternatives to dependence on earnings from South African traffic through Mozambique ports and South African purchases of Cabora Bassa hydro-electric power.

The FRELIMO Government made it quite clear that, over time, it planned to build a socialist political economy. If it successfully consolidated its ties with Tanzania and perhaps Zambia along these lines, this would lay the basis for a major structural transformation threatening South African-multinational corporate interests throughout the southern Region.

Angola

Angola presents a significantly different picture than that of Mozambique. Its population of about six million is somewhat smaller. It has, however, far more extensive known deposits of rich minerals. These have been increasingly intensively exploited since World War II by multinational firms based in a number of Western countries including the United States. South African firms, too, have extended their penetration there.

TABLE 14.2
SELECTED STATISTICS FOR ANGOLA

Population: 1970 Census in December: 5,673,046; mid-1973 estimate = 5,930,000
Urban areas: Luanda 1970 = 475,300

Wage Employment: Mining (1972) = 30,335
Health (1972) = 8,320
Education (1973) = 15,486
Manufacturing 1971 = 87,216

	1963	1972
GDP at Market Prices: (in million escudos)	24,528	59,325*

*Unofficial reports

SOURCE: Economic Commission for Africa, *Summaries of Economic Data,* Angola, 6th Year, 1974 (Mimeo).

Angola constitutes a rich prize for foreign interests. The United States, which established close ties with the neighbouring autocratic regime of President Mobutu in Zaire, became increasingly concerned with the outcome of the guerilla warfare that broke out there in the

1960s. The struggle over Angola became reflected in the emergence of divisive so-called liberation movements, developed in opposition to the guerilla forces of Movimento Popular Liberação de Angola (MPLA). Extensive evidence is now available that the U.S. CIA began to finance a splinter group, FNLA, as early as 1962, while President Kennedy was in office, in hopes of installing a friendly government in the event of Portuguese defeat. In the 1970s, the U.S. began to funnel vast amounts of armaments and financial assistance through Mobutu's regime to both FNLA and UNITA, which united in an uneasy alliance to oppose the new Government created by MPLA after independence. White South African troops advanced deep into southern Angola to strengthen the wavering FNLA–UNITA troops.

The justification offered by the United States and South Africa governments for their intervention was the fact that the Soviet Union was delivering modern weapons to the new MPLA Government. The fact that the Soviet Union had provided arms for MPLA guerilla fighters for years, while the U.S. and other Western Governments had shipped guns and planes to the Portuguese colonial administration through NATO was ignored.

It is not the purpose here, however, to examine the details of the claims and counter-claims of the contending forces in the post in-dependence strife in Angola. Rather, these few pages aim to outline the nature of the long-standing South African multinational cor-porate interests there which lay behind the post-independence in-tervention of the U.S. and South African governments.

At independence, Angola remained a typically warped, colonial-type of economy. Over 80 per cent of its exports were still sold in unprocessed form, mostly petroleum, $230 million in 1973; coffee, $205 million; diamonds, $80 million; and iron ore, $49 million. Most of its imports were manufactured goods. 10 The Benguela Railway, running 1,000 miles from Lobito on the coast to Zaire's copper belt, was built in the early part of the century with substantial sums of British capital, mainly to ship copper from Zambia's and Zaire's mines to the sea. In 1955, a branch line to the Zimbabwean frontier connected the Benguela line to the rail line running to the Mozam-bique port of Lourenço Marques, passing through the industrial and mining areas of Rhodesia.

Coffee, produced on Portuguese-owned estates employing im-poverished Angolan migrant labour, had been Angola's main export until the 1970s. Most of Angola's coffee was sold to the big coffee companies of the United States, an important hard currency earner for the Portuguese government.

Diamonds had been produced by Diamang (Companhia de Diamantes de Angola) which for over half a century operated mines under concessions spreading over a 45,000 square mile area. These fields are said to be the fifth largest in the world. In 1974, 3000 Europeans and 20,000 African miners were working there. In 1971, the Portuguese had turned the diamond concessions, formerly held solely by Diamang, over to a consortium, CONDIAMA, owned jointly by Diamang and De Beers. Diamang is reported to be owned by South African, British and Portuguese capital.[11]

Angola is also rich in iron ore. A West German consortium, headed by Krupps, joined the Portuguese in building a second 300 mile railroad from Cassinga to Lobito to ship out 2.5 million tons of ore annually to the Ruhr steel industry.

By the mid-1970s, however, oil had become Angola's main export. Most of it was produced by U.S. Gulf Oil which had begun in the 1960s to exploit the very rich reserves of Cabinda, the isolated enclave cut off from the rest of Angola by the coastal tip of Zaire. By 1975, Gulf was producing close to 160,000 barrels a day from 120 wells, the second largest operating field in black-controlled Africa. There were recurrent reports that Texaco had pinpointed petroleum deposits off-shore from Angola proper that made the Cabinda fields look small.[12] Texaco withdrew from Angola as independence neared. Gulf continued to produce oil until it reportedly was told by the U.S. State Department to close down rather than to pay royalties to the newly installed MPLA Government.

Angola's manufacturing sector is about 40 per cent larger than that of Mozambique, although its total output in 1972 was only worth about $420 million. As in Mozambique, most of Angola's manufacturing industries are concentrated in the production of foodstuffs (a third), drink and tobacco (15 per cent) and textiles, clothing and footwear (12 per cent).

Like Mozambique, Angola became increasingly enmeshed with the South African political economy after World War II, especially through the South African-dominated economy of Namibia, located between the two countries. About a fourth as many Angolans (20,000) as Mozambicans migrate annually. They go primarily to work on the South African and foreign-owned mines and farms in Namibia. The Portuguese also built a hydro-electric project, like that of Cabora Bassa in Mozambique, on the Cunene River in Angola to supply Namibia and South Africa with electricity. South Africa's Industrial Development Corporation set up a subsidiary, the South West Water and Electricity Corporation (SWAWEK) with an original share capital of $7.5 million, to implement the scheme in 1964. By 1970, the share capital had multiplied more than seven-fold to $50 million. The South African Government provided the entire investment, partly in the form of a long term loan, and partly as a non-reimbursable grant to the Portuguese Government.

The Anglo American Company had become involved in Angola with a total investment reported at $30 million by the 1970s. In Angola, as in Mozambique, Anglo's construction subsidiary, LTA, became one of the most important sub-contractors building the hydro-electric project. [14] Anglo also participated in Sociedade de Exploracões Minerais Africanas, which was prospecting for oil. It had another subsidiary, South African Angolan Investments, Ltd, ' which controlled a fishing company, Uniao Angolana de Pesca e Industria. [15]

As in Mozambique, Angola had a major interest in the Standard Bank/Totta Alianca subsidiary. In 1972, the Banco Espirito Santo e Comercial of Portugal, and the First City National Bank of New York, set up a bank, the Banco Inter-Unido, in Angola. The Portuguese Government had retained 10 per cent of the shares. [16]

Other South African companies were operating in Angola. GenMin owns 34 per cent of Ansa Petroleum, in which Anglo also owns shares, which has a 25 per cent interest in an oil concession in Western Cuanza. This company produced about 650,000 cubic metres of petrol in 1972 and in 1973. [17] GenMin had also established a company, together with Companhia Mineira do Lobito, for the exploration and exploitation of minerals, including nuclear materials, in two concessions. [18]

Two South African firms were engaged in manufacturing in Angola in 1969. One of these, African Oxygen Company, had invested in Angola African Oxygen with the British Oxygen Company, to operate an oxygen plant. Another South African firm, Amalgamated Packaging Industries, Ltd, has invested $4 million in a cardboard packaging plant, in partnership with Companhia União de Cervejas de Angola. [19] Other foreign investors in Angolan manufacturing include Firestone (U.S.), British American Tobacco, ICI, and British Leyland Co.

South African trade with Angola never became as important to South Africa's expanding industrial economy as did that of Mozambique. It had, however, also been increasing prior to the fall of the Portuguese. South Africa was only the sixth largest supplier of imports to Angola in 1973. Portugal remained the most important supplier, England was second, and the U.S., third. South African sales had risen, however, from about 4 per cent of Angola's 1970s imports to about 6.7 per cent of a much larger import bill in 1973. In absolute terms they had doubled, reaching $35 million in the latter year.

South African imports from Angola were far lower than her sales there. South African purchases had declined from 1.2 per cent of all Angola exports in 1970 to 1.1 per cent in 1973, although in absolute terms they had almost doubled to $8.4 million. South Africa still only ranked twelfth among buyers from Angola.

TABLE 14.3

ANGOLA'S FOREIGN TRADE BY REGION, JAN—JUNE 1974
IN ESCUDOS AND AS PERCENTAGES OF TOTALS

	Imports		*Exports*		*Balance*
	$000	*%*	*$000*	*%*	*$000*
Total	192,408	100.00	251,502	100.0	+ 59,094
Metropolitan Portugal	53,786	27.95	64,979	25.54	+ 11,193
South Africa	11,186	5.81	2,900	1.15	− 8,285
West Germany	24,775	12.88	13,802	5.49	−10,973
Britain	15,421	8.01	7,860	3.12	− 7,561
United States	15,690	8.16	68,531	27.25	+ 52,841
Japan	10,527	5.47	21,346	8.49	+ 10,819

Exchange Rate: 54.43 escudos = 1 U.S. dollar

SOURCE: Instituto Nacional de Estatistica, Delegacao de Angola, Dereccao Provincial do Servicos de Estatistica, *Boletim Mensal de Estatica,* December 1974.

Summary

The full story of the consequences of the fall of the Portuguese dictatorship for the peoples of the former colonies of Mozambique and Angola will be told elsewhere. In the context of the analysis being developed in this book, the fact that South African and multinational corporate interests had become increasingly involved in the pre-independence colonial economies has a two-fold significance. First, South Africa and its multinational corporate allies confronted the probable loss of increasingly important potential sources of labour and raw materials, as well as markets for their expanding manufactured goods production, if the new governments consolidated their political and economic independence. Second, the liberation of these countries and the creation of truly effective governments functioning in the interests of the masses of the people on South Africa's own borders constituted a real threat to the continued stability of the racist regime there.

These dangers spurred the South African Government to make every possible effort to extend its outreach and achieve its own brand of detente with its African neighbours to the north. The unfolding evidence in Angola indicated that, in these efforts, it enjoyed at least the covert assistance of highly-placed officials in the U.S. Government.

REFERENCES

CHAPTER FOURTEEN

1. B. Davidson, "South Africa and Portugal," in UN Unit on Apartheid, *Notes and Documents*, No 7/74.
2. *Economist Intelligence Unit, Quarterly Economic Review*, Third Quarter, 1974; African Research Bureau, Vol. 11, No. 9.
3. R. Nyathi, *South African Imperialism in Southern Africa*, (Dakar: ECA Institute for Planning and Economic Development, mimeo, 1974.)
4. Anglo American, *Annual Report*.
5. United Nations Document A/7623; Anglo American Co., *Annual Report*.
6. Tiger Oats and National Milling Co., *Annual Report*, 1973.
7. *Africa Today*, Vol. 17, No. 4, July, August 1970; Anglo-American, op. cit.
8. U.N. Document A/7023.
9. Cf. J. Saul, "Free Mozambique", *Monthly Review*, Vol. 27, No. 7. December 1975.
10. *African Research Bulletin*, Vol. 11, No. 4.
11. *New York Times*, December 28, 1975; See Economist Intelligence Unit, Ltd, *Quarterly Economic Review, Angola and Mozambique*, Annual Supplement, 1974.
12. Ibid.
13. Report of the Council for Namibia.
14. Ibid.
15. A/7623.
16. *Africa Today*, Vol. 17, No. 4, July-August 1970; Economists, *Quarterly Economic Review*, op. cit., No. 2, 1973, No. 4, 1972.
17. General Mining and Finance Corp. *Annual Reports*.
18. Economist, *Quarterly Economic Review*, No. 4, 1973.

Chapter XV

South Africa in Zimbabwe

The population of Zimbabwe (still called Rhodesia by the white minority regime that rules there) is about the same as Angola's. In 1972, it was almost 5.7 million, of whom 95 per cent were African. Over half the white settlers or their parents were born in South Africa. Although outnumbered by blacks 20 to 1, they have nevertheless attempted to impose an *apartheid* system like that of South Africa on the black majority. To further this end, they unilaterally declared independence from Britain in 1966. The United Nations voted for a total boycott of the Rhodesian regime in an effort to force them to allow Africans a greater degree of participation in the political economic structure. The Zimbabweans, themselves, began to organize guerrila forces to fight for liberation of their land.

South Africa, together with the Portuguese colonialists till their ouster in 1974, ignored the UN boycott. Their assistance was a primary factor in the Rhodesian regime's survival for the ensuing decade.

The aim of this brief chapter is not to analyze in detail the complex nature of the struggle for Zimbabwean national liberation. Rather it is to examine the structure of South African and multinational interests which have bound the Rhodesian political economy into a neo-colonial relationship with South Africa.

The Rhodesian Manufacturing Centre
Rhodesia, even prior to its illegal declaration of independence, had achieved the status of the second most industrialized country in sub-

Saharan Africa, next to South Africa itself. This was the result of a systematic colonial-settler policy of building up the Rhodesian manufacturing sector at the expense of the neighbouring countries, particularly Zambia and Malawi, prior to their independence. During the decade of the existence of the Federation of Rhodesias and Nyasaland (1953-1963)   the settler-dominated Southern Rhodesian Government had taxed the investible surpluses produced by the then Northern Rhodesian (now Zambian) copper mines and invested them to build up the white-controlled industrial sector in what is now Rhodesia.   At   the   same   time,   overcrowded,   under-developed Nyasaland (now Malawi) provided a source of low-cost labour for Rhodesian farmers and manufacturers. Both Zambia and Malawi were forced by Federation-imposed tariff walls to buy Rhodesian manufactured goods at prices often above those available on the world market. [1]

TABLE 15.1
INDUSTRIAL ORIGIN OF RHODESIA'S NATIONAL PRODUCT, 1967-1973

Sector	1967 US$ mn.	%	1970 US $ mn.	%	1973* US$ mn.	%	% Increase 1967-1973
Agriculture	249.2	19.7	273.5	16.1	380.6	16.5	53
Mining & Quarrying	78.5	6.2	114.2	6.7	153.5	6.4	95
Manufacturing	240.7	19.1	376.7	22.1	564.6	23.4	135
Construction	68.5	5.4	103.0	6.1	158.3	6.6	131
Electricity & Water	43.7	3.5	51.7	3.0	68.7	2.8	57
Commerce, Hotels & Restaurants	172.0	13.6	234.9	13.8	346.5	14.4	101
Finance	26.3	2.1	36.7	2.2	57.3	2.4	117
Transports & Communications	85.8	6.8	114.9	6.8	133.3	5.5	55
Other	298.0	23.6	393.9	23.2	531.8	22.0	78
Total (GDP at Current factor cost)	1,262.9	100.0	1,699.7	100.0	2,411.4	100.0	89.3
GDP at Market Price	1,353.2	107.1	1,840.1	108.3	2,583.1	107.1	90.9

SOURCE: Economic Commission for Africa, *Summaries of Economic Data Rhodesia.* Sixth Year, 1974.

NOTE: Converted at exchange rate of Rhodesian dollar equal to U.S. dollar.

* estimated.

The manufacturing sector of Rhodesia, in other words, had, by 1966, been built up as a sub-centre in southern Africa through the exploitation of Zambia and Malawi at the periphery. At the same time,

Rhodesia's settler economy was then, and is even more so now, a neo-colony of South Africa: South African and associated multinational firms invested there to take advantage of cheap labour and to obtain raw materials. They sold a significant share of their surplus manufactured goods in the Rhodesian market. A major share of the profits of this business has been siphoned out into South Africa. A significant share has been drained beyond into the coffers of multinationals based overseas.

In 1973, despite United Nations' sanctions, Rhodesia's national product at current factor cost was officially reported as $1,534 million, about $325 per capita, considerably above the per capita income of its Southern African neighbours, excluding South Africa and Zambia. The Rhodesian regime boasted a real rate of growth of 6.5 per cent in 1973. This was something of a decline from the 8.5 per cent rate of growth proclaimed in 1972, but nevertheless still high if the claim was valid. It should be remembered that there is no way of checking Governmental reports because Rhodesia shrouds its statistics in official confidentiality, allegedly for security reasons. The Smith regime is eager to present a picture of successful expansion in the face of the UN boycott.

Even at that, as one authority explains, 'Rhodesia has been able to maintain this growth only at the cost of increasing internal and international (mostly South African) indebtedness, and by increasing its volume of mineral and agricultural exports, the latter mainly to South Africa and Mozambique.'[2] A significant share of its exports, it might be added, have been sold outside of Africa to multinational firms, some of them based in the U.S., which are willing to conceal the source in a profitable business deal.

Growing debt has spurred internal inflation in Rhodesia as in South Africa. It was held down during the 1960s, but recently has been rising at an increasing rate. The official consumer price index for Africans, probably understated, showed a 6.1 per cent rise in the first six months of 1974, and a slightly higher rate of 6.4 per cent for Europeans whose luxury living standards require more imported goods, or an annual rate of over 12 per cent. This is a faster rate of price increases than for any full year in the last decade.

Confronted by UN sanctions, the Rhodesian regime has imposed an extensively interventionist form of state capitalism on the Rhodesian economy in close cooperation with domestic and South African business firms. It exercises complete control over foreign exchange which is in short supply due to difficulties in selling

Table 15.2

A. EXPANSION OF RHODESIAN MANUFACTURING
INDUSTRY, 1966-1973

	1966	1971*	1973*
Establishments (No.)	979	1240	...
Gross Output (in $US*)	$595m.	$1120m.	$1466m.
Employees	84,400	125,000	142,200
Wages & Salaries (in $US*)	$114	$189	$575
Net output (in $US*)	$223m.	$451m.	$576m.

B. Gross output by Sector

	1966 $000,000*		1973 $000,000*		% Increase 1967–1973
Foodstuffs	177.5	24.6	370.7	22.2	108
Drink & Tobacco	58.3	8.1	114.1	6.8	96
Textiles	61.4	8.5	174.1	10.4	183
Clothing & Footwear	56.8	7.9	112.9	6.7	99
Wood & Furniture	27.0	3.7	60.9	3.6	125
Paper & Printing	39.8	5.5	84.7	5.1	113
Chemicals, etc.	97.4	13.5	207.1	12.4	113
Non-metallic minerals	21.9	3.0	66.8	4.0	205
Metals & products	129.7	18.0	380.9	22.7	194
Transport equipment, etc.	45.4	6.3	81.9	4.9	80.4
Other	6.6	0.9	19.7	1.2	198.5
TOTAL	721.8	100.0	1673.1	100.0	132

SOURCE: Economic Commission for Africa, *Summaries of Economic Data Rhodesia*. Sixth Year 1973.
NOTE: Converted at exchange rate of one Rhodesian dollar equal to 1.7 U.S. dollars.

traditional exports on the world market. Rhodesian dollars are totally inconvertible.

Like South Africa, but even more strictly, the Rhodesian regime has given 'priority to the allocation of foreign exchange to industry rather than commerce'.[3] In 1965, before the Unilateral Declaration of Independence (UDI) and the imposition of sanctions by UN members, about half of all imports were utilized by the manufacturing sector. By 1970 the Association of Industry, dominated by the largest manufacturing firms, received about 70 per cent. The remainder was allocated to the Associated Chambers of Commerce, which spent 90 per cent on commerce connected with industry. Only 10 per cent was used to import finished consumer goods. Any project involving the import of over $150,000 worth of goods requires Government approval.

The introduction of hot-house state capitalism has, it is true, enabled Rhodesia to achieve a relatively high degree of self-sufficiency in manufacturing output. The *South African Financial Times*[4] describes the industries set up under this system, however, as 'backyard companies producing import substitutes'.

Not all South African 'assistance' proved unmitigatedly beneficial to Rhodesia under these circumstances, either. A significant problem confronting Rhodesian industries has been that they have been using second-hand machinery sold to them by South African firms. Much of it was apparently bought without adequate examination. A lot of it turned out to be in poor condition and by the early seventies required replacement. The South African firms had meanwhile taken their profits out of Rhodesia, and there was little foreign exchange available to buy new machinery[5]

Despite these drawbacks, manufacturing output reportedly was 50 per cent higher in 1970 than in 1966. Over 20 per cent of the growth was in chemicals, rubber and petrol, non-metallic mineral products and paper and printing industries.[6] Manufacturing employment grew from 15 per cent of the labour force in 1966 to 21 per cent in 1972.[7]

Whereas the manufacturing sector has benefitted from the protection imposed because of the UN boycott, the agricultural sector, dependent on export sale, has suffered. Rhodesia's white farmers have confronted serious difficulties because the UN sanctions have hindered sales of their crops overseas. The regime's tobacco board subsidized tobacco, the most important export, for about $30 million a year, but is unable to sell all that is produced. According to the report of the Government Commission of Inquiry into Agricultural Import Costs published in 1973:[8]

despite increased profit, capital expenditure and redemption charges have left farmers with less cash in 1972, in terms of current money values, than in 1965.

African Poverty

As in South Africa, one of the main reasons the Rhodesian whites seek to impose an *apartheid* system is to hold down wages and augment their profits. The evidence shows that they have indeed succeeded in keeping African wages low. A University of Rhodesia survey showed that more than 90 per cent of all Africans in commerce and industry earned less than $85 a month in 1971, 25 per cent less than the Poverty Datum Line in Salisbury for a typical family. In agriculture, where a third of all African wage workers are employed, the average wage was only $160 for the year. In domestic service, where more than 20 per cent of all African wage earners, and 40 per cent of those in Salisbury are employed, the annual average wage was about $317.[9]

Table 15.3

AVERAGE ANNUAL EUROPEAN AND AFRICAN WAGES IN
ZIMBABWE (IN U.S. DOLLARS)

	1965	1967	1969	1971	1965 dollars	Increase 1971 per cent
European	4,379	4,627	5,051	5,758		
African	418	445	476	535		

Distribution	Number of Earners	%
Under $17 a month	245,410	32.9
$17—34	172,610	23.1
$34—85	251,270	33.7
Subtotal	669,290	89.8
$85—153	63,170	8.5
$153—204	9,270	1.2
Over $204	3,800	0.5
Total	745,530	100.0

SOURCE: Kenneth Good, 'Settler Colonialism in Rhodesia', in *African Affairs,* Journal of the Royal African Society, Vol. 73, No. 290, January 1974. Converted into US$ at the rate of Rho $1.00 = US$1.70.

African unemployment is very high. Some 330,000 Africans left school between 1969 and 1973, but wage employment in that period increased only 197,000. As in South Africa, all Africans without paid jobs are forced to return to live on the overcrowded, infertile 'African tribal lands' which are restricted to about 40 per cent of the total national land area. The resulting unrest fostered the mounting guerilla resistance which has swept the country since the 1960s.

South African Support

White rule has been kept in place in Rhodesia by South Africa. If it were not for South Africa, the regime could not have survived the UN boycott.

Rhodesia does not publish trade statistics to avoid providing information about the effect of sanctions or the ways they are evaded. The United Nations Committee on Sanctions has, however, estimated that in 1972 total Rhodesian imports were worth some $415 million, equal to about a fourth of her national product. About 40 per cent of these were imported from within the South African Customs Union. While this estimate has not been broken down by sector, the South African *Financial Mail* characterizes the country's imports as 'machinery, oil, vehicles and vehicle spares'. This suggests that Zimbabwe has, perforce, constituted an important market for South African and multinational firms which have been expanding South African manufacturing output.

South Africa, together with Portugal prior to the independence of Mozambique, also provided a crucial conduit for the export of Rhodesian goods abroad. South Africa itself absorbed about a third of Rhodesia's exports, including asbestos and chrome, for its own use. When commodities allowed to pass through its ports to multinational firms beyond are included, South Africa probably accounted directly or indirectly for about half of Rhodesia's exports. 10

This is not to say that the United Nations boycott had no effect. On the contrary, the *Johannesburg Star* reported that, by April 1975, 'evidence is mounting that Rhodesia is facing its worst economic crisis... The most crucial factor appears to be the critical shortage of foreign exchange'. 11 This was one of the reasons for the significance of Union Carbide's success in lobbying for U.S. Congressional action to permit the import of Rhodesian chrome, ferrochrome and nickel in violation of the UN sanctions. (See pp. 212ff. below for details) From 1972 to 1974, these imports provided about $57 million worth of the foreign exchange which Rhodesia used to buy essential imports.

The Corporate Basis

An underlying reason for South African support of Rhodesia has been the extent of involvement there by South African firms, especially the Anglo American Group, and their multinational corporate allies. In an article entitled, 'The Extent of Dependence', the *Financial Mail* explained 12 that, over and above their trading limits, South African corporations are deeply intertwined in Rhodesia's company structure:

> Most of the important industrial companies, though operating as separate managerial entities, have ties with South Africa. As an indication: no less than five of Rhodesia's top ten industrials are either controlled by, or associated with, SA companies (Rhodesian Breweries, Hippo Valley, Premier Portland Cement, Plate Gass and BAT).

The biggest of these companies, Rhodesian Breweries, also holds the key to the country's food and liquor industries, and is its most ambitious hotel developer.

Anglo-American, through its Rhodesian subsidiary, is responsible for such key industries as steel (Risco), coal (Wankie), nickel (Trojan-Bindura) and has important stakes in sugar, citrus and timber.

Anglo, ICI and SA Manganese are leaders in mineral prospecting. Messina's Mangula is the country's biggest copper producer.

TABLE 15.4
SOME ANGLO AMERICAN SUBSIDIARIES IN ZIMBABWE (US $)

Name	Activity	1974 Market Value	1974 After Tax Profit
Anglo American Corp. Rhodesia	Holds Rhodesian interests of AAC & Charter. Widely diversified investments, including coal, nickel, steel, allied engineering industries, citrus, sugar & other agriculture, forestry, cement, flour-milling, property and merchant banking.	$73,775,000	$6,195,000
New Rhodesia Investments Ltd	Wholly-owned subsidiary owns entire capital of Anglo-American Corporation Services, Ltd, Anglo American (Rhodesian Services) Ltd, Appraised Securities Limited, Blue Skies (Private) Limited, Consolidated Mines Holdings (Rhodesia) Ltd and Orlop Investments Ltd. The group holds nickel mines at Bindura, Madziwa and Shangani, and has interests in many other Rhodesian and South African companies	*	*
Rhodesian Nickel Corp. Ltd	Owns Trojan Nickel Mind limited, Madziwa Mines Ltd and Bindura Smelting and Refining Company Ltd mines and refines nickel and copper in the Bindura/Shamva district	*	$4,379,200
Wankie Colliery Co. Ltd	Sales 1,974 1,971 Coal 000 tons 2,794 2,806 Coke 000 tons 267 237 Tar 000 litres 7,618 5,255	$7,913,500	$3,388,000
Clay Products Ltd	Owns a factory near Bulawayo producing a wide range of refractory products and earthenware pipes and fittings	*	$198,000

Name	Activity	1974 Market Value	1974 After Tax Profit
Hippo Valley Estates Ltd	Produces sugar, citrus and related products	*	$4,325,000
Anglo American Rhodesian Development Corporation Ltd	The company's main source of income is the hiring of rolling stock, originally purchased for $15.5 million (Rhodesian), to the Rhodesia Railways under long-term lease arrangements. It also administers the Mazoe Citrus Estates near Salisbury estates in the Eastern Highlands	*	*

SOURCE: Anglo American *Annual Report*, 1975.

NOTE: Anglo American has investments in many of the major Rhodesian companies.

*Data unavailable

The *Mail's* account only begins to scratch the surface of the empire dominated by Anglo in Rhodesia. Anglo's subsidiary, AAC Rhodesia holds Anglo and Charter interests 'in conjunction with other Rhodesian companies.' [13] It has 'a widely diversified portfolio of Rhodesian-based investments' in coal, nickel, copper mining, iron, steel, ferrochrome, and allied engineering industries, citrus, sugar, general agriculture, forestry and timber processing, flour milling, rolling stock hire, property, merchant banking and investment finance. It plays a dominant role in Rhodesia's corporate structure which, with intensified Government intervention, has become increasingly oligopolistically controlled in the last decade of UN sanctions.

AAC Rhodesia owned investments quoted on the South African stock exchange worth $43 million at market value in 1973, although book value was only about a third that. Its additional unquoted investments were reported worth about $32 million at book value. The company reported after tax profits of $3.5 million in 1973, over ten per cent more than in the previous year.

Another Anglo subsidiary, the Wankie Colliery Company, operates one of the biggest coal mines in Zimbabwe. It was originally established to sell coal to Anglo's copper smelting and refining plants in Zambia. After the Zambian Government, to comply with the UN boycott, forced Anglo to utilize coal from Zambia's own somewhat more expensive deposits, Wankie had to search for new markets. The company nevertheless reported sales of over three million tons of coal in 1973, somewhat more than in 1972, as well as 237,000 tons of coke and 5,255,000 litres of tar. How much of this was consumed in Rhodesia and South Africa is unknown. It seems not at all unlikely, however, that some, if not all, of the coal purchased by United States power companies for the first time in 1974 was in fact not from South Africa, but trans-shipped from Rhodesia. The Wankie Colliery reported after-tax profits of about $21 million in 1974.

Anglo, together with Anglovaal, holds a major direct interest in the Messina (Transvaal) Development Company mentioned in the *Financial Mail* article. In 1973, Messina's South African and Rhodesian operations, combined, produced 49,931 tons of finished copper at a before-tax profit of $32 million, over a third more than the preceding year's returns.

Still another Anglo subsidiary, the Rhodesian Nickel Corporation, owns 100 per cent of the Trojan Nickel Mine, the Madziwa Mines and the Bindura Smelting and Refining Company. These companies mine and refine Rhodesian nickel. Through the Rhodesian Nickel Corporation, Anglo owns shares (36.8 per cent) of the Shangani Mining Corporation which began developing a new nickel mine despite the UN sanctions in the early 1970s. Johnnies owns 55.2 per cent of the remaining shares. On completion, it was expected that the mine would produce between five and six thousand metric tons annually.

The South African chemical parastatal, AE&CI, has acquired a wholly-owned subsidiary in Zimbabwe which manufactures superphosphates at its Rhodesian factory near Salisbury. AE&CI Rhodesia buys phosphates from another AE&CI subsidiary. Dorowa Minerals, which mines it in Zimbabwe. In 1973, the companies were expanded at a cost of $3.6 million. AE&CI Rhodesia also owns 50 per cent of the Rhodesia Fertiliser Corporation which manufactures and retails fertilisers and crop chemicals, as well as 50 per cent of Prolux Paint Holdings. AE&CI sells explosives in Zimbabwe. [14]

The Rhodesian Chrome Issue

The U.S. multinational corporation, Union Carbide, which produces 20 per cent of South Africa's chrome, has valuable mineral deposits in Rhodesia, too. It has found its investments in the Rhodesian deposits profitable, despite their location in difficult-to-exploit narrow seams, primarily because of the availability of plentiful supplies of low cost labour. [15]

A powerful lobby led by Union Carbide, which owns chrome mines in Rhodesia, persuaded the U.S. Congress to vote year after year in the early 1970s to permit U.S. firms to buy Rhodesian chrome despite the fact that the U.S. Government officially supported the UN's international embargo.

Available evidence shows that Rhodesian imports were never really crucial to US security. [16] They could easily be replaced by supplies already in the national stockpile, or which could be obtained from other foreign suppliers. In 1974, for example, the United States imported from Rhodesia only 10.2 per cent of its national requirements of high-carbon ferrochrome, 2.9 per cent of its low-carbon ferrochrome requirements, and 7.4 per cent of its metallurgical grade chrome ore needs. The U.S. national stockpile alone contained enough metallurgical trade chrome ore to supply *all* domestic needs for almost four years, if not a single ton of chrome was imported. It would take about 52 years to use up the national stockpile of chromite if it were substituted for the small amounts imported from Rhodesia: about 18 years to use up the high-carbon ferrochrome; and 85 years to use up the low-carbon ferrochrome. Technological advances have further reduced the importance of metallurgical grade ore from Rhodesia. Any increase in the price of chrome ore that might result from reducing Rhodesian imports—though none seemed likely—would have an insignificant effect on the price of stainless steel, because chrome constitutes only a small fraction of the aggregate product. In short, Union Carbide's lobbying resulted from its own efforts to profit from the continued sale of the ouput of its Rhodesian mines, and to provide support for the Rhodesian Government, rather than out of a real concern for U.S. security.

Bishop Abel Muzorewa expressed the bitterness of the African population at this continued blatant U.S. violation of UN sanctions. [17]

In a few years or even a few months the government of Rhodesia will be black... We will not forget those who ignored out suffering, scorned our rights and in complicity with the facist regime of Mr Smith took our minerals, bestowing wealth to the white minority and sentencing the black majority to poverty and physical depravity. We will recall that when we demanded freedom, you took our chrome, when we asked for understanding, you demanded that we understand your need for chrome... you usurped our minerals to make the tools of war for your battles in Asia.

South African Pressure for Zimbabwean Detente

Zimbabwe's political economy had become, after a decade of illegal white rule, essentially a political and economic satellite of South Africa. After the collapse of Portuguese colonialism, it appeared likely that the guerilla fighters would step up their efforts to oust the Smith regime, using independent Mozambique as a base. South African Prime Minister Vorster began to meet with President Kaunda of Zambia, in a proclaimed effort to seek, instead, a peaceful 'solution'. He reportedly agreed to pressure Smith to come to terms with the African majority in the context with Vorster's refurbished outreach policy, allegedly to contribute to a regional detente.

There is no reason to believe that the South African and multinational firms were prepared to jettison their interests in Zimbabwe. It is far more likely that they perceived the installation of an amenable black African Government as preferable to continued military confrontation which might lead to a more radical outcome on the Mozambican and Angolan models.

From the South African-multinational corporate viewpoint, the important issue is how to preserve their corporate interests. To defend illegal white minority rule in the face of continued UN sanctions would be at best difficult and costly. At worst, continued guerilla warfare might, as it had in the Portuguese colonies, radicalize and unite the masses of the population.

An African victory achieved through military confrontation, in other words, would be far more likely to lead to the formation of a radical government which would seek to make the institutional changes required to utilize its industrial base to meet the needs of the Zimbabwean population. A truly self-reliant Zimbabwean government, united together with Mozambique, Tanzania, and perhaps Zambia, could provide the industrial foundation for rapid structural transformation throughout the entire southern region. This posed by far the more serious long-run threat to South African and multinational corporate interests.

REFERENCES
CHAPTER FIFTEEN

1. Richard Sklar, *Corporate Power in an African State* (Berkeley: University of California Press, 1975) p.16.
2. Africa Bureau (London) Fact Sheet No. 34, 'Rhodesia: Affects of the Sanctions War', February 1974.
3. U.S. House of Representatives, Subcommittee on International Organizations and Movements, *Sanctions as an Instrumentality of the U.N.: Rhodesia as a Case Study*, 92nd Congress, 2nd Session (Washington, D.C.: Government Printing Office, 1972).
4. 22 April 1970.
5. U.S. House of Representatives, op. cit.
6. Ibid.
7. Economic Commission for Africa, *Summaries of Economic Data, Rhodesia* 5th Year) Mimeo, 1972.
8. Quoted in Africa Bureau, op. cit.
9. Kenneth Good, 'Settler Colonialism in Rhodesia', in *African Affairs*, Journal of the Royal African Society, Volume 73, No. 290 (January, 1974).
10. *Financial Mail*, 23 October 1970.
11. *Johannesburg Star,* April 1975.
12. 23 October 1970.
13. Anglo-American Corporation, *Annual Report*, 1974.
14. AE&CI, *Annual Report*, 1974.
15. D.A. Brobstand Walden P. Pratt, eds, *U.S. Mineral Resources*, Geological Survey Professional Paper, 820. (Washington: U.S. Government Printing Office, 1973).
16. 'New African Realities', Washington Office on Africa, 1975.
17. Press Conference, June, 1975, cited in 'New African Realities', Washington Office on Africa.

Chapter XVI

Zambia's Response to the South African Outreach

Introduction

In the midst of Zambia's celebrations of the tenth anniversary of its independence, its President, Kenneth Kaunda, publicly proclaimed Vorster's outreach proposals as 'the voice of reason for which Africa and the world have waited for many years'.[1] The South African Government's apparent success in building a close relationship with Zambia was perhaps the most significant victory in its strategy of detente.[2]

The evidence suggests that the growing cooperation between the Zambian Government and the white South African regime was supported, if not actually arranged, with the behind-the-scenes assistance of United States officials. It certainly fits in with the stated aim of the Option No. 2 of the United States' Confidential National Security Council's Memorandum 39. More concrete is the known fact that Zambia's then Foreign Minister, Vernon Mwaanga, visited Washington to talk with the U.S. Secretary of State, Henry Kissinger, shortly after the post-coup Portuguese Government had announced its intention of granting independence to Mozambique and Angola. From the U.S., Mwaanga proceeded to visit South Africa to conduct secret negotiations with Vorster. The precise nature of the agreements there reached have never been published, but within a few months, the Zambian Government had begun to bring open pressure to bear on the

Zimbabwean liberation movements to end their increasingly successful guerilla warfare and negotiate with the white minority regime. Zambia's Foreign Minister, Mwaanga, played a leading role in convincing the Organization of African Unity's Council of Ministers, at the 1974 emergency meeting in Tanzania, to endorse Zambia's policy of peaceful negotiations with the Smith regime.[3] The reported *quid pro quo* was that South Africa would withdraw support for Smith and pressure his government to admit African participants.

Rhodesia's Prime Minister, Ian Smith, on the other hand, while agreeing to meet Zimbabwean liberation movement spokesmen, continued to repeat that he would not permit full African participation in the Rhodesian Government. 'The idea of one man, one vote, or immediate parity or handover', he reiterated, 'is a non-starter'[4]

President Kaunda, invited to Washington as a special guest of President Ford shortly after the Organization of African Unity meeting, continued to insist that 'Mr Vorster has shown a good deal of common sense in dealing with Rhodesia'. President Kaunda showed his own awareness of the United States' influence over South Africa, nevertheless, when he surprised the U.S. President's dinner guests by the bald declaration that the United States should 'stop treating South Africa like a colony'.[5] It would help, he asserted, if the Ford Administration would 'come out and clearly state that they are for majority rule – and once stated, act accordingly'.

The Zambian Government's position raised serious questions. Why did the Government compel the leaders of the Zimbabwean liberation movement to pursue policies of peaceful negotiations in the face of evidence that argued increasingly persuasively that these were doomed to failure? Was it realistic, or simply rhetorical, for Kaunda, evidently aware of the relationship of the United States Government with South Africa, to rely on after-dinner appeals to change U.S. policies?

A few months later, Zambia and President Kaunda were in the forefront of the African states supporting the US-South African backed movements in Angola. Again questions were asked: Why did Zambia seem to be swerving into the South African orbit?

These questions can only be answered by the unfolding of history. The purpose of this chapter is more simply to analyze the basically externally-dependent character of the Zambian political economy which ten years after political independence appeared to render it still susceptible to pressures brought to bear by South African and United States interests in line with the strategy suggested in Option Two of the U.S. National Security Council's secret Memorandum No. 39.

The Underlying Problem: Zambia's Inherited Externally Dependent Political Economy

The harsh truth is that Zambia's external economic dependence had not been significantly diminished despite a decade of national political rule.

Zambia is not a small country, geographically. Its land area is as big as that of Great Britain, Germany, Denmark, Switzerland, Holland and Belgium, combined. The colonial division of Central and Southern Africa during the notorious scramble at the end of the 19th century had, however, left its odd, butterfly-shaped land area completely land-locked in the heart of the continent. By the time Zambia attained political independence in 1964, its political economy had become firmly integrated with and dependent upon those of the white ruled nations to the South.

The new Zambian Government made major efforts to break its dependence on rail transport and other infrastructural ties to South Africa. Over time, it sought to extend governmental control of the dominant economic institutions shaped during more than a half century of British colonial rule. Yet careful analysis indicates that, despite these changes, the Zambian political economy remained externally dependent, still subject to pressures from South Africa and its allies overseas. To understand why, it is necessary to examine the inherited institutional structure and the limitations inherent in the particular sets of changes implemented by the new Zambian government.

Zambia has often been cited as a classic example of a dual economy.[6] A half century of outright colonial rule bequeathed to it a modern, technologically sophisticated 'Copper Belt' which employed about fifty thousand workers, one out of six Zambian wage earners, and produced a tenth of the world's copper. The nation's per capita income was the highest in independent sub-Saharan Africa, about $420 in 1970. The staple foodstuffs consumed by the miners and associated urban population were produced by some 30,000 African labourers working on about 700 large modern commercial farms strung out along 20 miles on either side of the railroad by which copper was shipped down through Rhodesia to South Africa. The rest of the food they consumed was imported, as were almost all the locally-consumed manufactured goods, from farms and factories in South Africa, Rhodesia, and Britain.

Away from the 'Copper Belt', the economy had, for the most part, been left to stagnate: almost no schools, hospitals, or even tarmac roads were constructed outside the narrow strip along the rail line. Scattered, sparsely settled peasant holdings cultivated with hoes, axes and cutlasses as of old, produced scarcely enough to provide a bare subsistence for the three-fourths of the population remaining in the more remote rural areas. The primary link between the rural population and the cities was the steady drift of younger men and women looking for work.

Contrary to orthodox Western theories, the explanation for the failure of any kind of multiplier effects to spread more productive activity from the export enclave on the 'Copper Belt' to the rural areas does *not* lie primarily in the conservative attitudes or traditional institutions in the rural areas. The fact that the mines did not serve as an engine of growth and development throughout the economy cannot be explained in terms of the peasant's lack of achievement. Rather in Zambia, as throughout Africa, the explanation lies in the sets of working rules and institutions—public and private—shaped in the colonial era to produce and sell copper needed by the mushrooming factories of Europe; and to buy, first British, and later South African and Rhodesian, manufactured goods.

It is simply not true that the rural inhabitants did not respond to 'opportunities' created by the expansion of the Copper Belt. The fact is that in Zambia, as throughout the Southern African colonies, the 'opportunities' created for Africans were sharply restricted to employment at low wages for long hours for the mine companies and the line-of-rail estates. A host of colonial rules and regulations affected practically all aspects of life.[7] Rationalized by the same myths of racial inferiority as in the rest of southern Africa, the entire institutional framework was shaped to relegate Africans to the inferior status of cheap, unskilled labour. Africans were, at first, forced to work through the imposition of poll and hut taxes, reinforced when necessary by the occasional burning down of the huts of those who refused to pay.

The possibility of earning cash to pay the tax by means other than wage labour was sharply restricted. African peasants had been pushed off the 20-mile strip of fertile land running along both sides of the rail line most accessible to the expanding market on the Copper Belt, to make way for the Government-supported white settler estates. Marketing organizations, either operated directly by the colonial government, or organized as settler-run cooperatives, assured priority to estate sales to the mines for rations for the mine workers. Africans seeking to sell crops for cash were paid discriminatory low prices, or excluded from the market altogether. A complex licencing system assured that aliens obtained the best locations for trade. African traders who managed to get licences found supplies restricted, and bank credit was difficult if not impossible to acquire. Africans seeking an education to obtain more skilled jobs were frustrated by lack of facilities in the rural areas, and, for the most part, excluded from those in urban centres. Africans were even prohibited entry to certain shops on the main street in Lusaka, the 'garden city' capital built by the colonial administrators in the 1930s.

Yet the Africans in Zambia, as in the rest of Africa, persisted in their attempts to benefit from the new opportunities and levels of living made possible by modern technology. Tens of thousands of young men travelled, often walked, hundreds of miles to find cash employment. Some came from as far as Malawi, Tanganyika, and Mozambique. As might be expected, they sought the relatively higher paid employment of the mines and urban centres. Given the low wages on the line-of-rail settler estates, it should be no surprise that the records are full of settler farmer complaints about the lack of adequate labour supplies.* A few Africans accumulated a little money to send their sons away to school or to technical institutions, often in Rhodesia. Some invested their sparse savings in tiny stores or bars in their home villages. But for most, the little cash they could earn in the mines or the commercial farms was barely enough to support their families, pay their taxes, and perhaps buy a bicycle or a little cloth.

The price paid by the rural areas for the steady drain of their most promising young men to work in the export enclave was high. In some villages, as many as 60 per cent of the men aged 20 to 40 years old were gone at any given time. In the north, traditional shifting agricultural techniques **required continual renewal of the land through leaving it to lie fallow while new areas were cleared and planted. This system was disrupted when men's labour, essential for heavy clearing of woods, was lost. In the Zambesi Valley in Western Zambia, extensive canals and irrigated lands, the heart of a flourishing, balanced agricultural system,[9] fell into disuse. Throughout the rural areas away from the line of rail, women, old men, and children had little choice

---

*Even in 1972, agricultural wages were still only a fourth of those in the mines.[8]

**The attitude of colonial authorities to traditional agriculture is illustrated by the fact that only the line-of rail commercial farms were listed as 'farms'. Traditional farmers were reported--if at all--as owning 'gardens.' Likewise, employment statistics list as 'employed', African farmers and their families are still employed in agriculture on their own farms.

but to plant and harvest over and over from the same tired, eroded patches of land. Production declined. Village elders complained that traditional institutions were undermined by returning young men seeking new ways; but isolated individuals, without know-how or funds, could do little to create new rural options. For the youth, the only escape from worsening rural poverty seemed to be permanent migration.

It was in this context that the two giant mining companies, Anglo American and Roan Selection Trust, emerged to dominate the Copper Belt. They were not built by the grit of a few valiant entrepreneurs risking their all to bring the remote treasures of Central Africa onto the world market. The Anglo American complex had, as Chapter 3 above shows, already emerged as a powerful mining finance house in South Africa. Roan Selection Trust eventually became affiliated with American Metal Climax, a large American firm with a growing business established in mines, smelters and refineries in the United States, and a growing African empire spreading from South Africa into Namibia and, more recently, Botswana.

The two companies had simply purchased 50,000 square miles of mining concessions from the British South Africa Company, which in those days still ruled Northern Rhodesia like a company holding. They built smelters and refineries to process their ore to a considerably higher level than that achieved even in the politically independent Latin American copper exporter, Chile. They sold their output directly to European and English fabricators, their fairly advanced level of processing permitting considerable flexibility in marketing. The low level of taxes and wages imposed by the Northern Rhodesian colonial government assured them profitable returns. By the time of independence, they had long since paid for their original investments out of profits, and continued to expand their output through reinvestment and loan capital. Over half the wages and salaries they paid went to European managers and skilled workers, about ten per cent of all mine employees. They continued to send a major share of the investible surpluses produced by the mines home to their shareholders in South Africa, England, and the United States.

As in most colonies, few linkages were built between the mines and the rest of the Zambian economy, aside from the essential and continuing flow of cheap labour.[10] By the 1970s, the mines were still importing about a third of their needed inputs, roughly $150 million worth of materials and equipment, mostly from South Africa and the United States. Most of the local inputs, about 40 per cent of them, were in the form of labour and by-products of metal mining itself.

Other inputs included electricity, water and timber, and some machinery and chemicals. On the other hand, if Zambians sought to purchase any of the wide range of manufactured goods produced from copper, they had to order them from South African or overseas factories.*

During the decades of colonial rule, some of the European traders and estate owners had tried to capture a share of the vast profits of the mining companies. Their persistence may help to explain why the southern-based mining firms appeared to prefer that Northern Rhodesia remain a direct British colony, rather than become more closely linked with the increasingly settler-influenced governments further South.

The establishment of the Federation of Northern Rhodesia with Nyasaland (now Malawi) and Southern Rhodesia (Zimbabwe) stemmed in large part from settler efforts in the three colonies to tax the mines' profits for expansion of the local economy for the benefit of the settler population, particularly in Southern Rhodesia.

The ten years of Federation [11] —1953 to 1963—saw a tax drain of almost $100 million from Northern Rhodesia (Zambia) to finance the infrastructure which provided the foundation of Southern Rhodesian industrial growth. Tens of millions of dollars more were drained from Northern Rhodesia and Nyasaland through the mechanism of higher-than-world prices charged for Southern Rhodesian manufactured goods in the tariff-protected Federation market. Manufacturing was so neglected in Northern Rhodesia that, at independence, even including industries serving the mines, it constituted only about six per cent of the national product.

Southern African and British firms had come to dominate the commercial and financial sectors of the Zambian economy to service the mining and settler farmer communities. Two major trading firms engaged in the import of consumer goods: ZOK (Zambia OK), part of a large South African chain, OK Bazaars; and CBC (Consumer Buying Corporation), an affiliate of the big British importing firm, Booker McConnell. Both had set up wholesale operations and retail trading outlets in the major urban centres, funnelling manufactured goods from their home factories into the Zambian market.

---

*The first wire and cable factory was only established several years after independence. It was built by the U.S. copper firm, Philips, and processed a tiny fraction, less than two per cent, of the mines' output. In fact, Philips also imported copper products which it sold in Zambia and to its neighbours, along with the products processed from Zambia's copper.

Three British commercial banks handled most of the colony's financial business: Barclays, with almost a third of its non-U.K. business in South Africa; Standard Bank, the second largest bank in South Africa; and National Grindlays. As mentioned in Chapter 9 above, these are the three banks with which the biggest U.S. banks have established increasingly close ties. The shipping and insurance operations were mostly provided by British, South African or Southern Rhodesian firms.

It has been estimated that, by the time of independence, the total cost of profits, interest, freight and insurance paid annually to the multinational corporations that dominated Zambia's export enclave was on the order of two thirds of its total foreign exchange earnings.[12] These funds might have been invested to train Zambian labour, build Zambian roads, and equip Zambian industry and agriculture with modern machinery. Instead they were shipped out of the country to the shareholders of the foreign South African, British and American firms that dominated Zambia's economy.

Herein, in the inherited institutional structure, lies the primary explanation of the causes of underdevelopment that characterized the empty rural expanse away from the line-of-rail when independence was achieved. This explanation sets the stage for examining the efforts of Zambia's newly politically independent Government to break from the South. The problem was not simply one of ending economic dependence on transport routes through Rhodesia, South Africa and the Portuguese territories. More critically, it was one of reshaping the entire set of public and private institutions created in the colonial era which linked the distorted growth of a narrow modern enclave in the Zambian economy to the profitable business of exporting copper to the factories of Europe.

An Evaluation of Post-Independence Zambian Policies

The Zambian Government officially adopted, as its basic philosophy, Humanism, which purports to focus on man and his well-being without regard to race or status. It holds that man can best realize his full value and dignity by cooperation and self-reliance. It does not pretend to be a blueprint for economic development.

As one leafs through various documents and speeches which have outlined Zambian governmental economic policy since independence, it becomes apparent that they were not, at the outset, designed to even attempt to deal with the fundamental aspects of the development problem posed above. A primary goal of the new Government was to train Zambians to take over key Government jobs as rapidly as possible. Beyond that the Government policies appeared to be founded initially on the fairly orthodox assumption that Government should redirect investible surpluses to expand social welfare and build the necessary economic infrastructure to attract private investors into productive activities. The primary difference between this approach and that of the former colonial government was the vast increase of Government expenditure on social infrastructure and facilities designed to open up opportunities for Africans to participate in the modern sector.

The First National Development Plan emphasized the training of manpower and the rapid expansion of social and economic infrastructure throughout the country. Its apparent success was financed by an unprecedented boom in world copper prices which pushed the national product upwards at the exceptionally high rate of 12 per cent annually. Coupled with new Government tax policies, this almost tripled government revenues by 1970 to $673 million. [13] Current expenditures for education were increased five times to $83 million, over 12 per cent of the budget in 1971. Funds for health were multiplied seven times to $37 million, over 5 per cent of the budget. Those for rural development rose from almost nothing to $82 million, almost as much as education. Tarmac and upgraded roads and schools and hospitals were built in remote areas long neglected by colonial administrators. Construction boomed. Employment in Government-sponsored community and social services outpaced all other sectors to provide 62,780 jobs by 1971—about twenty-five percent more than the total employment in the mining sector.

The multiplier effects of the investments made in the First National Development Plan failed, however, to stimulated productive activity significantly beyond the rail line. It is true that the output of the manufacturing sector tripled, and its contribution as a per cent of the national product more than doubled in absolute terms. Import substitution growth was also spurred by Zambia's attempt to reduce its dependence on Rhodesian factories after that country's white regime's illegal Unilateral Declaration of Independence (UDI) in 1965. Zambia's new industries were financed to a considerable extent by foreign private capital attracted by expansion of infrastructure, favourable tax policies, and protective tariffs. Seeking to maximize their global profits, rather than to restructure Zambia's economy, however, the multinational manufacturing firms invested primarily in production of luxuries and semi-luxuries for higher income groups associated with the mines and rail line development. They imported capital equipment and machinery, employing technologies utilized in their more developed homelands, but hardly appropriate in Zambia where mounting urban unemployment was already causing serious problems. They imported parts and materials from their South African and overseas affiliates to be processed in their Zambian plants rather than seeking to build Zambian intermediate industries using local materials. The beverages and tobacco industry tripled in size, outpacing the growth of all other industries. By the 1970s, it produced 40 per cent of the manufacturing value added, an exaggerated caricature of the typical pattern in developing economies. [14]

South African interests were deeply involved in this expanding Zambian manufacturing sector. [15] An Anglo-American affiliate was the largest firm engaged in the production and sale of beer in the flourishing beverages and tobacco sector. Other Anglo affiliates were engaged in the production of supplies and equipment for the mines, using parts and materials imported from South Africa. The list of leading Zambian manufacturers in several sectors reads like a Who's Who from South Africa. Some U.S.-based multinationals, already

TABLE 16.1

VALUE-ADDED IN MANUFACTURING IN ZAMBIA, 1965 AND 1972

	1965		1972	
Manufacturing industries	Million Kwacha	Per cent of total	Million Kwacha	Per cent of total
Food	6.6	13.7	23.6	14.3
Beverages and tobacco	13.0	27.0	67.9	40.7
Textiles and wearing apparel	3.9	8.1	12.6	7.6
Wood & wood products, including furniture	2.4	5.0	3.3	2.0
Paper, paper products, publishing and printing	2.1	4.4	6.5	3.9
Rubber products	0.8	1.6	5.4	3.2
Chemicals, chemical petroleum and plastic products	2.8	5.8	7.6	4.6
Non-metallic mineral products	6.1	12.7	10.6	6.4
Basic metal products	5.8	12.0	2.3	1.3
Fabricated metal products, machinery and equipment	4.4	9.1	24.4	14.8
Other manufacturing	0.1	0.2	0.3	0.2
Total	48.0	100.0	164.5	100.0

SOURCE: Calculated from Monthly Digest of Statistics (Lusaka), LX, 7, July 1973, Table 54. There was some change in the system of national accounts in 1970 so the 1965 figures are not entirely comparable. The exchange rate in 1972 was $1.56=K1.00.

established in South Africa, established last-stage assembly plants in Zambia, too. They did not produce much, however; rather they last-stage assembled and/or processed materials and parts imported from their plants in South Africa or in the United States.

In agriculture the Government at first granted millions of Kwacha to subsistence farmers to join in 'cooperatives' to clear land for new production in remote provinces. It loaned thousands more through the newly-created Credit Organization of Zambia. It set up a new marketing board designed to open market outlets for peasant produce. But lack of skills and necessary farm inputs hampered the peasants from early increases in output and sale of cash crops. The new marketing organization never adequately reached remote rural areas away from the line of rail. The 'cooperatives' remained little more than discouraged groups whose members eventually lost interest and returned to traditional farming methods or left the rural areas to seek employment on the line of rail.

Over time, top government civil servants and politicians began to obtain bank credit and buy up some of the larger rail line estates abandoned by white settlers. By the 1970s, unpublished data indicated that one out of five line of rail estates was in fact owned by well-to-do Zambians. Evidence began to surface suggesting that highly placed government figures were not averse to influencing agricultural policy to favour the estate sector in which they now owned a substantial share.

By the end of the 1960s, the marketing organization which had serviced the rail line commercial farms since colonial days, was combined with the new agency set up after independence to extend marketing services to African peasants to form NAMBOARD. [16] Marketing board purchases of maize, milk, beef and tobacco had declined in the immediate post-independence years, partly due to fears of the settler farmers as to their future under the Zambian government. Now the purchase of maize in the 1970s, at high prices subsidized by NAMBOARD, recovered to reach record heights, but the data shows that half to three fourths of it was purchased from the line of rail estates.

Government authorities seemed to become increasingly imbued with the myth that only large-scale, capital-intensive farms could adequately expand food output to ensure national self-sufficiency. Anglo American, with an eye to improving its public relations image in the independent African states, acquired thousands of acres and established a vast mechanized farm to produce maize and tobacco. The manager of Anglo's Zambian interests, a 'liberal' South African public relations man, was invited to participate in a Zambian governmental advisory committee on rural development, presumably in hopes that Anglo could recommend ways of attracting more foreign investment in agriculture. A man who was shortly afterwards appointed the new Minister of Planning and Finance published a widely read article heralding the new trend. [17] Republished in the local paper under the title, 'Let Them Come', it proclaimed the necessity of attracting foreign firms to the agricultural sector, promising them tax concessions and assistance to ensure profitable business, in order to expand agricultural output.

Despite the Government's declared redistributive policies and a rapid expansion of social welfare expenditures, income distribution in Zambia remained sharply skewed. Government officials and the press expressed widespread concern about rising wages and the growing urban-rural income gap. This tended to obscure the fact that by far the greatest share of the rapidly growing national wealth was going to swell the profits of the still predominantly foreign-owned firms and the high salaries of a relatively small portion of the urban population, now for the first time including members of a rapidly expanding African elite.

Wages rose, it is true, particularly those of the mine workers whose average wage was almost double that of other workers. But the fact is that, although earnings in all industries rose about 30 per cent from 1957 to 1970, rising prices in the urban centres cancelled out most if not all of the workers' gains in terms of real purchasing power. Wages and salaries declined as a proportion of the national product at market prices from 40 per cent in 1964 to 32 per cent in 1969, despite the increase in the numbers of wage workers employed. In other words, the wage earners' share of the total national pie declined as copper prices rose on the world market. A major share of this total wage and salary bill, furthermore, probably half, continued to go to the top ten percent of the wage and salary earners. These now included some Zambians, although most experts continued to be expatriate.

The Government's programme of Zambianization facilitated the entry of a limited number of Africans into the ranks of a rapidly forming high-income elite. Some obtained high government political and civil service posts with high salaries and fringe benefits. These salaries were originally claimed to be necessary to attract Europeans to the colonial service, but they hardly seem appropriate in a developing economy devoted to Humanism. Other Zambians were individually promoted to management posts in private and parastatal businesses. A few entered trade and speculative real estate where the more successful could reap profits as high as 70 per cent of investments.* A number, assisted by Government loans, purchased line-of-rail estates vacated by settlers upon independence.**

The orthodox policies adopted by the Zambia Government, in short, did little to change the basically distorted structure of the economy. The expanding manufacturing sector became increasingly concentrated along the rail line. The governmental agricultural institutions focused more and more on servicing the estate sector. A few fortunate Zambians joined the 'haves' among the managers and administrators in the public and private sectors.

The 'have nots' remaining in the rural areas, on the other hand, confronted stagnation perpetuated by the continued lop-sided externally dependent growth. Construction of new schools in remote provinces informed tens of thousands of new primary school entrants of the new levels of living made possible in urban centres by twentieth century technology. Nothing was done to increase productive employment opportunities for them in their home areas when they graduated. New tarmac roads brought lorries and buses to far-off provincial capitals for the first time, but their primary contribution was to bring skimpy lots line-of-rail manufactured goods for those few who had cash to buy them, and to transport back young men and women more eager than ever to break away from rural stagnation.

The rural-urban drift mounted into a tidal-flood: by the end of the 1960s, some 40 per cent of the nation's inhabitants were reported to be living in the cities, over half of them in 'squatter compounds' where they lacked city water supplies, sewerage, garbage disposal and electricity. About 20 per cent of the urban labour force was estimated to be unemployed and the figure was expected to double by the end of the Second National Development Plan. [19]

The Economic Reforms

As the First National Development Plan came to an end, President Kaunda announced a series of major economic reforms. These had two major thrusts: one was to Zambianize most internal trading establishments, thus enabling those few Zambian entrepreneurs with

*It has been reported that the larger of the African-owned taxi companies welcomed enforcement of licensing regulations as a means of reducing competition by smaller African taxi drivers (would-be entre preneurs) seeking to enter the business world at one of the few points where the required capital and skills are minimal. [18]

**These may well have been among the major beneficiaries of NAMBOARD's price subsidies designed to increase maize output.

cash and know-how to replace non-Zambians as private owners of retail trading establishments.

The second purported to give the Government a degree of partial control over what have become known in Africa as 'the commanding heights': basic industries, export-import and internal wholesale trade, and the banks. The implementation of these reforms had little impact in initiating the kind of fundamental reorganization of critical institutions suggested as essential by the explanation of the inherited patterns of underdevelopment existing in Zambia at the time of independence.

The Government did carry out negotiations to purchase 51 per cent of the shares of ownership, first of the major manufacturing and importing sectors of the economy and shortly afterwards, the mines. This, of course, is not to be confused with nationalization in the sense of a governmental takeover of 100 per cent ownership without compensation. Under the agreements reached,[20] the Government acquired controlling shares in exchange for fairly generous payment of compensation to the owners.*

In fact, however, Government's control over its new holdings remained indirect and distinctly limited. The holdings were placed under the overall supervision of a parastatal corporation, ZIMCO, in five subsidiary groups.[22] The first, INDECO, was responsible for eight sub-groups of 52 associated and subsidiary companies with assets totalling $260 million, the largest parastatal holding company of predominantly manufacturing industries in the former British African colonies. The second, MINDECO, was given responsibility

---

*The issue of compensation has been much debated. In the case of the mines, whose original investment had long since been recovered in the form of profits, the Government agreed to pay for book value which had been augmented by loans and reinvestment of part of the profits over the years. This meant that the Government guaranteed to pay about $40 million annually including interest to the parent companies of Anglo-American and RST until 1978; and to continue paying half that ($21 million) until 1982.

In the Zambian case lack of skilled Zambian manpower and the need to maintain overseas markets with the companies had contact, undoubtedly influenced the Government's decision to pay compesation.

In Chile, in contrast, after Allende's Government was elected, the Comptroller General had decided that, after deducting from the book value of the mines the *excess profits shipped* out of Chile from 1955 to 1970, the two U.S. companies, Kennecott and Anaconda, actually owed Chile $310 million and $68 million, respectively: hence the Chilean Government refused to pay any compensation at all. After the coup which outsted the Allende Government, the new millitary government, while retaining the very popular national ownership of the big mines, did agree to pay compensation to the companies. This, apparently, satisfied both the companies and the international lending agencies, who then proceeded to lend funds to the millitary dictatorship which they had previously denied to the elected Allende Government.

for the mines which reported net assets in 1972 of $922 million. The third, FINDECO, was given responsibility for the state insurance company, provident fund, and the Government's holdings in two small commercial banks. The remaining two held the National Transport Corporation and the National Hotels Corporation.

The foreign-owned commercial banks were originally to be included in the Government's proposals to acquire shares of ownership, but this measure was never implemented. Instead, they were merely required to incorporate locally, and to keep their reserves for their Zambian business in the country. To date they remain wholly foreign-owned with the exception of two very small banks: the Zambian Commercial Bank, in which the Government owns 60 per cent of the shares, and a wholly state-owned bank, the National Commercial Bank of Zambia, created by the Government along the lines of similar banks established in almost every former British colony, to extend at least some small amounts of credit to those areas formerly entirely neglected by the foreign banks. Their relative unimportance is suggested by the fact that the National Commercial Bank had, by 1974, opened only five branches in the main line-of-rail towns. In contrast, Barclays, Standard and National Grindlays, owned 51 branches mostly located in towns along the line-of-rail.

The parastatal corporations in Zambia are typical of those established to manage governmental holdings in all the former British territories. They are much like those established in South Africa. Essentially, they are perceived as the appropriate means of removing such holdings from the purview of the civil service, permitting their managers to exercise the autonomy required to enable them to function in a market economy much like any private enterprise.

In Zambia, the Government has continued, for the most part, to treat the much-expanded parastatal sector like private firms. The parastatal companies are expected to make their decisions with the primary goal of maximizing profits. Little attempt has been made to introduce other criteria for decision-making. Given the shortage of high-level Zambian personnel, the day-to-day management of the subsidiary companies is in almost every case still provided by the foreign partners. Not a few of the managers are South Africans. The Government did introduce a more vigorous policy of training with a view to accelerating Zambianization of higher level posts, but outside of this its actual control of the parastatals remains more of a future potential than a present reality.*

Examination of INDECO's holdings in 1972 illustrates the extent to which they were shaped, not by a conscious development strategy geared to restructuring the economy, but by short-term decisions in the context of profit-maximizing considerations reflecting the inherited distorted market in the country. INDECO Breweries had the largest number of employees, the largest turnover, and highest profit of any of INDECO's eight subsidiary groups. INDECO's new investment proposals, according to the Chairman, continued to be influenced primarily by import substitution possibilities, rather than consideration of the kinds of new industries which might more effectively contribute to restructuring both demand and supply in the context of a more integrated, nationally balanced economy.

The primary thrust of Government development policy in formulating the Second National Development Plan appeared to be a major expansion of copper production. It has been argued, in fact, that one of the main reasons for Government acquisition of a majority of shares in the mines was the leverage the Government might then exercise to require the companies to invest in expanded copper output.[23]

The Second National Development Plan announced that total copper output was expected to grow by 6.8 per cent a year, or about forty per cent by 1976. To attain this goal it would be necessary to invest almost $90 million annually; that is, in each year of the Plan, the amount invested would be equivalent to almost a third of the total existing assets of INDECO, significantly more than the annual Government expenditure on rural development. The Government apparently assumed it would continue to reap a high income from copper sales which it could then spend to expand other Government services, as it had during the period of high copper prices in the 1960s.

This policy was founded on two fallacies. First, it was based on an inadequate assessment of the heavy direct and indirect costs to Zambia of investing in copper expansion. These increased costs are likely to be rendered still more burdensome due to the fact that world copper markets may, over the long term, be unable to absorb expanded Zambian exports at a sufficiently high price to make the enterprise profitable to the Government.

---

*The Government has so far not even been able to exercise its control to influence parastatal salaries policies at the highest income level to bring them more in line with each other and other government posts. Yet the relatively high salaries paid in this sector tend to aggravate the difficulties of allocating Zambian high level manpower in accordance with some rational manpower planning scheme.

Secondly, and perhaps more critical, the policy seemed to ignore the fundamental structural causes of the problems of underdevelopment which continued to plague the nation.

The first fallacy relates to the inadequate assessment of the heavy direct and indirect costs to Zambia of expanding copper output. The concessions made by the Zambian Government to the mining companies to stimulate expanded copper output were very costly. Government revenues from the mines dropped from about $365 million in 1969 to an annual average of about $65 million in 1971-2. Four basic factors seem to have contributed to this precipitous fall. Their relative impact has been calculated in Table 16.2 showing the impact of each on the decline in government revenue.

TABLE 16.2

THE RELATIVE IMPACT OF THE FOUR MAIN FACTORS CONTRIBUTING TO THE FALL IN ZAMBIAN GOVERNMENT REVENUE, 1969 TO 1971−2 (AVERAGE) AS A PERCENTAGE OF THE TOTAL FALL

Contributing Factor	Percentage of fall in Government Revenue Caused
Fall in copper price	49%
Rise in Costs of Productions and sales	24%
Decline in effective tax rate from 73% to 28% of profits	21%
Decline in production	6%
Total fall in Revenue	100%

SOURCE: Ministry of Mines, Lusaka.

The agreements replaced the pre-existing royalty and export taxes (in essence the taxes on the production of copper) by a single mineral tax based on a percentage of gross taxable profit. Therefore, when the world copper price fell, as world supply outpaced world demand in the early 1970s, profits and hence tax revenue were sharply reduced. This factor accounted for over half the loss in revenue. By linking taxes to profits, in other words, the Government agreed to permit revenues to fluctuate with world copper prices. Had taxes remained as before, revenues would have fluctuated only with output and sales.

Secondly, the agreements provided for a reduction in the declared tax rate from 73 per cent of profits to an effective rate of 28 per cent by permitting the companies to write off 100 per cent of all investments for tax purposes in the year they were made. It has been estimated that this provision alone cost the Government about $70 million in tax revenues in 1971 and 1972.

Third, the cost of production reportedly rose about 20 per cent following implementation of the agreements, although the foreign firms continued to manage the mines. By further reducing profits, this reduced annual Government revenue by about $72 million more. The reasons for this sharp cost increase are not entirely clear. Wages and salaries, only about 20 per cent of direct total cost, appear to have been stabilized in 1969. It has been suggested, in fact, that one purpose of Government acquisition of shares was to ally Government with the companies in holding the line on wage costs. [24] The Mufulira disaster undoubtedly increased costs of the Amax-managed mine, although it should not have affected mines managed by Anglo; yet the costs of the latter rose by almost as much as the former. The import surcharge of 10 per cent on mining equipment could only have had a marginal effect. It is possible, however, that declining ore grades required more expensive capital equipment. Management fees, averaging about $6—7 million per year* paid directly to the companies under the agreements, were added as an operating cost, and to the extent that these exceeded pre-existing management salaries, would have contributed to rising costs. Import costs may have risen due to increased transport costs, but these were relatively stable in 1971-2. There is always the possibility that the companies over-invoiced imports from their own suppliers to reduce the reported share of profits accruing to the Government. [26]

The fourth factor reducing tax revenue was the fall of production, primarily caused by the cave-in at the Amax-managed Mufulira mines. The direct revenue loss attributable to the resulting decline in output has been estimated at only $18 million.

Additional costs to Zambia not included in the above estimate were incurred by the Government's efforts to use the agreements to expand copper production. Under the agreements, the companies were permitted to repatriate their profits, as well as the compensation payments made to them by the Government, without exchange control. They actually made a significant share of the investments by

---

*The management and consultancy fees of RST/Amax, at 3/4 per cent of the sales proceeds and 2 per cent of the consolidated profits before the income tax and after the mineral tax, totalled about $14 million for 1970 to 1973, an average of $3.5 million annually. [25]

borrowing abroad,* instead of reinvesting their share of profits. They were able to repatriate a major share of their profits after deducting less than 30 per cent for taxes. Hence total 'investment income' outflow, together with compensation payments, remained an added heavy burden on the current balance of payments. In the long run, the borrowed investment funds, too, must be repaid, along with a 7 to 9 per cent of interest, an additional cost factor as well as a burden on the future balance of payments.

To complicate matters and add to Zambia's balance of payments problems in 1973, the white minority Rhodesian regime denounced Zambia's Government for allegedly supporting the increasingly successful guerila forces of the liberation movement there. It declared the Zambian border closed, demanding that Zambia halt all support for the guerila forces. Rhodesians obviously hoped that the extra cost of shipping goods through alternate makeshift routes would be prohibitive, forcing Zambia to agree to end support for the guerillas.

The Rhodesians miscalculated. Significantly, it was the South Africa Government which pressured Rhodesia to re-open the border because Zambia had provided a major market for South Africa's manufacturing sector. Zambia consumed about 20 per cent of South Africa's textile exports and constituted a major customer for heavy mining machinery and equipment produced by South Africa's basic industrial sector.

President Kaunda immediately declared, however, that Zambia would under no circumstances resume shipment through Rhodesia, as long as it was illegally ruled by a white minority. He appealed for world funds to facilitate the shift of trade through neighbouring Zaire, Angola, Tanzania, Malawi and Mozambique. It was estimated that the cost of the shift would be over $150 million. [28]

The costs of imported goods began to soar, at least in part because of increased shipping costs. Delays at the ports in Tanzania and Angola due to overcrowding and, in 1975, the outbreak of civil

---

*As of 1972, RST reported it had borrowed $35 million from UK banks, led by Morgan Grenfell & Co.; $20 million from United States Export Import Bank, together with Barclays Bank to buy capital equipment in the United States; and arranged for bank and other loans amounting to $42 million—all at rates of 7-9 per cent. The NCCM reported it had borrowed $28 million through a consortium headed by Standard and Charter Banking Group for 3 years, plus contractor finance at $30 million from the U.S. Export Import Bank together with private U.S. banks and Barclays; $23 million under two agreements with U.K. Credits Guarantee Department, negotiated through Lazard Brothers and Standard; $37 million from a German Bank for German equipment; and $15 million from Mitsui and Mitsubishi for Japanese equipment. In all, these loans totalled some $213 million primarily to finance the new investment in capital equipment and machinery. [27]

war in Angola, contributed to shortages of imported consumer goods. The mine companies began to air-lift heavy machinery and equipment from South Africa. Internal inflation further aggravated Zambia's financial strain.

In late 1973, as the world copper price rose, the Zambian Government sought to obtain greater control over the mining sector and increase its revenues by paying off, in full, the bonds it had pledged as compensation to the companies for acquisition of 51 per cent of the shares.[29] The remaining total it owed for these was $262 million. Once this was paid off, the Government assumed the agreements would be abrogated, ending restrictions on the Government's right to alter the tax structure and control repatriation of company profits, as well as granting the Government the power to manage the mines and market their output.

The redemption of the bonds led almost immediately to increased government revenues as a result of the imposition of a new tax regime. The Government's 1974 mine revenues rose to almost $500 million. The Government had, however, utilized a major share of the windfall profits and foreign exchange reserves that had accumulated, when the copper price temporarily sky-rocketed in 1973-4, to pay off the bonds. It borrowed the remainder, about $150 million, on the Eurodollar market for a high floating rate of interest, then about 15 per cent. Over the grace period before repayment ended, the cost of interest, alone, would create an added balance of payments and tax burden of about $22 million a year.

The Government had apparently been in error when it assumed that, after paying off the compensation in full, it would be able to take over management and marketing of copper from the companies. A crucial section of the hitherto secret* agreements, apparently withheld the right of management and marketing from the Government even after the full compensation had been paid. Further negotiations led to about $90 million in additional payments to the two companies over a three year period to enable the Government to acquire the full control of the management-marketing functions. In effect, this increased the initial compensation costs to the Government by about a third. The Government then found it necessary for the most part, because few

---

*Ironically, the agreements, assumed to be confidential and hence not available to top Zambian civil servants, had been made available years earlier through the Securities and Exchange Commission to shareholders of American Metal Climax in the United States.

Zambians had been trained at that level, to hire the same company personnel who had handled these functions before.

The cost to Zambia of these efforts to expand copper output may be only partially measured in terms of current revenues lost and the impact of the outflow of profits, interest, fees and compensation on the current and future balance of payments. Zambia's payments balance and entire economy is also affected by the world price prevailing for its copper, a price which is fundamentally determined by the supply of copper in relation to the demand for it on the world market. These are factors over which Zambia, by itself, can exercise no control. Throughout the 1960s, Zambia had a balance of payments surplus because of the high world copper price. As world copper production outpaced world demand and copper prices dropped in the early 1970s, Zambia began to experience serious balance of payments deficits as both visible and invisible imports continued to increase.* The Government had to resort, for the first time, to drawing on the International Monetary Fund.

Worse yet, Zambia's expanded copper exports, together with those of other copper producers all eager to earn more foreign exchange, created the danger of a chronically depressed copper price. The Second National Development Plan projected a world price of $1,150 a ton, well below the March, 1970, peak of $1,950. But within a few months, world prices had plummeted to a low of $1,085/ton. The average price for 1972 remained depressed. In 1973, copper prices tended to rise rapidly, apparently reflecting uncertainties as to the impact of the closure of the Rhodesian border on Zambia's exports, and the effect of a Belgian copper refinery strike. By mid-year, a prolonged miners' strike in Chile had halted all that country's exports for a time, and world copper prices sky-rocketed to an all-time high. This price increase, aggravated by speculation on the London Metal Exchange, proved to be only temporary. In 1974, the international monetary crisis and economic depression in the Western industrialized nations sharply reduced the world demand for copper. World Bank estimates indicated that copper demand could be expected to remain

---

*The nation still had a balance of trade surplus of $115 million at the end of 1971, but its payments for services (including the outflow of investment income, almost $90 million, contract, salary and gratuities transfer, almost $90 million more, and 'other' unrequited transfers for unspecified reasons, $70 million) totalled $420 million—more than half of the country's total export earnings. About a third of these 'invisible' items were transport costs ($134 million) reflecting the increased volume of imports and exports. The combined effect of these factors was to leave Zambia with a current balance of payments deficit at the end of 1971 of $305 million — about 40 per cent of its total export earnings.

at less than the supply expected as a result of the efforts of all exporters to expand output at least until 1980.[30]

Zambia, together with other members of CIPEC, sought to take joint action to stabilize world copper prices. The potential effectiveness of this mechanism was diminished by the fact that CIPEC represented only Zambia, Zaire, Chile and Peru, which produce only about 60 per cent of all exported crude copper, and less than a third of world crude copper production. A major share of the copper consumed in Europe and the United States, about 40 per cent, furthermore, is provided by re-cycling copper scrap. Big companies, like Anglo American and Amax, have been exploring for and investing in new copper mines in Australia, Canada, and South and East Asia, as well as in the African countries, like Botswana, Zaire and Mauritania. Some have begun to hedge their bets by buying shares in companies producing aluminium, a close substitute for copper.

In 1974, CIPEC members agreed to cut output by ten per cent in an effort to halt the continuing depression of copper prices. Zambia's Minister of Planning and Finance observed that he had little optimism as to the short-run effect of this policy.[31] In late 1975, the CIPEC countries nevertheless announced plans to reduce output by 15 per cent.

In other words, Zambia, having already paid a heavy price for its efforts to create the necessary conditions to expand copper output, confronted the likelihood that the collapse of world copper prices would altogether wipe out anticipated compensating gains. To hold world copper prices up by stockpiling copper is expensive and obviously does not restore the losses incurred to augment copper production. It also aggravates unemployment in the exporting countries. There is another way to look at the Government's strategy of increasing investment in copper, namely, from the point of view of opportunities foregone to develop other sectors of the economy. The explanation of underdevelopment in Zambia advanced in the first section of this chapter suggests that the Government needed to make fundamental institutional changes to permit the formulation and implementation of a long-term industrial and agricultural strategy, say over twenty years, to increase productive employment opportunities in all sectors of the economy. [32] Such an approach could contribute directly to raising the levels of living of the broad masses of the population in the rural areas away from the line of rail as well as in the urban centres. It would reduce the nation's dependence on expanded copper production, and increase the economy's self-reliant production of a growing share of productive inputs and consumer necessities for the needs of the population in the country itself.

This is not, by any means, to argue that the copper mines should be neglected. On the contrary, the necessary institutional changes should be made to ensure that the foreign exchange and tax revenues which the mines ~produce make an important contribution to the implementation of an appropriate alternative development strategy. That contribution could be maximized within the framework of a realistic analysis of the world market, and in close cooperation with other copper exporting nations to adjust output to consumption and stabilize world copper prices. Further backwards and forwards linkages between mines, the industries producing inputs and fabricating the mines' outputs, and the rest of the economy could be forged within the framework of the overall strategy. Copper output should be sold overseas in an increasingly processed form in so far as markets could be assured to maximize returns from given output. Attention should be given to the potential uses of the resulting processed copper products in Zambia's own industrial development. In other words, this alternative approach would emphasize the necessity of planning the mines' contribution to ensure the carefully planned overall development of industry and agriculture designed to create an increasingly self-reliant, integrated, balanced national economy.

Instead, the Zambian Government emphasized expansion of mine output in hope of reaping increased government revenues and foreign exchange earnings in the future. It failed to develop policies directed to overcoming the inherited structural and institutional causes of underdevelopment. As a result, it increased the nation's dependence on copper exports at the very time when world copper prices had begun to fall.

The Crunch

By 1974, Zambia's externally dependent economy was caught in a squeeze which rendered it difficult to resist pressures to accept South Africa's version of detente for Southern Africa. Rising import costs, a heavy and costly international debt, and falling copper prices created a serious domestic financial crisis. The nation was compelled to rely on further external borrowing simply to finance current imports.[33] At the same time, the fall in copper prices slashed tax revenues. The 1975 mine revenues were expected to plummet to only $202 million, less than half of the sum received in 1974. Despite the introduction of new taxes on other sectors of the economy, including a sales tax on locally manufactured goods, the anticipated 1975 government deficit was $177 million, almost 15 per cent of planned expenditures.[34]

The Government planned to finance the deficit by further internal and external borrowing. Expansion of internal borrowing, especially short-term, could be expected to aggravate internal inflation. Continued external borrowing would inevitably saddle the nation with heavier future payments abroad, particularly if the Government resorted to Euro-dollar loans.

The Minister of Planning and Finance, A.B. Chikwanda, estimated that, in 1975, Zambia's balance of payments deficit would total $150 million, or about 11 per cent of the total value of exports in 1974. He concluded his budget speech as optimistically as possible by declaring:[35]

> the economic future of Zambia is tied to the fortunes of our mining industry. While the world is going through a recession I cannot see a happy future for copper prices—certainly not in 1975. As I have said, I cannot predict the severity of the recession nor can I forecast its duration. All I can say at this stage is that while the recession lasts the problems of foreign exchange and revenue will be with us. We must, therefore, tighten our belts even more.

To put it bluntly, Zambia's continued dependence on the sale of copper in the world market condemned its Government and people to a bleak future of increased internal and external debts, inflation and growing unemployment.

The economic consequences of Zambia's post independence policies are visible in the statistics and government reports. Another less evident but politically probably more significant result of the development strategy adopted by the Zambian Government has been that it has enable a small group of Zambians to move into key positions in the expanding governmental bureaucracy. The perpetuation and expansion of the inherited civil service and the mushrooming parastatal base has created for them a powerful institutional and financial base. They wield enormous power and influence by virtue of their newly-acquired status in the bureacracy. At the same time, they are linked through the complex parastatal holding company structure with the South African-multinational corporate mining, manufacturing and financial firms which still dominate the nation's economic life. Their salaries are high, fifty times those of minimum wage-earners. They have begun to invest heavily in real estate and trade. Often utilizing credit provided by the big foreign banks, they have purchased about one out of five of the line-of-rail estates. When they choose to retire from government, they are assured of lucrative posts in the private sector, utilizing the contacts they have made while in government to ensure the success of projects with which they became associated.

Significant elements in this powerful emergent group had, by the 1970s, begun to exert pressures at critical points in the nation's political-economic structure. This appears to have become a powerful factor operating behind the scenes to change the nation's stance vis á vis the liberation movements in Southern Africa to a more positive response to South Africa's outward reach.

This, then, was the political-economic climate within which Zambia's Government opened negotiations with South Africa and its powerful behind-the-scenes western allies after the fall of the Portuguese colonial empire. The stage was set for the implementation of the kinds of pressures envisaged in the U.S. National Security Council's Memorandum. Zambia, in 1975, was in a position which made it difficult to respond unfavourably.

*Sir Michael Blundell, in his revealing book, *So Rough a Wind*, anticipated the likelihood that the emergence of this kind of group would help to ward off structural change in Kenya. His book was essentially a plea to Kenyan settlers to accept Kenyan independence and majority rule because they could not expect English taxpayers to continue to finance the anti-guerilla warfare which had already cost tens of millions of pounds sterling. He expressed the hope that emergence of a group of well-to-do African farmers and businessmen as well as politicians and highly placed civil servants would given the impracticality of maintaining white domination — assure continuation of the *status quo* 'by other means'[36]

REFERENCES

CHAPTER SIXTEEN

1. G. Hovey, *New York Times*, 25 March 1975.
2. Hovey, *New York Times*, 16 April 1975.
3. *New York Times*, 16 April 1975.
4. *New York Times*, 31 May 1975.
5. *New York Times*, 20 April 1975.
6. W.J. Barber, *The Economy of British Central Africa, A Case Study of Economic Development in a Dualistic Society* (California: Stanford University Press, 1961), p. 6.
7. The way these were imposed and their consequences for the population of the then Northern Rhodesia are described in L.H. Gann, *A History of Northern Rhodesia, early Days to 1953* (London: Chatto and Windus, 1964).
8. E.g., see Central Bureau of Statistics, *Monthly Digest of Statistics*, (Lusaka), December 1973, p. 5.
9. L. Van Horn, 'The Agricultural History of Barotseland, 1840—1974', in N. Parsons and R. Palmer, eds., *The Roots of Rural Poverty* (Heinemann: forthcoming).
10. J. Fry and C. Harvey, 'Copper Production in Zambia', (Lusaka: University of Zambia, mimeo. 1972).
11. Cf. W.J. Barber, C. Leys and C. Pratt, 'Federation and the Distribution of Economic Benefits', *A New Deal in Central Africa (London: Heinemann, 1960)*.
12. Barber, *The Economy of Central Africa*, op. cit.
13. All statistical data relating to Zambia's post independence revenues and expenditures, employment, prices, gross domestic product, and balance of trade and payments, unless otherwise specified, are from the Central Bureau of Statistics, *Monthly Digest of Statistics* (Lusaka).
14. E.g., for comparison, see A. Seidman, *Comparative Development Strategies in East Africa*, (East African Publishing House, 1972), pp. 38, 101, 114, 122-3.
15. Data available at Company Registry in Lusaka, compiled in an unpublished study by students under directorship of R. Bottomly, University of Zambia.
16. See T. Ocran, *Marketing Boards in Zambia* (Wisconsin Ph. D. thesis, University of Wisconsin, 1969).
17. A.B. Chikwanda; *Times of Zambia*, Lusaka.
18. A. Beveridge, *Converts to Capitalism: The Emergence of AfricanEntrepreneurs in Lusaka, Zambia* (New Haven: Ph. D., Yale University, 1973).
19. Unpublished data prepared by Manpower Planning Office, Ministry of Planning and Finance, Lusaka, 1974.
20. For an analysis of the Agreements, see C. Harvey and Bostock, *Copper and Zambian Economic Independence,* (New York: Praeger, 1972).
21. CALA Newsletter (Madison, Wisconsin, 1973), Vol. 2, No. 2.
22. For structure and assets of the parastatals, see their annual reports published in Lusaka. For an analysis of the parastatals operating in the parastatals, see A. Seidman, 'The Distorted Growth of Import-Substitution Industry: The Zambian Case', *Journal of Modern African Studies*, Vol. 12, No. 4 (1974), pp. 601-631.
23. Harvey and Bostock, *Copper and Zambian Economic Independence*, op. cit.
24. Conversation of author with the then Chairman De Beers of Anglo-American in Zambia, 1973.
25. C.M. Ushewokunze, 'The Legal Framework for Copper Production in Zambia', in A. Seidman, ed., *Natural Resources and National Welfare: The Case of Copper* (New York: Praeger, 1975).
26. Evidence as to the impact of over-invoicing of imports of developing countries is summarized in L. Turner, *Multinational Companies and the Third World*, (London: Allen Lane, 1973), esp. pp. 53ff.
27. See annual reports of NCCM and RCM, Lusaka, 1973.
28. United Nations team which studied cost of shifting transport links.
29. For analysis of the impact of this change and its cost to the Zambian Government, see Ushewokunze, 'The Legal Framework for Copper Production in Zambia', op. cit.
30. K. Takeuchi, 'Copper: Market Prospects for 1974-1985', in A. Seidman, *Natural Resources and National Welfare: The Case of Copper*, op. cit.

242

31. A.B. Chikwanda, *Budget Speech, 1975*. (Lusaka: Government Printing Office, 1975), p. 3.
32. Cf. A. Seidman, 'The Distorted Growth of Import Substitution Industry: The Zambian Case', *op. cit.* and also see A. Seidman, *Planning for Development in Sub-Saharan Africa)*Dar es Salaam: Tanzania Publishing House, 1974), esp. Parts II and III.
33. Chikwanda, *Budget Speech, 1975,* op. cit., p.4.
34. Ibid., p. 11.
35. Ibid. p. 5.
36. *So Rough a Wind, The Kenya Memoirs of Sir Michael Blundell* (London: Widenfeld and Nelson, 1964), p. 178.

Chapter XVII

Post Script: Towards the Transformation of Southern Africa

The foregoing evidence may appear, on the surface, to portray the overwhelming might of a white minority regime, wielding a powerful military machine and increasingly backed by giant U.S.-based multinational corporations.

The aim of this portrayal is not at all to imply that all is hopeless, that the superpower of the multinationals assures permanent hegemony of white rule in Southern Africa. On the contrary, the purpose of formulating a model to explain the internal contradictions of the South African regime and the implications of its outreach to its neighbours is to facilitate formulation of effective strategies to defeat it.

At the level of the neighbouring independent nations, the strategy suggested by the model and the evidence, presented in the foregoing parts of this book, is not new. [1] The analysis of the inner dynamic of South African state capitalism, today increasingly allied with U.S.-based multinational corporations, does, however, lend added force to the argument. It is essential for newly independent peoples of southern Africa to formulate development strategies designed to reduce their nations' external dependence on multinational corporate interests, and to build internally integrated, balanced economies capable of providing expanded productive employment opportunities for the masses of their populations. To achieve this, they need to create political institutions designed to ensure that their governments represent the interests of the working people and the peasantry, rather than a narrow elite linked through complex bureaucratic structures and parastatals to multinational corporate concerns.

While achieving this political prerequisite, the government needs to formulate and implement a long-term development strategy to restructure the national political economy. This requires that it gain control of what Tanzania's President Nyerere has termed the 'commanding heights': basic institutions, especially the banks. Only if the government has established firm control in these crucial areas will it be able to capture and direct all available investible surpluses to the development of integrated, balanced national economies designed to meet the needs of the entire population.

Tanzania has, for some years now, been attempting to shape the necessary new institutions to transform the political economy along these lines. FRELIMO, the liberation movement which assumed the reins of Government in Mozambique upon attainment of independence, announced its intention of pursuing the same course. This is not to suggest that the transformation is easy, but that two southern African nations are already seeking to achieve it. MPLA in Angola also appears to be moving in this direction.

The potential of this approach would be greater if the independent nations of the region could cooperate in formulating and implementing a regional strategy,[2] linking their national economies to attain development along these lines. To assert this is not to propose a common market, typically recommended by orthodox western economists as necessary to attract essential foreign investment. On the contrary, as the experience of the South African Customs Union and the Federation of the Rhodesias and Nyasaland illustrate, the multinational corporate investments made within the framework of common market arrangements tend to concentrate in the more developed areas, aggravating lop-sided regional dependencies. This experience has been replicated, too, in the East African Common Market since independence. That is the underlying reason for the precarious status today of that fragile East African cooperation which seemed to hold such promise a decade ago.

Regional cooperation, if it is to contribute to more balanced, self-reliant regional development, requires that the participating states exercise sufficient control of the commanding heights of their respective economies to ensure that they can effectively implement a long-term plan to allocate resources to interlinked, regional industrial and agricultural development. The potential, as well as the problems, may be influenced by considering the possibilities opened up if Tanzania, Zambia, and Mozambique could develop the essential coordinated strategy and make the necessary institutional changes, to implement it.[3]

The establishment of the Tanzam pipeline, the Tanzam road, and the Tazara railroad provide an infrastructural base which could, facilitate extended trade between Tanzania and Zambia. These initial steps would need to be followed up by joint formulation and implementation of plans to build basic industries to take advantage of the enlarged markets of the two countries. This would require sufficient control of the banks and financial systems to ensure that all available investible surpluses are invested in agreed-upon projects, and that credit continues to be available as needed. It necessitates, too, sufficient control of import and internal wholesale trade institutions in both countries to ensure that they purchase agreed-upon products from each other, rather than from (sometimes initially cheaper) outside sources such as South Africa. In short, it would require significantly greater control of the commanding heights of the economy of the participating nations than has as yet been attained in Zambia.

The Governments of Tanzania and Mozambique have agreed to discuss allocation of future basic industries together at the ministerial level. If they extend this initial agreement to the formulation and implementation of a joint long-term plan for industrial poles of growth linked to the necessary agricultural and mineral raw material development, they should be able to make significant joint progress. If Zambia should agree to join with them in working out a long-term perspective plan for a still larger region, and make the necessary institutional changes to implement it, the three countries between them could restructure the regional economy and initiate a dynamic which could have an impact throughout the entire southern third of the continent. The potential for attaining a balanced, integrated economy in southern Africa, building on these already existing foundations, is extensive. Tanzania, Mozambique and Zambia, alone, cover a land area the size of western Europe. Their hinterlands contain extensive mineral riches. Some of these are known and are already developed: Zambia's copper mines are among the largest and most technologically advanced in the world. Many more remain to be discovered in the extensive land areas which are only now beginning to be adequately surveyed. Tanzania has known iron ore and phosphate deposits. All three countries, together, have a wide range of soils and climates suited to produce practically every variety of agricultural raw material and foodstuff needed in a modern economy. Their existing hydro-electric capacity centered in Mozambique's Cabora Bassa dam and Zambia's Kafue project, linked into a regional electrical grid, could electrify the regional economy. In 25 to 50 years, the region could boast of integrated industrial and agricultural growth sufficient to transform the levels of life of the entire population of the area.

This is not to argue that such a regional economy should seek to become autarchic, cut off from the rest of the world. Rather, joint control of export-import and internal wholesale trade would ensure that the benefits of the export of existing minerals and cash crops would be directed to providing expanding productive employment opportunities throughout the regional economies. Machinery and equipment at appropriate levels of technology would be imported in exchange for traditional exports.

The realization of joint planning and development among the three countries would provide new avenues of escape from South African-multinational corporate domination for the other nations of Southern Africa. Botswana could begin to plan infrastructural and industrial linkages with Zambia and, through Zambia, with the integrated and rapidly growing regional economies of the three countries. Angola, too could reduce its dependence on the multinationals by planning to develop its rich resource potential to build a domestic industrial complex complementary to that of its neighbours to the east. Landlocked Zimbabwe, after ousting the white minority regime, would be able to build upon its already existing industrial base in the context of the growth of regionally planned political economy. Malawi would eventually be able to break its dependence on South Africa and participate in the advantages to be attained through the transformation of the regional economy.

To focus on the vast potential for extensive planned regional development among the already-liberated nations of Southern Africa is not to ignore the people in South Africa and the captive satellite nations still enmeshed in South Africa's outward reach. The wealth and power of the South African regime, and its support from the multinational corporate world, have, it is true, prolonged the rule of the white minority. The South African Government seeks to institutionalize the age-old tactic of divide-and-rule at home by 'granting' separate 'tribes' the 'right' to rule their own 'homelands,' tiny fragmented Bantustans on some 13 per cent of the least fertile, most eroded lands of the country. Increasingly, multinational corporations, particularly those from the United States, are encouraged to invest in the South Africa's *apartheid*-ridden economy, to contribute modern technology to reduce the nation's reliance on African labour.

The people of South Africa, itself, have long been organized and struggled for their own liberation. The African National Congress of South Africa, founded in 1912, was the first national liberation movement in Africa and continues to give leadership to the struggles there. Hundreds of political opponents have been jailed. Many have been killed. Yet growing unrest and strikes continue to threaten South Africa's self proclaimed 'industrial peace'.

There can be little doubt that, in the long run, the South African people will win the right to rule in their own homeland, in South Africa itself. Superior military technology is not decisive, as the prolonged but ultimately victorious struggles, not only in Vietnam, but also in Mozambique, Guinea Buisseau, and Angola have proven.

The duration of their struggle will be shortened, however, to the extent that peoples of the neighbouring nations, through their own unity build up their own independent, balanced, integrated regional economies and thwart the penetration and rejuvenation of South African-multinational corporate interests based in the regional centre. It will be shortened, too, to the extent that the peoples of the United States and other western nations join the growing world-wide protests against multinational corporate investment in and support of the oppressive South African regime.

Once South Africa is fully liberated, its peoples will be able to direct its powerful industrial machine and extensive mineral resources to make a far-reaching contribution to the complete transformation of the southern third of the continent to provide all of its inhabitants with levels of life as high as anywhere in the world.

REFERENCES

POSTSCRIPT

1. A. Seidman, *Planning for Development in Sub-Saharan Africa* (Dar es Salaam: Tanzania Publishing House, 1974).
2. The necessity of economic integration is spelled out in R.H. Green and A. Seidman, *Unity or Poverty? The Economics of Pan Africanism* (London: Penguin African Library, 1968). The difficulties of realizing the continental perspectives there set forth have been illuminated by experience in the intervening years since that volume was published. The basic advantages of economic integration still hold. If they cannot be achieved on a continental basis in the immediate future, there is nevertheless a valid argument for attempting to set in motion a dynamic towards its realization on a regional basis.
3. This possibility has been outlined more fully in A. Seidman, 'Alternatives for Regional Economic Integration', Wingspread Conference, Background Paper, 19-22 October 1975, Racine, Wisconsin.

Index

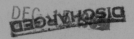